Coleridge's American Disciples

The Selected Correspondence of James Marsh

Coleridge's American Disciples

The Selected Correspondence of James Marsh

Edited by John J. Duffy

The University of Massachusetts Press, Amherst 1973

Library of Congress Catalog
Number 72-90497
Printed in the United States of America

Published with the support of
The American Council of Learned
Societies under a grant from
the Andrew W. Mellon Foundation, and
the Vermont Historical Society

Designed by Richard Hendel

The University of Massachusetts Press
Amherst, Massachusetts 01002

Contents

All letters are written by James Marsh or addressed to him unless otherwise indicated.

Preface

James Marsh (1794–1842) was a professor of philosophy, president of the University of Vermont (1826–33), and leader of the Vermont branch of the Transcendental Movement. A transitional figure and a mediator, he is easily overlooked by historians of American culture in favor of men whose impact on the first half of the nineteenth century has been more completely documented. But he reveals more fully than many of his contemporaries in the Transcendental Movement the tension between the heritage of the Puritan mind and a new sensibility formed by the Romantic revolution. Thus the letters collected here help to elucidate certain lines of continuity within American culture during the first third of the nineteenth century.

This selection from James Marsh's correspondence would have been impossible without the conscientious work of two people. The late William Parmelee Marsh catalogued and filed the papers and letters which had been passed down through the years from James Marsh's son, Joseph, and his granddaughter, Gertrude Marsh Hall. Mrs. H.E. Peterson carried on the work of her uncle, W.P. Marsh, and generously assisted in the transcription of her great-grandfather's letters. I am especially grateful to Mrs. Peterson.

I must also here acknowledge and thank for their encouragement the custodians of the James Marsh Collection, the late Mrs. Laura Jensen, and W. Knowlton Hall.

The help of T.D. Seymour Bassett, John Buechler, Elizabeth Lovell, and David Blow, and the resources of the Wilbur Collection, Guy W. Bailey Library, University of Vermont, continued generous and unstinting throughout the course of preparing these letters for publication. For that help, encouragement, and cooperation I am particularly grateful.

Publication of this book was assisted by the American Council of Learned Societies under a grant from the Andrew W. Mellor Foundation. The Vermont Historical Society, the American

Philosophical Society, the University of New Hampshire and, in the early stages of preparing this selection of letters, the University of Maryland generously assisted my work with research grants-in-aid. To Charles T. Morrissey of the Vermont Historical Society, George W. Corner of the American Philosophical Society, Deans Trevor Colbourn and William Drew of New Hampshire, and Professor Lewis Lawson of Maryland, I wish to express my appreciation.

Other important help was provided by, and I am grateful to, Marcus McCorison of the American Antiquarian Society, George W. Bricker of the Philip Schaff Library at the Lancaster Theological Seminary, the Honorable Louis Wyman, David Swift, Ian Fletcher, Herbert Schneider and A. H. B. Coleridge.

For their permission to publish Marsh's correspondence I am grateful to the following: Mrs. Laura Jensen and W. Knowlton Hall, Mrs. Virginia Shropshire, the University of Vermont, Dartmouth College, Yale University, the Massachusetts and Pennsylvania Historical Societies, the University of Texas, A. H. B. Coleridge, and Ronald Wells. I am also grateful to Kenneth W. Cameron for permission to reproduce two letters from George Ripley to James Marsh which I first published in *The Emerson Society Quarterly* (Winter, 1968), and to the Vermont Historical Society for permission to use portions of my article "James Marsh's Search for Unity," *Vermont History* (Winter, 1970).

For her endurance and fine work, I must also thank Stephanie Ackerman who prepared the manuscript of this edition of letters.

For her patience, I thank my wife Barbara.

Editorial Principles and Abbreviations

Readability, sometimes, but not often, at the expense of consistency, has been my first concern in transcribing these letters. The following editorial principles have been observed:

1. Ellipses in the body of a letter, unless otherwise noted by square brackets, are reproduced from the source. Ellipses in notes are my own.
2. Most abbreviations have been expanded, except such familiar ones as Mr., Mrs., Dr., ms., Co., and p. (for page). Names of some of Marsh's correspondents have been expanded in order to fully identify them. Names of publications, ampersands, and most numbers have been expanded.
3. In all letters I have normalized the date, address, and closing, adding brackets only when the date is an editorial conjecture.

The correspondence of James Marsh has been gathered from the various places indicated in the headnote for each letter. Joseph Torrey's *Memoir* was based on Marsh's journal, now lost, and approximately fifty letters, now also lost except for the fragments which Torrey used. Some of those fragments are reproduced here.

The following abbreviations have been used to designate in the headnotes the source of each letter:

UVM:	Guy W. Bailey Library, University of Vermont
Dartmouth:	The Baker Library, Dartmouth College
Yale:	Yale University Library
Wells:	Ronald Vale Wells, *Three Christian Transcendentalists* (New York, 1943).
Brown:	Samuel Gilman Brown, *The Life of Rufus Choate* (Boston, 1870).
Remains:	Joseph Torrey, ed., *The Remains of Rev. James Marsh, D.D. Late President and Professor of Moral and Intellectual Philosophy in the University of*

Vermont with a Memoir of His Life (Boston, 1843).

JMC: The James Marsh Collection.

A complete set of photocopies of the James Marsh Collection, which is now in the estate of the late Mrs. Laura Jensen, is deposited in the Guy W. Bailey Library, University of Vermont.

Chronology

July 19, 1794	James Marsh was born in Hartford, Vermont.
1812	Attended William Nutting's Academy, Randolph, Vermont.
1813	Entered Dartmouth College.
1815	Took part in religious revival at Dartmouth.
August 7, 1815	Made a public profession of religious conversion and joined the church at Dartmouth.
1817	Received the Bachelor of Arts degree from Dartmouth.
November 1817	Entered Andover Theological Seminary.
1818	Returned to Dartmouth as a tutor.
September 1820	Visited Cambridge and Harvard and attended evening lectures.
November 1820	Returned to Andover to complete ministerial studies.
February 21, 1821	Entered in his journal: "Of my progress in the German language, I . . . begin to feel as if I had conquered it."
May 1822	Visited New Haven, New York, Princeton, and Philadelphia.
July 18, 1822	Published "Ancient and Modern Poetry" in *North American Review*.
September 1822	Completed ministerial studies at Andover.
December 1822	Completed translation of Bellerman's *Geography of the Scriptures* at home in Hartford, Vermont.
January 6, 1823	Left Hartford to join John Holt Rice at Richmond, Virginia.
February 25, 1823	Appointed tutor at Hampden-Sydney College in Virginia.
May 1823	Returned to Hartford.

October 1823	Visited John H. Rice in Albany, New York, and arranged for another teaching appointment at Hampden-Sydney.
December 1823	Arrived at Richmond on his way to Hampden-Sydney.
Summer 1824	Travelled by horseback over the Cumberland into Ohio and southwestern Pennsylvania to visit his brother Roswell.
October 12, 1824	Ordained in Hanover, New Hampshire.
October 14, 1824	Married Lucia Wheelock.
October 30, 1824	Arrived back in Hampden-Sydney as professor of languages and belles lettres.
Summer 1826	Published translation of Herder's *Spirit of Hebrew Poetry* in *Biblical Repertory.*
October 1826	Appointed president of UVM.
August 18, 1828	Lucia died.
March 1829	Published review of Moses Stuart's *Commentary on the Epistle to the Hebrews* in *Christian Spectator.*
Winter-Spring 1829	Published nine articles on popular education in *Vermont Chronicle.*
November 1829	Published "Preliminary Essay" and first American edition of Samuel Taylor Coleridge's *Aids to Reflection.*
1830	Awarded honorary doctor of divinity by Columbia College.
May 1830	Published *Select Practical Theology of the Seventeenth Century.*
1830	Married Laura Wheelock, Lucia's sister.
1831	Published first American edition of Coleridge's *The Friend.*
1833	Awarded honorary doctor of divinity by Amherst College. Resigned presidency of UVM. Appointed professor of moral and intellectual philosophy at UVM. Completed two-volume translation of Herder's *Spirit of Hebrew Poetry.*

1837	Published translation of D. H. Hegewisch's *Introduction to Historical Chronology*.
August 12, 1838	Laura died.
Winter 1841–42	Seriously weakened by tuberculosis.
July 3, 1842	James Marsh died.

Introduction

At the unveiling of the bust of Samuel Taylor Coleridge in 1885 in Westminster Abbey that great Victorian gossip, Richard Monckton Milnes, recalled a visit that he and Arthur Hallam had made to Coleridge in the early 1830s while they were still students at Cambridge University. Coleridge had received them "as Goethe or Socrates might have done." "In the course of the conversation the poet asked if either of us intended to go to America. He said, 'Go to America if you have the opportunity; I am known there. I am a poor poet in England, but I am a great philosopher in America.'"[1] Coleridge's American reputation as a philosopher was launched by James Marsh. In 1829 Marsh edited, with his own "Preliminary Essay" and extensive notes, the first American edition of Coleridge's *Aids to Reflection*,[2] the book that introduced two important Coleridgean ideas—Reason and Understanding—to Emerson and others in the formative stages of the Transcendental Movement.[3]

Marsh was well regarded by some of the major figures among the transcendentalists in Boston and Concord. The first meeting of this group, originally called the Hedge Club, but soon after known as the Transcendental Club, was held at the home of George Ripley on September 19, 1836. Bronson Alcott, Ripley himself, Emerson, Orestes Brownson, James Freeman Clarke, Convers Francis, and Frederic Henry Hedge, after whom the club was first named, met and discussed with excitement Coleridge's and Marsh's distinction between Reason and Understanding, a distinction that Emerson had told his brother in a letter two years before was "a philosophy itself."[4] Years later Frederic Henry Hedge recalled the brief meeting in 1836 that preceded the first formal meeting of the Hedge Club at which "the writings of Coleridge, recently edited by Marsh, and some of Carlyle's earlier essays . . . had created a ferment in the minds of some of the younger clergy of the day. There was a promise in the air of a new era of intellectual life."[5]

Even before that first meeting of the Boston transcendentalists, in an 1833 review of Marsh's "Preliminary Essay" and edition of *Aids to Reflection*, Hedge had presented to the intellectuals of New England a "vindication of German metaphysics" and the first American "respectful recognition of the claims of Transcendentalism."[6] But as early as 1826, when he assumed the presidency of the University of Vermont, Marsh had already been developing many of the fundamental ideas of the "Essay" and *Aids to Reflection*. In fact, by 1833 he had been successfully teaching them at Vermont for seven years. As his Inaugural Address demonstrated, Marsh had returned in 1826 to Vermont from Hampden-Sydney College in Virginia, where he had been professor of languages and belles lettres, with the intention of building a curriculum along Coleridgean transcendental lines. Within three years he and Professors George Wyllys Benedict and Joseph Torrey, as well as Solomon Foot, a tutor, who together made up the complete faculty of four, had thoroughly reformed the curriculum of the University of Vermont. The scheme for reform was set forth in detail in a pamphlet entitled "An Exposition of the System of Instruction and Discipline pursued in the University of Vermont" (1829),[7] an essay generally well-received by other educators, though few of its readers could have realized that Marsh's pattern was the *System of Universal Knowledge on a Methodical Plan Projected by Samuel Taylor Coleridge*.[8]

In 1837, a year after the Hedge Club's first meeting and eight years after the publication of *Aids to Reflection*, George Ripley was preparing to publish his *Specimens of Foreign Standard Literature*, a "philosophical miscellany" in fourteen volumes which would introduce to New England (and here we see the care taken in selecting a title) not "new" literature from the Continent (for the orthodox might call it heretical), but *standard* German and French intellectual and literary fare.[9] Ripley wrote to Marsh, telling him that his plans were to secure as contributors to the series some of New England's "most distinguished students of continental literature."

. . . [I] have already engaged the services of several, on whom I place great reliance. It would give me great

pleasure if you would consent to undertake the translation of such work in theology or philosophy, as your taste may suggest, illustrated with an introduction and notes, similar to your valuable commentaries on Coleridge.[10]

While Marsh never accepted this invitation, he and Ripley seem to have met more than once after 1837, perhaps at the homes of George Ticknor, George Bancroft, Washington Allston, or the Danas where Marsh sometimes visited during school holidays or on money-raising trips for UVM. In another letter Ripley expressed regrets for failing to meet Marsh "again during our Commencement Week."[11] He went on to discuss the forthcoming Brook Farm venture and the recent appearance of *The Dial.* Again Ripley invited Marsh to contribute something from his pen to this new publication of the Boston group. Confessing "large sympathies with ideal conservatives in church and state," Ripley felt that Marsh's "views in theology or metaphysics would always be welcome in the pages of the 'Dial.'"[12] But again Marsh failed to accept Ripley's invitation.

By 1840 the first volume of Ripley's "philosophical miscellany" had been in print for almost two years. There is a suggestion, however, that the textbook of logic based on a translation of Jakob Friederich Fries's *System der Logik* which Marsh used in his philosophy course at UVM after 1832 might have been intended for Ripley's "miscellany." In 1841 Marsh expressed his dissatisfaction with Boston transcendentalism, coming down especially hard on its failure to develop a logical system:

The whole of Boston Transcendentalism I take to be rather a superficial affair; and there is some force in the remarks of a friend of mine that the 'Dial' indicates rather the place of the moon than of the sun. They have many of the prettinesses of the German writers, but without their manly logic and strong systematizing tendency. They pretend to no system of unity, but each utters, it seems, the inspiration of the moment, assuming that it all comes from the universal heart, while ten to one it comes from the stomach.[13]

Despite his influence on the Boston transcendentalists, through his "Essay" and introduction to

Coleridge, and Ripley's high regard for him, Marsh, the "ideal conservative" from Vermont, was acutely critical of ideas he heard from the transcendentalists of southern New England during the late 1830s and the last few years before he died in 1842. What he himself had to say was instead directed to sympathetic listeners beyond the small circle of subscribers to *The Dial*. *Aids to Reflection* was more than a book read and valued only by a Boston coterie. Though not readily accepted by everyone in the early 1830s, by the end of the decade or by the early '40s, Marsh's edition of Coleridge's book was difficult to keep stocked in some bookstores. At Andover, for instance, where Marsh had studied German scriptural scholarship with Moses Stuart, many students at the seminary turned to the "Preliminary Essay" and Coleridge for guidance "in the formation of a Manly Character," despite the rejection of Coleridge by their professors, including Stuart.[14] In 1853, eleven years after Marsh died, W. G. T. Shedd published the first collected American edition of Coleridge, including the "Preliminary Essay." Shedd was simply finishing a job begun under Marsh's tutelage, a task that the poet's literary executor, Henry Nelson Coleridge, had originally planned for Marsh. Shedd's edition, only now being superseded, was to become the standard American text of Coleridge for more than a century.

As Shedd's work suggests, Marsh's students at Vermont during his sixteen years there were deeply influenced by him. At the semi-centennial celebration of the University in 1854, twelve years after Marsh's death, the Reverend Aaron G. Pease professed the "literary and philosophical creed of the Vermont alumnus." Pease clearly expressed the debt that his former students felt for their late professor and president as he read Article Four—"He believes in Coleridge"—and Article Five:

> *He believes in Professor Marsh . . . for whenever one of these great names is pronounced, the other is not a great way off. He believes in Professor Marsh as the man whom the University and the cause of education in this country, and his own mind, are more deeply indebted than to any other man. . . .*[15]

What seems to have attracted students to Marsh and what historians of American ideas will find interesting in him is a way of looking at the world that both shares certain assumptions with and diverges from the Boston-Concord group. Marsh, like many other New England thinkers of the early nineteenth century, attempted a synthesis of nature and spirit, but a synthesis informed by traditional Christian faith. Marsh's mind was aroused to know the world of nature as well as ideas. John Dewey, while recognizing the danger of labels, called him an Aristotelian Kantian.[16] Foreshadowing Thoreau's concern for nature and Emerson's belief in ideas, Marsh delivered the transcendentalist message in a context of intellectual rigor and revitalized Christianity. The entire Transcendental Movement was insistently religious in impulse, "a religious demonstration," as Perry Miller has reminded us.[17] While the men in Boston and Concord in the mid-1830s were only beginning to demonstrate, Marsh up in Vermont had been having his own religious demonstration since his years at Dartmouth when he first attempted to instill the experience of both common life and serious philosophy with a new spirituality. He saw the problem to be a need for reforming the old orthodoxy without destroying certain features of it or denying the natural world it existed in. For Marsh, nearly all contemporary thinking about religion failed to have any meaning. Christianity had not been best expressed in modern form, as far as Marsh was concerned, by the voices at Harvard, Andover, or Yale, but by some "old" voices of seventeenth-century England and some "new" philosophers of late eighteenth- and nineteenth-century Germany and England. The goal of his demonstration, in his own words, was to show that a thinking man "has and can have but one system in which his philosophy becomes religious and his religion philosophical."[18]

In reaching for this goal, moreover, Marsh continues to be interesting for us because, in his attempts to become a thinking man whose philosophy was religious and religion philosophical, he found himself caught up in the tensions between the danger, on the one hand, of reducing orthodox Christianity to a speculative system in the manner of Unitarianism, and, on the other, through emphasizing personal, subjective religious experience, the danger of losing his faith in what he saw as the power of Christianity to make over the world. The effects of this tension on a mind that wanted to see the universe and all of life as a whole, a mind that ranged freely over German philosophy and biblical studies, English, German, French, Italian, and classical literature, as well as natural science, perhaps best explain why his personal bibliography is not very large, while his learned reading was most substantial for his time and place.

During his years at the University of Vermont and for many years after his death in 1842, Marsh was recognized in his home state as the leader of the group which came to be known as the Vermont Transcendentalists and, among his academic and other contemporaries throughout the country, as a leading student and proponent of German and Coleridgean Idealistic philosophy. Marsh's first interest in Coleridge and German philosophy developed in 1819 when as a tutor at Dartmouth he read the English poet's *Biographia Litereria*. When it first appeared in New York in 1817, Coleridge's book presented to American readers, as it had earlier that year in England, a new and controversial theory of the imagination based on a distinction between Reason and Understanding which Coleridge had found in German Romantic literature and philosophy. Marsh told Coleridge in a letter written in 1829:

> *From my past knowledge of your "Literary Life" some ten years ago, I have sought, as my opportunities would permit, a more intimate acquaintance with your writing, and with your views on all the great and important subjects which you have treated.*[19]

It is now difficult to say specifically whether Marsh's reading in Coleridge then led him to German philosophy, especially to Kant's *Critique of Pure Reason*, or whether his reading in Madame de Staël's famous *De L'Allemagne* (New York, 1814) originally provided the impetus to his German studies. At any rate, sometime between 1815 and 1819, Marsh dove into what his friend Rufus Choate called "that ocean of German theology and metaphysics." "Marsh, you may swim on alone in that if you will," Choate scolded, "and much good may it do you."[20]

The ultimate effects of Marsh's dive into that German ocean were larger, however, than Choate and Marsh's other friends from Dartmouth, or perhaps even Marsh himself, could then foresee. After assuming the presidency of UVM in 1826 and, during the following year, persuading Torrey, a good friend from undergraduate days, to leave his congregation in Royalton and join him in Burlington, Marsh directed the reorganization of UVM's government and curriculum. Twenty-five years after the reformed curriculum had been adopted, John Wheeler, another friend from Dartmouth and Marsh's successor as president of UVM, described the new system of instruction in a way that, by emphasizing certain central ideas of organic unity, process, and development, clearly pointed to the reformer's debt to German and Coleridgean ideas. The new course of study sought, Wheeler said,

> *to give a coherence to the various studies in each department so that the several parts shall present, more or less, the unity not of an aggregation nor of a juxtaposition, nor of a merely logical arrangement but of a* development and a growth, *and therefore, the study in it, rightly pursued, should be a growing and enlarging process to the mind of the student.*[21]

Wheeler's description of the system implicitly acknowledges the distinction on which Marsh and his colleagues organized the full course of study. It was "not a merely logical arrangement" based only on the simply logical capabilities of the Understanding, but went beyond the limitations of the Understanding and by enlarging the students' minds allowed them to develop their higher power of Reason, what Emerson called "the soul itself."[22]

The extent of the influence of Vermont's curriculum and, perhaps even more importantly, the personalities of these men, especially Marsh, is suggested by the eighty-one students from Marsh's era who went on from UVM to become teachers throughout the country. With many other Vermonters during and after the 1830s, alumni of the University migrated west and south, carrying what they called "Marsh's philosophy." Marsh's sons, James, Sidney, and Joseph, for example, all UVM alumni, migrated as far west as Oregon, where Sidney was president and Joseph professor at Pacific University as well as mayor of the town; and even Hawaii where James was assistant minister of education, a member of the Hawaiian parliament, and publisher of the first Hawaiian language newspaper.

Moreover we can probably conclude from the continued reprinting of Marsh's "Preliminary Essay" and notes to *Aids to Reflection*, especially in W.G.T. Shedd's long-standard 1853 edition of Coleridge's works, that the results of Marsh's interests in German studies and Coleridge were felt well into the nineteenth century. Yet we are still only dimly aware of the full meaning of this, for its time and place, unique expression of intellectual and emotional concern. Expressions of gratitude to Marsh came, of course, from among the Boston-Concord transcendentalists.[23] But the debt to Marsh was also acknowledged in the most concrete way by less prominent figures. In 1842 Emerson noted in his journal a report from Edward Washburn at Andover that "whole shelvesful" of *Aids to Reflection* were being sold there yearly to the students. In the 1880s when he was living in England, Moncure Conway, one of Hegel's first American followers, recalled that long before he had come to reside in Bedford Park, an "esthete's Elysium" near London, he had carried in his saddle bag and studied Marsh's edition of *Aids to Reflection* during his years as a Methodist circuit rider in Ohio.[24] As an undergraduate at Vermont in the late 1870s, John Dewey had been a close friend and student of Professor H.A.P. Torrey, Joseph Torrey's nephew, and in later years at Columbia University Dewey acknowledged to Herbert Schneider and others that the influence of Marsh's lectures on psychology and Coleridge's *Aids to Reflection*, which were used as texts in the younger Torrey's philosophy courses, were still sufficiently meaningful in the 1870s to shape irrevocably the thinking of many undergraduates there, including in some ways Dewey himself.[25]

However far-reaching the effects of Marsh's studies, the beginning of his story is in Hanover, New Hampshire, at Dartmouth College, and in part concerns at least three other men. James Marsh, John Wheeler (1796–1862), Joseph Torrey (1797–1867), and Ebenezer Tracy (1796–1862) all attended

Dartmouth between 1812 and 1819. Torrey and Wheeler, the latter the son of the Dartmouth benefactor, John B. Wheeler, took their degrees in 1816, the year before Marsh; and Tracy graduated two years after him in 1819. Rufus Choate was one of their group, but after graduating from Dartmouth in 1819 and then serving as a tutor while rooming with Marsh, he went on to read law, eventually becoming a prominent lawyer in Massachusetts and a member of Congress. George Perkins Marsh, Class of 1820, philologist, conservationist, diplomat, cousin of James Marsh, and son of Charles Marsh, a prominent Vermont lawyer, Congressman, and Dartmouth trustee, was also in their circle. From this group of Dartmouth men, three were to become presidents of UVM: Marsh, from 1826 to 1833 (he refused the first offer of the presidency in 1821 while still at Andover); then Wheeler from 1833 to 1849; and finally Torrey from 1862 to 1866. After tutoring students at Dartmouth for two years, Marsh completed his ministerial studies at Andover in 1822. Tracy attended Andover for one year, 1821–2, and returned to the Seminary in 1830 to edit *The Journal of Humanity* until 1833, when he went back to Bellows Falls to resume the editorship of *The Vermont Chronicle*, a Congregationalist newspaper founded by Wheeler. Of the three Dartmouth men who served at UVM, only Marsh never served a congregation other than the University. Torrey served at Royalton, Vermont, from 1824 until he accepted, over the objection of his congregation, an appointment to the faculty of the University in 1827. Wheeler served the congregation at Windsor, Vermont, from 1821 to 1833 when, as Marsh's choice, he assumed the presidency of UVM.

Dartmouth during these years, as all of her alumni and some legal historians recall from Daniel Webster's plea, was indeed a small college. From 1816 to 1820 only 157 degrees were awarded. Nearly half of those graduates became clergymen, for, like other early American colleges, Dartmouth had deep religious roots. With an intense religious tradition, it was perhaps inevitable that the beginning of the controversy which resulted in the Dartmouth College Case and Webster's tear-compelling plea to John Marshall and the United States Supreme Court for his small, beloved college would have a religious, as well as political and personal source. The whole affair began in 1804 with the appointment of Roswell Shurtleff as professor of divinity and pastor of Hanover Congregational Church against the wishes of President John Wheelock, son of Dartmouth's founder, Eleazer Wheelock. Shurtleff fostered the revivalist tradition at Dartmouth during the Second Great Awakening in the early nineteenth century; in one month in 1815, the year Francis Brown replaced John Wheelock as president of the college, 120 students and townsfolk, including James Marsh and his future wife, Lucia Wheelock, John's niece, were formally accepted into the church as a result of Shurtleff's sermons on such texts as "the harvest is past, the summer is ended." Shurtleff, Torrey recorded in his *Memoir* of Marsh, was their "beloved pastor," as well as professor of divinity.

By 1817 the controversy between ex-President Wheelock and the board of trustees of the college over Shurtleff's appointment had developed into a personal and political dispute which resulted in the Legislature of New Hampshire establishing a rival university and prohibiting faculty and students from entering or using the buildings of Dartmouth College. Factions formed among the students; some violent battles were fought over the possession of the libraries of several student societies; and litigation, as it will, engendered further litigation.[26] Yet at least six students—the two Marshes, Torrey, Wheeler, Tracy, and Choate—were able to resist the distraction of intra- and extramural conflict by regular meetings in a small discussion group or literary club which had been formed in 1813–14, Marsh's first years at Dartmouth. Choate's biographer, Samuel Gilman Brown, believed that "the students were stimulated by the unusual circumstances."[27] It seems just as likely, however, that Marsh's small group with its weekly meetings for readings and discussions, having been formed prior to the "unusual circumstances" of 1815–17 as a response to the inadequacies of Dartmouth's formal curriculum, was available to fill the void created by the dissolution of academic and intellectual life at the college.

While it would not be until 1832 that a professional educator could be heard publicly saying that the object of education was to bring young people "as early and as rapidly as possible to *self instruc-*

tion, *self-government*, and *self-education*,"[28] Marsh had already discovered the value of independent study, perhaps even before entering Dartmouth. According to his family's plans, his older brother Roswell was originally intended for Dartmouth, but because he refused to carry a leg of mutton to Hanover as partial payment for his board, their father instead sent James, then eighteen years old, to William Nutting's academy in Randolph, Vermont, for one year of preparation for Dartmouth.[29] Entering college at nineteen in 1813, he was old for a freshman by comparison to the sophomore Torrey, who was then sixteen, and Wheeler, who was only fifteen. By 1819, however, he had made up a great deal of lost ground. As a tutor in 1818–19 Marsh was reading not only the standard college fare of the period in classical literature (his Latin grammar text from Nutting's academy survives with evidence of plenty of hard use) as well as Hebrew and French, but he had also become proficient in German and Italian—when he left Dartmouth for the last time in 1820 his Italian grammar was passed on to Washington Choate.[30] He was, as Torrey later remarked, a skillful and fluent reader. His accomplishments in languages by 1822 surprised Edward Everett, the editor of *The North American Review*, who told George Ticknor that Marsh's review-essay "Ancient and Modern Poetry," published during that summer by *The North American Review*, must have been written by someone with first-hand experience of Europe.[31] While Ticknor had travelled throughout Europe and had been a guest in Milan of Ludovico di Breme, the young Italian liberal and author of the book for which Ticknor recommended Marsh as the reviewer, the longest trip Marsh ever made would be in 1824 to Brownsville, Pennsylvania, in order to visit his brother Roswell who had migrated west in 1813.[32]

Marsh's intellectual life and literary interests apparently grew in spite of Dartmouth. From 1815 to 1819 the five-man faculty of the college provided instruction in the arts and sciences. In philosophy, however, Locke, Butler's *Analogy*, Stewart's *History of Philosophy*, and Edwards on the Will, all, except for Edwards, stressing the rational aspects of human experience and knowledge, failed to satisfy Marsh and his friends. While teaching at Hampden-Sydney

College in Virginia in 1826, Marsh expressed his dissatisfaction to George Ticknor, another Dartmouth man and a generous friend who had long since gone to the fountainhead of German philosophy. Having studied in Germany and then travelled in Europe from 1815 to 1819 before assuming the Smith Professorship at Harvard, Ticknor in 1826 was in the midst of his ultimately unsuccessful attempts to reform the curriculum at Harvard when Marsh told him:

. . . for several years now . . . I have been fully convinced that very essential changes were necessary in our whole course of early instruction. In many cases I have no doubt the present system is rather an injury than a benefit to the scholar since it confirms and flatters with the appearance of learning many who if left more to themselves would sooner become their own teachers.[33]

In the litigious atmosphere of Hanover, Marsh and his friends became their own teachers. They purchased books for the library of their club and met regularly to read and discuss papers written by individual members. The full membership included at various times James and George Perkins, Marsh, Torrey, Wheeler, Tracy, Choate, and perhaps Jonathan Cushing (1793–1835), Class of 1817, president of Hampden-Sydney College during Marsh's three years there and head of the household of bachelors where Marsh stayed in his first winter term in Virginia as a tutor in 1823. But the leading figure in the group was certainly James Marsh: in 1821 Rufus Choate told Marsh that he had long since given up his German studies for he felt like a cuttlefish following Marsh's wake through a German ocean of metaphysics, theology, and criticism. Wherever Marsh went to study or teach—at Dartmouth, Andover, Hampden-Sydney, or Vermont—in his wake a school formed like the one at Dartmouth. In 1823 he wrote from Hampden-Sydney:

I was kept up last night till 12 o'clock, by a discussion in a society we have formed here, and which by the excitement and interest it is producing, reminds me of Hanover more strongly than anything of the kind I have enjoyed since the days of my tutorship.[34]

"The excitement and interest," Torrey pointed out, was generated by Marsh himself and "seldom failed to be spread by his simple, earnest words, whenever he spoke upon any subject with which his own mind was full."[35]

At Andover, too, he had found the academic routine just as unsatisfactory as Dartmouth's, and so he ignored regular classes in order to study alone. He told Lucia Wheelock that he found nothing "more profitless . . . than the constantly recurring routine of formal assemblies of any kind."[36] At Dartmouth during his tutorship he had also found especially annoying another feature of collegiate education as it was then practiced. Marsh objected to "some who seem to know no way of managing young men, but by the terror of authority . . . a method [which] tends to break down all the independent spirit and love of study for its own sake, which I thought it of so much importance to cherish."[37] Torrey, however, in later years apparently had difficulty accommodating himself to Marsh's liberal "notions" about studying: perhaps Marsh's "method of allowing and encouraging young men to use unlimited freedom in the choice of their studies," Torrey remarked, "would have proved incompatible with any regular system of discipline calculated on the average want of the youthful mind."[38] The most recent historian of the University of Vermont, Julian Lindsay, has pointed out that in fact disciplinary practices at Vermont became increasingly authoritarian after Marsh stepped down from the presidency in 1833, even rigorously so after his death in 1842.[39] But, even though Marsh himself later expressed some doubt about the success expected from the newly-established free elective system instituted at Harvard in 1841,[40] his own independent habits of study twenty years earlier had been fruitful. In February 1821 he recorded in his journal:

Of my progress in the German language, I have been more conscious than ever before, and begin to feel as if I had conquered it. In Spanish, too, I have done something, and will conquer it within the year. My Hebrew I have some fears about, but I think I shall master it. . . . At the club on Friday, I was rather surprised to find

> *that though I had devoted but half a day to the subject [the Apostolic Fathers], my knowledge of them was as good as anyone's. I do not make this record from vanity, but the fact is to me proof of the superiority of my system.*[41]

By 1822 he was sufficiently confident of his command of German to join with Richard Cary Morse, son of Jedidiah Morse, the geographer, and then a licentiate at Andover Seminary, in a translation of the geographical sections of Johann Bellerman's *Handbuch der biblischen Literatur.*[42] Their professor, Moses Stuart, assured them of a market for the book among his students. Soon after this project Marsh also began a translation of J. G. von Herder's *Vom Geist der ebraischen Poesie* for serial publication in *The Biblical Repertory.*

The two prominent facets of Marsh's sensibility—the one concerned with objective, intellectual matters, what in himself he called "the mere scholar," and the other personal, subjective, private, and inward-turning—he continually sought to integrate after the crucial spring and summer of 1815 when he experienced the first major conflict of his life of thought and life of feeling. The goal of that search, though cast in terms perhaps now unfamiliar, he repeatedly formulated in the phrase "to make religion philosophical and philosophy religious." In the spring of 1815, during one of Roswell Shurtleff's more fruitful religious revivals, Marsh became interested in another student's expressions of religious faith. In turn he probed his own mind in an effort to find the spiritual center of his life. But his first efforts were unsuccessful, and Marsh was soon verging on despair. "I envied those around me," he wrote, "whom I looked upon as in a more hopeful condition than myself, and my heart rose in opposition to the divine sovereignty."[43] He seems to have found some temporary consolation in an unnamed friend. But while studying Euclid one night, Marsh soon relapsed into despair, appalled by the seemingly mechanical nature of life. "As I proceeded in the demonstration," he wrote, "all my faith in things invisible seemed to vanish, and I almost doubted the reality of my own existence."[44]

Exactly how Marsh made his way out of the Center of Indifference in which he found himself during the summer of 1815 is now difficult to determine, for his journals, diary, and commonplace book are lost. Clearly Shurtleff's evangelical fervor played a part; and a letter written six years later to Lucia Wheelock suggests that she was also present at that critical moment. After mildly complaining about the lack of a letter from her during another revival at Hanover in 1821, Marsh quickly assured her that his complaint did not suggest doubts in "the system of faith which we professed together before the altar."[45] But whatever the avenue of his conversions and almost despite the traditional and orthodox language of it, the thrust of Marsh's search for a meaningful emotional and intellectual unity in a bleakly mechanical world was distinctly modern. Moreover, his three most important published works in the 1820s—a long review-essay in *The North American Review* on Ludovico di Breme's defense of Romantic literature, a review of Moses Stuart's *Commentary on the Epistle to the Hebrews* for *The Quarterly Christian Spectator*, and the "Preliminary Essay" and notes for *Aids to Reflection*—all exhibit Marsh's continuing efforts to satisfy his own need for an integrated sensibility and at the same time bring into the theological and philosophical disputes of New England in the 1820s and early '30s a method of reconciling the disparate parties and their arguments.

While Roswell Shurtleff's appointment at Dartmouth in 1805 generated a controversy which was finally settled more than ten years later by a United States Supreme Court decision, the appointment of Henry Ware also in 1805 as Hollis Professor of Divinity at Harvard similarly initiated a dispute which irreparably divided the Congregational Church in New England. Although Jedidiah Morse, Eliphalet Pearson, and other theologically conservative divines had objected to Ware's alleged liberalism, Unitarians became dominant at Harvard by 1808 and in the meantime had instigated as a conservative reaction the establishment of Andover Seminary. The dispute between the two schools continued for thirty years. While both camps accepted the Bible as revelation, they differed on the role of the human mind in finding the truth of that revelation. Leonard Woods, one of Marsh's professors at Andover, succinctly expressed the conservative objection to relying on the human intellect, especially as he found that reliance demonstrated in the sermons of William Ellery Channing and Coleridge's *Aids to Reflection*, when he thanked Marsh for presenting him with a copy of the book soon after it was published by reminding Marsh that "philosophy of religion is, after all, worth but little."[46] Meanwhile, a third camp had appeared in Connecticut where Nathaniel Taylor of Yale attempted to revise Calvinistic theology in a way that would reconcile liberals and conservatives.

When Marsh was closest to these disputes—at Andover and, for a short time in the fall of 1820, at Cambridge—he was least attracted to joining one side or the other. He had tried a few weeks of classes at Harvard Divinity School in October 1820 but found the glacial quality of Boston and Cambridge Unitarians somehow unsettling, despite the friendly company of Ticknor and others whom he would continue to visit during the next twenty years; and when he was graduated from Andover in 1822, he was, as he told Richard Morse, happy to have put behind him the contentious and boorish atmosphere of that place.[47] His essays in *The North American Review* and *The Quarterly Christian Spectator*, as well as the famous "Preliminary Essay," are good indications of his attitude during these years.

Ostensibly a review of a book by Ludovico Gattinara di Breme defending modern Romantic literature, the essay entitled "Ancient and Modern Poetry" exhibited a sensitive and broad understanding of how an emerging modern sensibility resulted from a new relationship between faith, reason, and imagination. Marsh defined the medieval and modern sensibilities in a way which led him, as it did his German sources, to describe the modern as indebted to the medieval in two ways: first, for an inward turning of the "powers of the human mind, [which] removed the center of its thought and feelings from 'the world without' to 'the world within'," and, second, for a "boundless faith in connexion with the world of invisibles" which "carried the mind . . . to express feeling, and the deepest feeling, on objects purely spiritual."[48] In conflict with this passionate inward turning of the mind, however, the modern, post-Lockean sensibility also finds its "thoughts disciplined and guarded on every side by the fixed laws of philosophical inquiry."

Modern education enforced this conflict:

We are taught to exclude the influence of feeling, and reduce the operations of the whole soul to the measured movements of a machine under the control of the will. We suffer no idea to take possession of us more fully, or to produce any greater effect upon our feelings, than prudence and cool reason dictate. (123)

Developing an idea he had found in an essay by Moses Mendelsohn, Marsh complained, as he would at Hampden-Sydney and again when revising the curriculum at Vermont, of how we had become enslaved by the written text:

The preacher does not converse with his church, he reads or declaims to them a written treatise. The instructor from his desk reads a written pamphlet. All is dead letter, with none of the spirit of living intercourse. We love and hate by letters. We wrangle and are reconciled by letters. . . . Our whole being depends upon our alphabet, and we can hardly conceive how it is possible for a child of this world to form and perfect his character without a book. (127)

Yet, in a pre-Gutenberg world, religious rites and rituals "were themselves a species of record full of meaning, . . . while they aroused the heart to religious feelings . . . carrying the imagination to objects of the other world" (126). For medieval minds, "faith was coextensive with the world of their imagination, it had vastly more influence upon their feelings and actions" (128). In effect, the medieval mind was essentially poetic: "They had not learned to *write* their poetry, but they lived it" (128). Just as slightly more than one-hundred years later T. S. Eliot would hear the last unified sensibility speaking to him from the seventeenth century, so Marsh heard it, though it spoke to him from the nonconformist "imagination of Bunyan." Faith, reason, and imagination had existed then for the last time in organic unity.

Reason and philosophy gradually distinguished from each other the worlds of faith and imagination, before so intimately blended, and as our sober ancestors turned all their poetry into religion, we are in danger of turning all our religion into poetry. (131)

Marsh's first published essay demonstrated that as a student at a decidely conservative New England seminary—Moses Stuart himself incurred heresy investigations for introducing German scholarship into his courses—Marsh had a knowledge of European literature unique for his time and place and an attitude toward contemporary American culture at odds with other regular contributors to *The North American. The North American Review* spoke for Unitarian Boston and, for all its scholarly virtues, as Van Wyck Brooks pointed out, was hostile to the philosophical forms of feelings which characterize the Transcendental Movement of the 1830s and '40s. Richard Henry Dana, Sr., Marsh's good friend and perhaps the first real literary Romantic in New England, had broken his relationship with the magazine in 1819 because other members of the editorial board had objected to his championing Wordsworth, Byron, and Coleridge.[49] Early in 1823 Alexander Hill Everett attacked Schiller and by 1829 had repeatedly published attacking reviews of German, French, and English philosophical and literary Idealism in the pages of *The North American Review*.[50]

What sets Marsh off from both *The North American Review* and Andover is best seen in the uncertainty of his tone and style in "Ancient and Modern Poetry." Where he sounds most like the conventional early-nineteenth-century historian, relying heavily on secondary sources in his analysis, his style is pure *North American*, lifeless and turgid; but when he speaks most independently of others, relying completely on his own experience of a life of dissociated thought and feeling in which neither Andover nor Harvard was satisfactory, he is vital and almost passionate. Sentences superficially neoclassical in balance become filled with feeling as he decries a life in which "We love and hate by letters."

Between the publication of "Ancient and Modern Poetry" and his review of Moses Stuart's *Commentary on the Epistle to the Hebrews*, Marsh published in *The Biblical Repertory* a translation of Herder's *Vom Geist der ebraischen Poesie*. The serial publication of his translation of Herder seems, however, to have made only a mild impression in the quarters where Marsh hoped it would do the most good. Charles Hodge, then the editor of the *Repertory*, a magazine which Marsh himself seems to have suggested to the Princeton group, knew little about German criticism and scholarship in 1826. He told Marsh that he was open to suggestions and contributions on German scholarship to his magazine.[51] Even in 1830, writing to Marsh in protest over the publication of *Aids to Reflection*, Hodge, despite having studied in Germany during the interim, continued to confess ignorance of German philosophy, especially Coleridge's German sources, though he was certain that Marsh was disseminating heresy.[52] By the late 1830s, however, Hodge, Albert Dod, and James W. Alexander, all of Princeton, were battling alongside Andrews Norton of Harvard against "the latest form of infidelity," Transcendentalism's "German insanity," as Norton called it.[53] Only after the Burlington publisher, Edward Smith, had brought out Marsh's two-volume edition of Herder in 1833 was a voice heard commending Marsh for presenting the German book to American readers. Writing for *The Christian Examiner* in 1835, George Ripley acknowledged a debt to Marsh for "the literary enterprise and industry of an American scholar undertaking and completing such a task."[54] Ripley found Marsh's translation valuable because it brought to New England an idea Herder had extended from Schleiermacher and which Ripley found especially remedial to the stagnation of religious thinking in the 1830s—"the soul's sense of things divine" and "the reason gazes immediately on eternal realities."

In early 1829, however, when Marsh wrote the review of Stuart's *Commentary on St. Paul's Epistle to the Hebrews* for Nathaniel Taylor's *Christian Spectator*, strong resistance formed against Marsh's introduction of German concepts and Coleridge's terminology. In a sermon delivered at New Haven in 1828, Taylor had attempted a refutation of both the liberals at Boston and the conservatives at Andover. Against the Unitarians he argued the inadequacy of the theory of a *felix culpa* to support the doctrine of Redemption. Against Andover he argued that man's nature is only the occasion of sin, not the cause. Taylor had hoped to revitalize Jonathan Edwards's theory of the Will and reconcile Unitarians and Congregationalists at least on that question. Instead, as Marsh predicted to Coleridge,

Taylor further undermined whatever authority Edwards still had at Yale, generated another controversy out of the original Harvard-Andover dispute and, just as in the earlier controversy, instigated by reaction the establishment of another seminary at East Windsor, Connecticut.[55] Marsh felt that the confused state of theology in New England resulted from the failure of the disputing factions to think out the consequences of their arguments. He told Ebenezer Tracy and Torrey that in his review of Stuart's *Commentary* he had hoped to introduce some ideas from Coleridge and the German theologian Tholuck in order to "awaken among our scholars a taste for more manly and efficient mental discipline."[56]

Marsh's review of Stuart's *Commentary* presented a basically Coleridgean and German view of the doctrine of Redemption. "I made a free use of your language," he told Coleridge;[57] but Taylor had objected, even deleted a note of credit to Coleridge, and added five concluding paragraphs of his own correcting Marsh's suggestion of certain subjective elements in the doctrine of Redemption which Stuart incorrectly defined. Marsh told Torrey that Stuart failed to comprehend what Marsh was even talking about.[58]

With the publication of his review of Stuart, the form and method of Marsh's search for a unifying system gained its first large public expression outside Vermont. But Stuart failed to understand him and Taylor suppressed and corrected part of the review because Marsh was arguing from a distinction which neither was able to understand at the time, although Marsh's students at Vermont would have recognized it immediately. Revelation, the basic material of doctrine, Marsh asserted, "may be *above* the comprehension of our *understanding*, but it cannot *contradict* the unbribed and unequivocal voice of *reason*."[59] Stuart's study of St. Paul's epistle failed, Marsh felt, in that his discussion of the doctrine of Redemption tried to extend scholarly and critical methods of analysis of the text of *Hebrews*, basically an exercise of the Understanding, to an analysis of the "inward and subjective nature" of Redemption, and thus into that area where Reason operated. Cautiously, almost timidly, for he was after all correcting his former teacher, Marsh differed with Stuart on whether there was a mechanical cause-effect relationship between Redeemer and redeemed of the sort that Stuart analyzed and whether terms such as Atonement, sacrifice, or satisfaction, all hallowed terms in Calvinist orthodoxy though they were, adequately taught "the inward and subjective nature" of the doctrine (147). Given the linguistic modes and rituals, essentially the cultural milieu, of the Apostles, the terms might have once been meaningful; but, Marsh said,

for us—for those who have the whole of the new testament in their hands, and read it aright, and feel its power, the language of the apostle ought to mean more, than these metaphorical representations, literally interpreted, could express, either to the Hebrews, or to ourselves. (148)

As an heir of Puritan piety, Marsh emphasized that a critical commentary must also serve an end of "great practical importance"—"the growth of our churches in knowledge and piety." The best application of the critic's analysis would be accomplished in Marsh's conception of the ideal sermon, "of which the commentaries of Leighton, the practical writings of Howe and other divines of the same age [the seventeenth century], furnish the most perfect examples" (122). Unlike Coleridge, whose *Aids to Reflection* consisted largely of extracts from Archbishop Leighton's works, Marsh implied, Stuart's commentary was weakened by his failure to acknowledge the subjective elements in the Redemption which extended beyond the comprehension of the Understanding.

While Stuart and Taylor either could not understand or simply rejected Marsh's use of the distinction between Reason and Understanding, Emerson and others were ready to accept it totally. When Marsh brought out *Aids to Reflection* in late 1829 with those terms used, though sometimes equivocally, in both Coleridge's text and his own notes and "Preliminary Essay," Emerson avidly read it and took notes from it in his journal. Although it came from the quarter in which he might have least anticipated it, this was the response to the book Marsh had looked for in 1829.

A group of letters survives to show that Marsh in fact mounted a campaign to prepare a favorable reception for a series of seventeenth-century religious treatises, including the works of Howe, More, Bates, Baxter, Leighton, and *Aids to Reflection* after Taylor's suppression of part of his review of Stuart. He solicited pre-publication support and advice from Archibald Alexander at Princeton, John Rice at Hampden-Sydney, and, after publication, asked for reviews and opinions from Francis Wayland, the President of Brown University, Leonard Woods at Andover, and a layman's opinion from Rufus Choate. Alexander's response to Marsh's proposal of what he seems at first to have conceived of as a series of volumes of seventeenth-century theological treatises, prominently including a full volume of Archbishop Leighton, has unfortunately not survived. But the editorial policy of anti-Idealism adopted by *The Biblical Repertory* with Alexander's son James and Charles Hodge as editors during the 1830s suggests what the elder Alexander might have said to Marsh. Rice, while he could give Marsh good practical advice, still saw little value in philosophical theology of any kind; Wayland was apparently sympathetic, but felt unqualified to comment publicly, as did Rufus Choate. Woods wrote a lengthy critique of Coleridge's ideas, finding them essentially threatening to Andoverian orthodoxy. He warned Marsh:

> *. . . if the peculiarities of [Coleridge's] metaphysical and religious opinions should ever take hold on the attention and feelings of ministers and students in general, and even of Presidents and Professors, as you seem to think desirable, I should look for consequences unutterably gloomy and dreadful.*[60]

Among his close friends, only Ebenezer Tracy could be helpful. Torrey and Wheeler were in Europe, where Wheeler became the only Vermont transcendentalist to see Coleridge plain. Tracy, who had not yet returned to Vermont to resume the editorship of *The Vermont Chronicle* at Bellows Falls, wrote from Andover to promise whatever help he could muster. He was compelled to remind Marsh, however, that support could not be expected from religious periodicals like Taylor's *Christian Spectator* or any of the literary quarterlies or reviews. Tracy wanted to write a review of *Aids to Reflection* for *The Christian Spectator*; but, as he pointed out to Marsh, Taylor and his followers "will be a little careful about publishing any other heresies than their own."[61] He passed some small encouragement on to Marsh by emphasizing that once *Aids* had "the attention of thinking men fixed on [Coleridge's] distinction between the reason and the understanding you will have done enough to reward the labor of a life."

As Tracy's letter implies, Marsh's purpose in republishing *Aids* was basically didactic, as it was intended for those "who wish for instruction, or assistance in the instruction of others" (*Aids*, viii). He knew, of course, that the book contained ideas inconsistent "with much that is taught and received in our theological circles. . . . and it may appear novel, stange, and unintelligible, or even dangerous in its tendency" (xi). He knew already from Nathaniel Taylor's reaction and would soon discover from Leonard Woods and Hodge, that forceful opposition would come, on one hand, from "those who, instead of *reflecting* deeply upon the first principles of truth in their own reason and conscience and in the word of God, are more accustomed to *speculate* . . ." and, on the other hand, from the theological school which "seeks that which will best comport with the simplicity of the gospel" (xii). Philosophy without religious feeling and religious zeal without philosophy were both symptoms of the dissociated sensibility. Only by properly comprehending the meaning of Reason and its superior relation to Understanding could the perfection of human unity be accomplished. Reason, moreover, can only realize itself or be fully conscious of its own nature by embodying its own principles in a reconstructed physical and social reality. Resisting the temptation to leave Reason to operate in the realm of pure speculation, and thus significantly modifying Kant, Marsh argued that Reason must terminate in action. To limit its operation to the realm of speculation or to ignore it altogether were perversions of Reason.[62]

The question of the Marsh–Coleridge relationship is interesting at this point because it shows how the native American mind of Marsh, indebted as it was to the New England heritage of ethical and theological concerns, turned to the new voices of Coleridge and Germany, first to Kant and then to

Tholuck, Fries, and others, in an effort to combat the then popular mixture of Lockean and common sense philosophy of materialism. In a letter to Lucia written in 1821, Marsh had made a remark that implied the central impulse of his thinking as it would eventually develop:

> . . . this *I know, that . . . such a devotion to the things of God and the things of an invisible future . . . are most rational in themselves.*

Coleridge's convictions that Christianity was a system of truth which is identical with the truth of philosophy itself, if only men would reflect and feel about it appropriately, was what appealed to Marsh in *Aids to Reflection*. And so, in 1829, he had come quickly to that same point in the early pages of the "Preliminary Essay": "Christian faith is the perfection of reason." Marsh frequently returned to this idea in his essay, always in conjunction with his other central idea that a thinking man "has and can have but one system in which his philosophy becomes religious and his religion philosophical." For Marsh, as for Coleridge, the truth of Christianity was essentially rational. In order to comprehend its rationality, however, modes of knowing must be distinguished by Reason and Understanding. Marsh does not clearly draw this distinction in the "Preliminary Essay" although he does refer to the terms as necessary for a full comprehension of human knowledge and action.

More than one student of nineteenth-century thought has wondered whether or not Marsh's source, Coleridge, was correctly drawing these distinctions, which he variously claimed were based on Kant and the Cambridge Platonists.[63] The precise relationship between the Cambridge idealists and the German transcendentalists is still an open question; but for Marsh, in the 1820s, the Germans had revived ideas that could be found in the writings of Archbishop Leighton, Henry More, and Bacon.

The accuracy of Marsh's interpretation of these terms is of some importance, then, in light of the role they played in his reorganization of Vermont's curriculum, his attempts at formulating an integration of religion and philosophy based on them, and the alacrity of Emerson and other transcendentalists in assimilating them into their own thinking.

Early on in the "Preliminary Essay" Marsh said that he hoped *Aids* would correct the then popular misconceptions of Reason. Owing to the prevalence of the philosophy of Locke, Reason "considered as a thing differing in kind from the understanding, has no place in our metaphysics. Thus we have only *understanding*, 'the faculty judging according to sense,' a faculty of abstracting and generalizing, of contrivance and forecast, as the highest of our intellectual powers." One of Marsh's objectives in introducing Coleridge to an American audience was "to direct the reader's attention to the science of words, their use and abuse, and the incalculable advantages attached to the habit of using them appropriately, and with a distinct knowledge of their primary, derivative and metaphysical senses."

In 1829 Marsh apparently believed that he understood Coleridge's distinction and saw its parallels in both Kant and "those profound thinkers and unrivalled masters of language, the great English Philosophers and Divines of the Seventeenth Century." Henry Pochmann has carefully examined Marsh's published literary remains and has shown how, in fact, Marsh, after a too heavy reliance on Coleridge's interpretation of Kant, then came to realize the dilemma facing him when he finally attempted to develop a psychology based on Kantian concepts of Understanding and Reason. The whole of Pochmann's analysis need not be recounted here, but certain points of it are important for indicating the direction of Marsh's thinking between the publication of *Aids to Reflection* and his death in 1842.

In his edition of Marsh's *Literary Remains* Joseph Torrey printed his friend's "Remarks on Psychology." The unfinished final chapter of "Psychology" reveals that Marsh's dilemma arose when he tried to define Reason and Understanding. Reason, he discovered, could be defined as either a kind of sophisticated Understanding or, because of problems in terminology, a kind of free intuition. Neither of these definitions would conform to Kant, he realized; and, by the mid-1830s, he also seems to have realized that Kantian terminology was inadequate for what he had to say. Pochmann believed that Marsh "found in the end the same insuperable chasm between matter and mind that Emerson was to discover when he sought to graft upon his essay on *Nature* another to be entitled Spirit."[64] However, no early nineteenth-century philosopher had a language adequate to Marsh's task. He had originally been drawn to Coleridge because of the Master's "habit of using them [terms] appropriately." Torrey said that Marsh waited "in hopes of deriving some assistance in respect to language from Coleridge's promised 'Elements of Discourse.'"[65]

In view of Marsh's personality, it would have been singular if he depended solely on Coleridge to supply a short cut to Kant, when he could have resumed his own first-hand study of the German idealist. But a letter to Ticknor in 1829, in which he asked the Harvard reformer to purchase for him in Boston a copy of Kant's *Vermischte Schriften*, suggests that Marsh was still working directly on Kant as late as perhaps even 1831. In 1832, Charles Follen urged Marsh to construct a psychology based on Carus and Fries. But Marsh must have discovered that Kant and Fries were irreconcilable. Coleridge died in 1834; and Kant, or at least Kant as Marsh tried to use him, finally failed to give him a way of validly establishing the three Christian ideas of God, immortality, and the free will, though Marsh continued to feel in his heart the truth of these three concepts.

Despite the dead end that he could have been drawn into by relying heavily on Kant and Coleridge, Marsh's correspondence and reading during the last few years before his death indicate that he continued seeking a synthesis of ideas and experience that would confirm his faith. Had he not died in 1842, the evidence suggests, he might have gone on to become not only the first prominent American investigator of Kantian thought, but also one of our first native critics of Hegel. Julian Lindsay first discovered in the early 1950s the evidence of Marsh's studies of Hegel, but never published the fact.[66] Three volumes of Hegel belonging to Marsh, with some marginal notations apparently in Marsh's script, survive in Marsh's library at UVM, waiting for the scholar who will piece them together with Marsh's acquaintance with Frederick Augustus Rauch's *Psychology*, the first book in English bearing that title and one used in courses at UVM during the 1840s.

Rauch had overcome the very problem that Marsh had found insurmountable in the late 1830s. He clearly distinguished Kant's Understanding and Reason and carefully employed a terminology suitable for explaining Hegel's ideas. Appearing in 1840, Rauch's *Psychology* could have been helpful to Marsh. Rauch said that his book was designed to "unite German and American mental philosophy" in a system of "Hegelian realism" that would "give the science of man direct bearing upon other sciences, and especially religion and theology."[67] Though the full extent of Marsh's connection with Rauch and Hegel's thought is presently difficult to determine, there is still the suggestion that Hegel, as the Christian philosopher might have interpreted him, could have played an important part in Marsh's unification of his Christian faith with a complete philosophical system.[68]

The implications of Marsh's thinking through a Kantian, and then a Coleridgean, definition of Reason as a basis for his theory and practice of education also become clear when we realize that Marsh, while preparing his edition of *Aids to Reflection* for the press, was also writing a series of articles on education for *The Vermont Chronicle* which outlined a reconstructive role for schools in society; had only recently completed the reorganization of UVM's curriculum on the basis of the distinction between Reason and Understanding and would revise it again in 1830–31; and in that same year sketched the outline of his theory of education in a sermon delivered at the dedication of the new chapel at UVM:

> . . . *the legitimate and immediate aim of education, in its true sense [Marsh said early in the sermon], is, not by the appliances of instruction and discipline to shape and fit the powers of the mind to this or that outward condition in the mechanism of civil society, but by means corresponding to their inherent nature, to excite, to encourage, and affectionately to aid* the free and perfect development of those powers themselves.[69]

Education, as Marsh saw it, was far from Gradgrind's utilitarian drilling into conformity. Indeed, he argued, if the sole purpose of education were to fit students for "success in the world, as merchants, for example or civil engineers, or as professional men, the results will be such a cultivation of their minds only as will . . . make their powers serviceable."[70] The point of the Dedication Sermon of 1830 suggests the actual end which Marsh's personal search for unity in Coleridge and the Germans ultimately served. He drew a comparison between the ostensibly admirable powers of the Understanding exhibited by great warriors and politicians like Napoleon and Talleyrand, on one hand, and a simple Yankee, doubtless a Vermonter, whose "powers of understanding are . . . but imperfectly cultivated, but who, instead of rushing eagerly and unreflectingly into the pursuits of worldly interest and ambition had turned his thoughts to the knowledge of himself; who has communed with his own heart and cherished the powers of reason and self-consciousness . . . he is the man in whom we recognize essential and inherent worth. In him we find unfolded the true and distinctive principles and character of our humanity."[71]

Marsh's most productive and publicly expressive years, from the mid-1820s to the mid-30s, were difficult times in America. The determinism of a Newtonian world-view only partially satisfied the intellectual and emotional needs of a people who had recently given birth to a form of government based on the principles of a free and self-governing community. At the dedication of the new chapel in 1830 Marsh outlined his idea of a university in such a society as being essentially an instrument of cultivating the community, by which he meant bringing to the fullest development the powers of the individual members of that self-governing community.

As some historians have recently and pointedly reminded us, at the advent of the Industrial Revolution, Americans floundered between the two worlds of the disappearing frontier and civilized progress, powerless to be reborn.[72] Their yearnings for a simple transcendent unity, as Charles Sanford has remarked, were expressed in government by the Monroe Doctrine, in the arts by the repeated use of the themes of a return to nature and antiquity, in religion by the revivalistic version of a new heaven and new earth. Yet they lived in a society experiencing the strains of a multiplicity of competing self-interests of the kind associated with Justice Marshall's decisions defining, like the Dartmouth Case, the sanctity of contracts and private property.

Marsh, like his world and time, was in need of an ideology that could give form to and ritualize a common world of experience, a community of experience; and he intensely and personally felt the need to be reborn into such a world from the crucial summer of 1815 onward. His turn to Kant and Coleridge was perfectly expressive of that need; and in Kant he could find an elaborate metaphysics showing how human knowledge of a world determined by the fixed laws of Newtonian physics might be compatible with human freedom.

Eighteen thirty, however, was the peak of the public period of his search to satisfy that need. During the '30s he would become intensely engaged in a debate within Vermont over the impropriety and theological weaknesses of the New Measure revivals led by Jedidiah Burchard. And in 1837–38 what he saw as mindless behaviour in his fellow Vermonters' responses to the Canadian Rebellion exercised his critical powers. But even with the help of the family of his father-in-law, James Wheelook, who came to live with him in Burlington shortly before Lucia's death in 1828, and his marriage to Lucia's sister Laura, who would also die in 1838 of tuberculosis, from the early '30s Marsh was seriously weakened by ill health. His control of the University's affairs waned soon after 1830, and the school again suffered financial troubles. Resigning the presidency in 1833 to his chosen successor, John Wheeler, he attempted to find a new position at some other college and was even offered professorships at Bowdoin and Dartmouth, as well as honorary degrees at Amherst and Columbia. But then he continued as professor of philosophy at UVM; after 1835, he may have even thought of moving to southern Ohio to found a cooperative community with Zenas Bliss, a former student, and David and Emily Read, his sister and brother-in-law, and others. His only publications in the 1830s were brief prefaces to Coleridge's *The Friend* and to his two-volume translation of Herder, a biographical introduction to his own one-volume selection of treatises by seventeenth-century English divines—promised subsequent volumes never appeared—and a translation of a German textbook of historical chronology. His letters frequently speak of lack of time and strength to complete the large projects suggested in his surviving lecture notes. Visits to Boston with Ticknor, Channing, and his other friends doubtless came as a relief from the rigors of life in Vermont. While still active and thoughtful in 1840–41, by June 1842 his weakened condition was so critical that rumors of his death reached New York City and one newspaper there published his obituary even before he died.[73] It was read to him on his deathbed at the home of his sister Emily Read in Colchester.

On the one-hundredth anniversary of the publication of *Aids to Reflection* in Burlington, John Dewey sensitively recognized in Marsh "a pure personality, gifted in scholarship, ever eager for more knowledge, who wished to use scholarship and philosophy to awaken his fellowmen to a sense of the possibilities that were theirs by right as men, and to quicken them to realize these possbilities in themselves." His transcendentalism, Dewey concluded, "is the outer form congenial in his day to that purpose. The underlying substance is a wistful aspiration for full and ordered living."[74] Well into the 1940s Dewey continued to gratefully admit that his own thinking had been formed as an undergraduate at the University of Vermont in the 1870s when Marsh's influence there was still discernible—and after being so formed had little changed. Herbert Schneider recollected in 1967 that he gave Dewey a copy of Coleridge's *Aids to Reflection* at a birthday party late in the philosopher's long life. Asked if Coleridge's book reminded him of anything, Dewey said, "Yes, I remember very well that this was our spiritual emancipation in Vermont. . . . This *Aids to Reflection*, in Marsh's edition, was my first bible . . . I never did change my religious views."[75] That Marsh has a place of importance in American intellectual history is thus glaringly apparent. These letters should aid in defining that place more precisely than it has been in the past.

1. Quoted in Thomas W. Reid, *The Life, Letters, and Friendships of Richard Monckton Milnes* (London, 1890), II, p. 432.
2. Samuel Taylor Coleridge, *Aids to Reflection, in the formation of a Manly Character, on the Several Grounds of Prudence, Morality, and Religion: illustrated by select passages from our elder divines, especially from Archbishop Leighton.* First American edition, from first London edition, with an appendix and illustrations from other works of the same author; together with a preliminary essay and additional notes by James Marsh (Burlington, Vermont: Chauncey Goodrich, 1829). Hereafter cited as *Aids to Reflection.*
3. For Emerson's references to Marsh and Coleridge see *The Journals and Miscellaneous Notebooks of Ralph Waldo Emerson*, ed. Alfred R. Ferguson (Cambridge, Mass., 1964), IV, p. 30; *The Letters of Ralph Waldo Emerson*, ed. Ralph L. Rusk (New York, 1939), I, pp. 412–13. H. C. Goddard's *Studies in New England Transcendentalism* (New York, 1908), p. 110, concisely records the acknowledgements by major figures in the Transcendentalist Movement of their debt to Coleridge: Channing "owed more [to Coleridge] than to the mind of any other philosophic thinker"; Alcott said that Coleridge "arrested him out of the Aristotelian-Platonic dilemma"; Parker "bore testimony to Coleridge's service to New England in helping emancipate enthralled minds"; Margaret Fuller said that Coleridge's benefit to the age was "as yet incalculable."

Henry Pochmann has argued that Emerson was not very much concerned with Coleridge until 1835. However, Ferguson's edition of *The Journals* contains evidence that as early as 1830 Emerson had been carefully reading *Aids to Reflection* in Marsh's edition (*Journals*, IV, 163–69).
4. *The Letters of Ralph Waldo Emerson*, ed. Rusk, I, p. 412.
5. James Eliot Cabot, *A Memoir of Ralph Waldo Emerson* (Boston, 1887), pp. 244–45.
6. F. H. Hedge, "Coleridge's Literary Character," *Christian Examiner*, 14 (1833), 108–29.
7. *An Exposition of the System of Instruction* . . . was revised in 1831.
8. Julian I. Lindsay, *Tradition Looks Forward: The University of Vermont, 1791–1904* (Burlington 1954), p. 138; see also J. I. Lindsay, "Coleridge and the University of Vermont," *Vermont Alumni Weekly*, 15 (1936), nos. 13–15.
9. George Ripley, ed., *Specimens of Foreign Standard Literature* (Boston, 1838–42).
10. Letter dated February 23, 1837.
11. Letter dated October 17, 1840.
12. Ibid.
13. Letter to Henry J. Raymond dated March 21, 1841.
14. A slightly distrustful sketch of the popularity and influence of Coleridge in American schools in the first half of the nineteenth century was Noah Porter's "Coleridge and His American Disciples," *Bibliotheca Sacra*, 4 (1847), 117–71. In 1842, however, Emerson recorded in his journal: "Edward Washburn told me that at Andover they sell whole shelvesful of Coleridge's

Aids to Reflection in a year" (VI, 266).
15. John Wheeler, *A Historical Discourse at the Celebration on the Occasion of the Semi-Centennial Anniversary of the University of Vermont, With an Account of the Proceedings at the Celebration* (Burlington, 1854), p. 117.
16. John Dewey, *Problems of Men* (New York, 1946), p. 364.
17. Perry Miller, *The Transcendentalists: An Anthology* (Cambridge, Mass., 1950), p. 8.
18. "Preliminary Essay," *Aids to Reflection*, p. xx.
19. Letter dated March 23, 1829. Other than letters owned by the Marsh family or contained in various libraries, Joseph Torrey's *The Remains of Rev. James Marsh, D.D., Late President and Professor of Moral and Intellectual Philosophy in the University of Vermont with a Memoir of His Life* (Boston, 1843) is the only extant source of biographical information on Marsh.
20. Samuel Gilman Brown, *The Life of Rufus Choate* (Boston, 1870), pp. 24–25.
21. *A Historical Discourse by Rev. John Wheeler, D.D. . . .*, p. 37. "The highest department, that of philosophy [i.e., Marsh's department] . . . should be . . . the oscillating nerve [to] connect the various studies, during the analytical instruction . . . ; and . . . the embosoming atmosphere, that should surround and interpenetrate the whole . . ." (p. 38).
22. *The Letters of Ralph Waldo Emerson*, I, p. 413.
23. See my "Transcendental Letters from George Ripley to James Marsh," *Emerson Society Quarterly*, 50 (1968), 20–24.
24. Lloyd D. Easton, *Hegel's First American Followers* (Athens, Ohio, 1966), p. 126.
25. "Many years ago, when I was beginning to work on the history of American philosophy, Dewey handed [me] a volume [*Remains*] with the remark, 'This was very important to me in my early days and is still worth reading'." Herbert W. Schneider, *John Dewey. A Talk Delivered by Professor Herbert W. Schneider in the Ira Allen Chapel, the University of Vermont, on October 26, 1949* (Typewritten Ms. The University of Vermont, 1949), p. 5.
26. On these and earlier years at Dartmouth, see Fred. Chase, *A History of Dartmouth College* (Cambridge, Mass., 1891).
27. Samuel Gilman Brown, *The Life of Rufus Choate* (Boston, 1870), p. 15.
28. Quoted in Russell B. Nye, *The Cultural Life of the New Nation, 1776–1830* (New York, 1960), p. 167.
29. William Parmelee Marsh, *The Descendants of President James Marsh . . .* (Typewritten Ms.: Winchester, Mass., 1941), p. 13.
30. Ms. letter from Washington Choate to Rufus Choate, November 4, 1820; Baker Library, Dartmouth College.
31. Letters from George Ticknor to Marsh, April 16, 1822, and to Leonard Marsh, April 27, 1822.
32. *The Descendants of President James Marsh*, p. 13.
33. Letter dated February 3, 1826.
34. Letter to Lucia Wheelock, December 1823, in Torrey, *Remains*, p. 67.
35. Torrey, *Remains*, p. 69.
36. Letter dated December 1820, in Torrey, *Remains*, pp. 34–35.

37. Letter dated September 1820, in Torrey, *Remains*, pp. 25–27.
38. Torrey, *Remains*, p. 26.
39. Lindsay, *Tradition Looks Forward*, pp. 150–65.
40. Letter to Henry J. Raymond, March 1, 1841.
41. Torrey, *Remains*, pp. 37–38.
42. Johann Joachim Bellerman, *Handbuch der biblischen Literatur*. Zweite vermehrte . . . Auflage. 4Thle (Erfurt, 1787–98).
43. Torrey, *Remains*, p. 18.
44. Ibid., p. 20.
45. Letter dated July 1, 1821, in Torrey, *Remains*, pp. 47–48.
46. Letter from Leonard Woods, Sr., January 11, 1830.
47. Letter dated October 6, 1822, Yale.
48. "Ancient and Modern Poetry," *The North American Review*, 22 (July 1822), 124.
49. Van Wyck Brooks, *The Flowering of New England* (New York, 1952), pp. 117–21.
50. "History of Intellectual Philosophy," *North American Review*, 29 (1829), 109 ff., and "*Sartor Resartus*," *North American Review*, 41 (1835), 454 ff., are good examples of Everett's witty hostility to philosophical Idealism.
51. Letter from Charles Hodge to Marsh, April 28, 1826.
52. Letter from Hodge to Marsh, November 22, 1830.
53. Norton published, under the title *Transcendentalism of the Germans and of Cousin and Its Influence on the Opinion in this Country* (Cambridge, Mass., 1840), a reprint of two articles by Alexander, Dod, and Hodge, from *The Biblical Repertory* of January 1839.
54. *Christian Examiner*, 38 (May 1835), 170.
55. On the "Great Taylorian Controversy," see Frank Hugh Foster, *A Genetic History of the New England Theology* (New York, 1907), pp. 369 ff.
56. Letter from Marsh to Joseph Torrey, who was then travelling in Europe, February 14, 1829: ". . . have used [*Aids*] much in reviewing Stuart, and have spoken of him in a note in terms which will seem extravagant to those who are not well acquainted with his worth."
57. Letter dated March 23, 1829.
58. Letter dated July 16, 1829.
59. "Review of Stuart on the Epistle to the Hebrews," *The Quarterly Christian Spectator*, 1 (1829), 122.
60. Letter dated January 11, 1830.
61. Letter dated October 28, 1829.
62. Kant's Practical Reason produces three postulates, God, freedom and immortality, which are necessary as conditions for true moral action. Marsh, like Coleridge, was interested in religious knowledge as well as principles of morality; and so, with Coleridge, he saw Reason as both cognitive *and* volitional. While functionally distinguishable, Practical and Pure Reason worked in harmony. The thrust of Marsh's educational practice was thus more Coleridgean than Kantian, in that it sought to develop or cultivate "undivided reason, neither merely speculative or more practical, but both in one" [Coleridge, *Statesman's Manual*, ed. W. G. T. Shedd (New York, 1884), p. 462].
63. Three of the more important studies on the Coleridge-Kant relationship are Rene Wellek's *Immanuel Kant in England* (Princeton, 1931), Alice D. Snyder's

Coleridge on Logic and Learning (New Haven, 1919), and Gian Orsini's *Coleridge and German Idealism* (Carbondale, Ill., 1969).

64. Henry Pochmann, *German Culture in America* (Madison, Wisc., 1957), p. 140.

65. Torrey, *Remains*, p. 118.

66. Hegel's *Encyclopadie der Philosophischen Wissenchaften* . . . , 2nd ed. (Heidelberg, 1827) and *Wissenschaft der Logik*, 2 vols. (Nurnberg, 1816) have been identified by Julian Lindsay as owned by Marsh but not in the collection of his books given by the Marsh family to UVM in 1944.

67. While in the 1830s Theodore Parker was probably the first native American really sympathetic to Hegel's ideas, Rauch, a German political refugee, was actually teaching them at Mercersburg Seminary and Marshall College in Pennsylvania. Hegel is said to have spoken English with Rauch.

68. Sometime after 1828 Marsh also became interested in the biblical scholarship of another of Hegel's followers, F. A. G. Tholuck. Marsh's library contains Tholuck's *Commentar zu dem Evangelie Johanis* (Hamburg, 1828) and *Blüthensammlung aus der morganländischen Mystik* (Berlin, 1825). John Dewey first drew attention to certain Hegelian features of Marsh's fragmented "Psychology" in 1941.

69. Torrey, *Remains*, p. 589.

70. Ibid., p. 590.

71. Ibid., p. 593. Marsh here also resembles another German who similarly developed from a Kantian base. Wilhelm von Humboldt founded his social and political precepts on the untranslatable German word "Bildung," by which he meant, like Marsh, the fullest, most harmonious development of the potentialities of the individual, the community, and the human race. Cf. Humboldt's *The Limits of Social Action*, trans. J. W. Burrow (Cambridge, 1970), Ch. II.

72. For example, see Charles L. Sanford, *Quest for America: 1810–1824* (New York, 1964), pp. vi-xxix, and, especially, his *The Quest for Paradise: Europe and the American Moral Imagination* (Urbana, Ill., 1961).

73. Marsh was said to have given his "characteristic smile" on the day before he died when a friend read to him his own obituary, entitled "Another Light Extinguished," from the June 1st number of *The New York Commercial Advertiser*.

74. Dewey's address at UVM in 1929 was published twice later: in *The Journal of the History of Ideas*, 2 (1941), and in *Problems of Men* (New York, 1946).

75. Corliss Lamont, *Dialogue on John Dewey* (New York, 1959), pp. 15–16.

A Young Romantic 1819–1826

James Marsh's first interest in Coleridge and German romanticism developed, he told Coleridge in 1829, during his post-graduate years as a tutor at Dartmouth College (1818–20) with his reading of Madame de Staël and the *Biographia Literaria*. At the same time he was, as the fragments of some surviving early letters show, reading Wordsworth and Byron. By late 1826 he had completed his ministerial studies at Andover Seminary (1822), published a long review-essay entitled "Ancient and Modern Poetry" in the *North American Review* (July, 1822) on George Ticknor's invitation, married Lucia Wheelock of Hanover, New Hampshire (1824), and translated J. G. von Herder's *The Spirit of Hebrew Poetry* for Princeton's *Biblical Repertory* (1826). He was then ready to carry the romantic message to the small impoverished northern New England college optimistically called the University of Vermont.

Text: *Remains*, pp. 24–25

[Dartmouth College]
[1819]

. . . you will soon be tired of him[1] as an example, but he seems to me to live more than other men. He has conceived a being in his imagination of stronger powers, of greater capacity for suffering and enjoying, than the race of mortals, and he has learned to live in him. "It is," he says,

"to create, and in creating live
A being more intense, that we endow
With form our fancy."[2]

How vastly does everything of a religious nature swell in importance, when connected in our minds with a being of such capacities as Byron seems to us to be! When I speak as I do of this author, I know you will not imagine that I can ever intend to approve his moral feelings, or commend the moral tenor of his works. But why should not the disciple of Christ feel as profoundly, and learn to express as energetically, the power of moral sentiment, as the poet or the infidel? It is this, that I aim at in my devotion to Byron. I love occasionally to hold communion with his spirit, and breathe its energy. It gives me new vigor, and I seem in reality to live a being more intense. . . .

1. Byron.
2. *Childe Harold's Pilgrimage*, Canto III, Stanza VI.

Text: *Remains*, pp. 41–42

[Andover]
[February 1821]

. . . There is in them[1] a power of thought that enlarges and strengthens the intellectual power, while it elevates the whole soul, and fixes it in calmer seats of moral strength. It is the poetry that, of all, I would prefer to make my habitual study. Nor would I study it as I used to study poetry, but with a direct practical purpose, to nurse my own faculties, to imbibe its spirit, to breath its purity, and recurring constantly to the Gospel, the still purer fountain from which it derives its characteristic excellencies, to form that exalted character which should be the aim of every christian. . . .

1. Torrey said that Marsh "had now, in a great measure, lost his admiration of Byron, and become attached to Wordsworth, and other poets of the same class" (*Remains*, p. 41). A list of household goods sold when Marsh left Hampden-Sydney includes a copy of Wordsworth's *Lyrical Ballads*. The effects of his reading in Wordsworth continued at least into his first years at UVM. The peroration of his *Inaugural Address* (1826) is capped with a quotation from the "Intimations" Ode ("truths that wake to perish never") which illustrates the goals of education as Marsh conceived them.

To George Ticknor[1]
Ms: Dartmouth

Andover
March 30, 1822

My dear Sir

I did not intend to trouble you again respecting the review[2] which you encouraged me to write till I should send it to you. But circumstances induce me to send you a line on the subject. I soon found after

I saw you that it would be impossible to prepare it for the number of Review[3] now coming out and so postponed it to more necessary business with the resolution to have it in season for the next. It is nearly ready and shall be sent to you in the course of a few days I think this week but a friend has suggested that as the editor is in no want of matter there may be some danger even now that it will be excluded from the next number.[4] If it should be thought worthy of admission at all as from your very flattering remarks upon the original MS. I hope it may be. It will be of some importance to me to publish it soon and I write to secure an admission so far as circumstances allow. I am aware that it cannot be done fully till the editor[5] has seen it and perhaps then would be an indelicacy in saying a word to him on the subject. Your former kindness has encouraged me to use this freedom and as I am unacquainted with the editor to request your interference if you should think it proper or likely to be serviceable. I intended to finish it before this but have been dipping into some of the original writers of the Middle Age[6] and made myself more labour than was perhaps necessary. I wished however to assure myself of the correctness of my views as far as possible and still more to do some justice to the flattering opinions of my friends and the kindness which permits me to subscribe myself,

Yours etc.
James Marsh

1. George Ticknor (1791–1871), Dartmouth Class of 1807, studied in Germany (1815–19), and was professor of French, Spanish, and belles lettres at Harvard (1819–25). His *History of Spanish Literature* (1849) was a long-standard text in Hispanic studies.

2. The full title of this review-essay was "Present literature in Italy: Art. VI. Intorno all' ingiustizia di alcuni giudizii letterarii Italiani. Discorso di Lodovico Arboria Gattinara di Breme, figlio." 8vo. Milano, 1816. [Running title: "Ancient and Modern Poetry"], *North American Review*, 22 (1822), 94–131.

Marsh's essay clearly demonstrated how extensively he had been reading since his years at Dartmouth. He draws on a wide variety of sources in historical scholarship. His reliance on the German scholars, Grimm, Eichhorn, Schlegel, and Mendelsohn, indicates a close familiarity with the most important schools of cultural history in Europe at the time. In addition, his reading in contemporary literature, including Byron,

Wordsworth, Coleridge, and Madame de Staël, as well as a knowledge of medieval love poetry, Dante, the *gestes* of Charlemagne, and, of course, the works of the early fathers and classical Greek and Roman writers, indicates a familiarity with ancient and modern literature almost amazing for a young man who had studied only at a very rustic Dartmouth and the conservative seminary at Andover where Moses Stuart's classes were suspected of heresy for using German biblical scholarship.

3. *The North American Review*.

4. A member of the editorial board in the 1820s, John Gallison, who was also a lawyer and a newspaper editor, recalled more than forty years later that the board met weekly in one of the member's rooms, decided on articles for the next number, and "solicited articles upon particular subjects from literary friends at a distance."

5. Edward Everett (1794–1865) was editor of *The North American Review* in 1822. Everett's appointment was made over the objections of Richard Henry Dana. Dana, who resigned in 1819 after Everett's appointment to the editor's chair, seems to have made few friends on the editorial board and among the *Review's* readers because he championed the new Romantic poetry which Marsh discusses in "Ancient and Modern Poetry."

6. Marsh refers to the following medieval texts in "Ancient and Modern Poetry": Dante, *Inferno*, Canto 3, line 17 (p. 96); Otfried, *Bib. Vet. Pat.*, tom. xvi, p. 764 (p. 126); Walafrid Strabo, "de Rebus Ecclistiasticis," *Bib. Vet. Pat.*, tom. xv, p. 194 (p. 127).

To George Ticknor
Ms: Dartmouth

Andover
April 5, 1822

My dear Sir

I return you at length the books, with which you have so long and obligingly favoured me, with many thanks for the use of them. You will find in the bundle the MS. very different from what it was and probably as different from your expectations of what it would be as it is from mine. I wrote the long introduction because I could think of no better way of introducing the author and the more abstract discussion that follows. I wished for an opportunity too to say something about the history of the controversy[1] and introduced larger extracts from Breme than I should have done partly to obtain this and partly to make some distinctions in the principles and opinions relating to the discussion. But with that part I was not after all very well satisfied and perhaps the extracts will seem to come in at last only by way of intersecture though I believe they all have some relation to this subject and aimed to insert them so as to preserve a connected train of thought. I might have translated them but as the discussion is one likely to interest only "Buchs-lebenmenschen"[2] I supposed the editor might choose to publish the original. In discussing the causes I adopted the arrangement which seemed likely to be most perspicuous though it occasions a little apparent repetition or at least a recurrence to similar views. It obliged me too to make less use of the former MS. than I had expected and this is in fact almost wholly new. Your own hints and the passage referred to in Mendelsohn led me to bring out more fully the institutions of the Middle Age.[3] It now seems to me the most interesting topic of the whole and I had found time and place to dwell more upon it. You will perceive I think at once that if there is any justice in the view I have taken it will admit of being extended much farther and that a rich field of illustration is opened. The general principles relating to the change in the relation of faith and imagination touched upon in the last page and once before was not stated in the former MS. and seems to me though I may be mistaken a very important one and founded in philosophy.[4] I have supported it though not in its whole extent by the opinions of Grimm and Schlegel.[5] This point too like the former seems to me to open a wide and interesting field but I could only touch upon them. I was unable to give the piece in its present limits all the unity I could have wished and am far from being satisfied with it as a whole. But I have no more time to devote to it and must send it as it is. I had intended to write more notes and references as I might easily have done, but have observed that few are usually published in the Review and it is perhaps best on the whole there should not be. I have only thrown in a few in haste to be disposed of as shall be thought proper of course. I have only to say in addition that I should be very glad to thank you in person for your goodness but for the present am too much employed to deliver it and can only enjoy the pleasure of again subscribing myself your much obliged

and humble servant
James Marsh

1. In "Ancient and Modern Poetry" Marsh discusses the opposing arguments in the eighteenth and ninteenth centuries' debate between classical and modern philosophies of art. Di Breme's discourse was itself concerned with defending modern romantics against classical partisans, especially the French. Marsh says that the controversy has become one in which "They whose ancestors, five or six centuries ago, arranged themselves with shield and spear under the banners of the emperor and the pope, now gird their loins, like Dominie Sampson, and engage in the classic and romantic war, for the rival claims of Homer and Ossian. . . . Where Dante was sentenced to be burned, his too exclusive admirer, Mad. de Staël was sentenced to be reviewed" (p. 98).

2. The editorial board of *The North American Review* and its contributors included some of Boston and New England's prominent *Buchslebenmenschen* in the 1820s: Nathan Hale, Richard Henry Dana, E. T. Channing, Dana's cousin and the brother of William Ellery Channing, and Jared Sparks, a Harvard tutor who became editor after Everett stepped down to seek election to Congress in 1823. Contributions to the number for July 1822, along with Marsh's, were articles on Rousseau's life and Mirabeau's speeches by Alexander Everett; a review of Sismondi's *Julia Severia* by Edward Everett; another review by Edward Everett of *Bracebridge Hall*; and William H. Gardiner's review of Cooper's *The Spy*. Yet Everett, whose reputation was as a scholar and orator, never really brought the *Review* anywhere near the quality of *The Edinburgh Review*, one of the journals it hoped to equal. Twenty years after Everett had given up the editorship, one of his less friendly readers remarked, "What a wonderful journal it might have been if only the poet Dana had been made editor back in 1820."

3. Mendelsohn had observed that Jewish rites and rituals served to communicate both religious feeling and meaning, a conclusion which Marsh similarly drew from his reading in medieval writers on Christian rite and ritual. Specifically, Marsh said, "They addressed the senses . . . carrying the imagination to objects of the other world" (p. 126). Marsh continued his exposition of the romantic defense of imagistic and picturesque aesthetics with further support from Mendelsohn: "We fatigue and refresh, instruct and amuse ourselves by writing. —The preacher does not converse with his church, he reads or declaims to them a written treatise. . . . All is dead letter with none of the spirit of living intercourse" (Mendelsohn, *Jerusalem oder ueberreligiose Macht und Judenthum*, p. 125; quoted on p. 126). The argument becomes a familiar one in the nineteenth century, appearing later in Arthur Hallam's neoromantic defense of Tennyson in 1831 and achieving its greatest effect in English and American poetic theory after William Butler Yeats had read Hallam's essay in the early 1890s.

4. Marsh traces the development of the modern sensibility to its sources in medieval Christianity. In an argument that would become familiar

in later nineteenth- and twentieth-century literary criticism, Marsh stated that medieval man lived poetry because his "faith was co-extensive with the world of [his] imagination, it had vastly more influence upon [his] feelings and actions" (p. 128). Though neither of the terms appear explicitly in this essay, Marsh is arguing in the direction of the romantic myth of a "dissociated sensibility" developing in western civilization after the Renaissance and, at another point in the essay, suggests the outlines of the theory of "objective correlatives," an idea he had found in Coleridge's *Biographia Literaria* and would develop further during the 1830s in his lectures on psychology. Both of these basically romantic ideas play important roles in Marsh's discussion of how the modern poetic sensibility has turned to an ultimately inward self for the material of literary expression.

5. He draws on Schlegel's *Poesie der Greichen* and Grimm's *Ueber de Entstehung der Altdeutschen Poesie und ihr Verhaltnis zu der Nordischen.*

From George Ticknor
Ms: JMC

Boston
April 16, 1822

My dear Sir

The Editors of the North American are very glad to have your Review and will print it next time. For myself, I do not think they have ever printed a better one.—They will, however, be obliged to you, if you will translate the Italian Extracts from di Breme: —that being a custom; and therefore, I should like to have you come in and call at my office and take it, as I have no means of sending it to you except the Coach. You will, of course, return it again soon. You will find a few alterations in it; but all, I believe, which they propose to make.

I have only told one of them your name, and shall keep you incognito, unless you authorize me to announce you.

Yours truly
Geo. Ticknor

To Leonard Marsh
Ms: JMC

New York
April 27, 1822

My dear Brother

After receiving the line which I sent to father

from Bridgeport you will be surprised to find me now in New York.[1] We arrived here on Friday after a fine ride. The approach to the city through Hell Gate is superior to any thing which I have met with in elegance and taste. The shores on both sides are lined with country seats richly ornamented and the water covered with vessels sailing in every direction. I have a lodging at present in Pearl Street and have spent most of my time in running over the city and in visiting the acquaintances I find here. I have letters to strangers but have not yet delivered them. The city is in many respects vastly superior to Boston and the interest much more various. But I soon become tired of seeing the outside of things however splendid they may be and would rather have an hour's conversation with a man of intelligence than see all the magnificence of Broadway.

I spent an hour or two in Eastburn's[2] bookstore on Saturday and was so fortunate as to engage him most of the time in conversation. He is a man of extensive reading and knows more of books I suspect than any other bookseller in the country. I called also on the converted Jew[3] with whom I became acquainted in Andover and went with him to the Synagogue of his deserted people. He was himself formerly a rabbi and as he stood by the reading desk observed it was the first time he had been there since he himself officiated. He is an interesting man of three or four and twenty and an ardent christian.

On leaving him I went to find Major Howard.[4] I met first with cousin Sarah with whom when she was a romping girl I used to ramble over the hills. I only recollect her from the family resemblance and when I introduced myself she was much surprised at the change which had taken place in her young gallant. She is no less altered in the most important respects yet no less interesting than when I loved her so much in my boyhood. We became old friends in a minute and I have seldom spent an hour more happily. She is all heart and soul—loves her husband, loves her children, and what is more prays for them all with a very ardent love for the religion which she would have them also enjoy. Such a sight is to me extremely interesting and I have never had higher notions of the happiness which a minister of the gospel *might* enjoy with his parishioners than from conversing with her. I felt I am sure for once that I would prefer it to any other which the world might afford. Her children are taught with great care and are beautiful girls. I believe you once mentioned to me your admiration of Julia. Major Howard I think too an interesting man though I have seen him but a few moments and suspect from some circumstances he is seriously disposed. The general state of religious feeling in the city is highly interesting and I shall hope to spend some time here with great profit, after I return from Philadelphia.

I shall go from here to Princeton tomorrow and go on to Philadelphia after a few days to return here by the middle of May so as to attend the meeting of the American Bible and the Jews Society. Jadownisky as it happens and a Mr. Stewart[5] formerly of Princeton and now devoted to the Sandwich Mission will go in the same stage. I have yet become acquainted with none of the clergymen of this place and thought it best to defer offering my letters till I return when I shall make a longer stay and have a better boarding house than at present. Maj. Howard and his family will then be boarding out in the house where they now live in State St.—by the battery, the very finest situation in the town and I shall go into the same house.

I shall write to some of you every week and tell you my progress in my travels though it is not to be expected that my journal will be vastly interesting. I have not learned the art of Sir John Carr[6] yet of finding poetry and all manner of interesting objects in my port folio. They hardly find their way to my head and are not apt to get out again when they do. Of this place you know as much I suppose as I can tell you. Hereafter I shall be on the terra incognita and when I return here shall try to find something more than appears at first view.

I had by the way a very pleasant visit to Boston and Cambridge and should inevitably become a Unitarian if the difference in the attentions which I received in the headquarters of the two sects could make me so. The Andover professors are the most ungentlemanlike and almost hoggish fellows that I ever met with. None of them except Dr. Murdock[7] ever ask a scholar to call on them or scarcely to sit down when they do call—at least that is the mode in which they have treated me. At Boston and Cambridge it is exactly opposite—Ticknor treats me with the most flattering attention and has even asked me to come and spend some time with him in his study. I called at Professor F. and Mr. Higginson[8] to whom with several other gentlemen I was introduced and treated with much attention. I do not consider it all as personally flattering but it shows the character of the men and most strongly contrasts with the manners of the Andover professors with whom indeed I have long been out of all patience, as have many of the most respectable of my brethren at Andover.

Of the review by the by which I had sent, Ticknor said it was the best that had appeared in the work and that Everett said that evidently he—Ticknor—wrote it as he did not suppose any one who had not been to Europe could know any thing of the subject of it. This is altogether more flattering than my own vanity would have suggested and must not be repeated out of the family as I would not be found circulating it myself. I have sent another piece to the Christian Disciple which I value nearly as much though it is a good deal shorter.[9]

Give my love to all our dear family and let me find a letter here from you when I return from Philadelphia. My health is much better than when I left Andover and I hope to find you all—and be found myself in good health and spirits in about six weeks. I must go to my old work of wearing out these stone pavements or my boots, so good morning—my friend is waiting.

Yours heartily
Jas. Marsh

1. After an arduous winter of studying and writing the article for *The North American Review*, Marsh travelled to Boston, New York, Princeton, and Philadelphia. While intended as a trip into the spring warmth of the middle Atlantic states in order to restore his health, Marsh's visits to Princeton and Philadelphia also established his relations with men, like the Alexanders and Hodge of Princeton Seminary, who would in the mid-1820s help him find employment and encourage him in his studies, but then become the harshest critics of his Coleridgean and German philosophical interests.

2. James Eastburn, the Broadway bookseller.

3. Bernard Jadownisky was

Nearly the same want of system prevailed in the other Colleges in the state. When a regular arrangement of classes and of studies was introduced so many difficulties arising from established habits and especially from the reluctance to study the language were found in the way that it was thought best to make some exception where the feelings of those concerned were very decided and thus the irregular class has been formed. The studies which they omit are generally the Greek and Latin and as a compensation in regard to time they attend the scientific studies of two classes. They are not candidates for a degree and have rather been considered a little remnant of the ancient chaos than as a part of the regular system having any specific organization. They are a monument of the entire neglect and disgrace into which the study of the classicks had fallen in the state and still I believe often do much injury individually by discouraging others who are engaged in their studies. As they are at present managed we find some difficulty also in conforming their studies to those of the regular classes so as to keep them constantly employed and we generally find them more in danger of becoming irregular in habits as well as studies than the other students. We consequently wish and advise all to take the regular course. I have been thinking however of late whether in adapting our system to the want of the country something more might not be made of this class of students and the course of studies which they usually call for arranged for a separate class. It would be attended I think with much perplexity at least unless we had more instructors than could be supported at present. In New England the demand would be supplied by a separate establishment like Partridge's Academy or the Rensselaer School or the Gardiner institution and here it probably will be by the University as soon as it becomes well organized and secures the confidence of the publick.[2] But the whole subject of education is attended with many more difficulties in the slave holding than in the free states and some of them of a nature that I much fear is incurable whatever system may be adopted. The young men have in most cases received so little early discipline that it requires all our skill and the most constant attention to keep them steadily engaged in the pursuit of any regular course of study and in the languages especially it is difficult to make them do more than is strictly required for the examination and for obtaining a degree. These we have succeeded in making very important in the eyes of the students and for two or three weeks previous to the publick examinations they voluntarily do their utmost and accomplish as much perhaps as in the whole term previously. I am myself well aware that our present plan admits of many improvements but such are the means and the materials put into our hands that improvements must be introduced gradually and in the mean time I hope we are accomplishing something worthy of our time and labour. But I beg your pardon for dwelling so much on the subject and will thank you after seeing our laws, studies etc. to suggest any thing that you think may be useful. Give most affectionate regards to Mrs. Ticknor and believe me with very high esteem yours always.

Jas. Marsh

1. Jonathan Peter Cushing (1793–1835) graduated from Dartmouth with Marsh in 1817. After studying law in New England, he left for the south to establish a practice. During a stopover in Richmond on the journey south, Cushing was persuaded to replace a tutor who had fallen ill at Hampden-Sydney and remained there until his death in 1835, serving as professor of chemistry from 1819 and seventh president after 1821.

2. Alden Partridge (1785–1854), Dartmouth Class of 1802, West Point Class of 1809, rose to acting administrator of the Military Academy at West Point before he was replaced by Sylvanus Thayer. Reputedly lax in his adminstration of the Academy, Partridge clashed with Thayer after being replaced by him, was court-martialed on charges of neglect, and resigned from the Army in 1818. Returning to Vermont in 1819, Partridge established the American Literary, Scientific, and Military Academy which, after a number of moves to Connecticut and back to Vermont, eventually became Norwich University.

Rensselaer Polytechnic Institute had been founded on November 5, 1824, by Stephen Van Rensselaer in Troy, New York, and took in its first students in January 1825. The Legislature of New York granted the school a charter in 1826.

John Sylvester Gardiner, rector of Trinity Church, Boston, prepared students for Harvard. Ticknor called him a good scholar and one of the best teachers in New England.

The first buildings at the University of Virginia were completed in 1824.

1819–1826 To George Ticknor
Ms: Dartmouth

Hampden-Sydney College
February 3, 1826

My dear Sir

I should at least have thanked you for your kindness in sending me your pamphlet[1] and the accompanying letter before now. But when I received them I delayed with the expectation of receiving in a few days the books which you ordered and of which I wished to give you some account. The books, however, proved at last to be only a smaller parcel ordered before and the delay has been prolonged from week to week till the present time. In the mean time I have not been unmindful of the pamphlet or uninterested in it and the subject of which it treats and hope it is not yet too late to express with propriety my congratulations that you have so far succeeded in your wishes for the reform of the University.[2] Publick opinion though blind and necessarily uninformed as to the System to be adopted yet reasonably demanded some change that should produce a more efficient application of the means of knowledge accumulated at Cambridge. The same demand as their means accumulate will be made of our other Colleges for I am convinced that with the present modes of instruction additional means will not be attended with such corresponding improvement as the publick will have a right to expect. Indeed for several years and nearly from the time of leaving College when I found myself compelled to begin again at the very foundation I have been fully convinced that very essential changes were necessary in our whole course of early instruction. In many cases I have no doubt the present system is rather an injury than a benefit to the scholar since it confirms and flatters with the appearance of learning many who if left more to themselves would sooner become their own teachers. I am glad as every unprejudiced friend of literature in the country must be that the effort to place Harvard, where considering its immense superiority in point of means it ought to be, foremost in such a course of improvement has at last been successful and hope the new system may be carried into practice in the spirit that has originated it. But it is hardly to be supposed and I presume was not expected by the friends of reform that all the benefits of it could be realised at once or that either instructions or pupils would at once fall into that practice of thorough analysis and bring their minds to that close and intimate intercourse with each other on which, as you remark I have no doubt with perfect justice, the beneficial results must after all depend. This indeed is comparatively easy in the abstract sciences and requires in an instructor only a clear head and a little practice. But in teaching languages, morals and metaphysics such thorough knowledge and analysis of the subjects, such clear perceptions of the relations not only of ideas but of words and withall so ready a tact in penetrating the mind of the scholar is necessary that I fear it will be long before our colleges are supplied with instructors who will realise in practise all that is reasonable in theory. In the languages especially, if I may judge from the little experience I have myself had, it will always be difficult in a College at least to give the habit of thoroughly analysing words and sentences and constructing them again, as in Thiersch's Grammatic[3] for example, to boys who have already learned at an Academy all which they suppose it necessary to know of these matters. Still I am convinced that there is no other method of teaching languages that will produce the characteristick results to be aimed at and as matters now are in this country it must be first done in our Colleges unless we had enough such men as your friends at Northampton[4] to do it at an earlier period. I hope the experiment at Cambridge will be thorough and effectual.

I am obliged to you for your flattering request of remarks on your pamphlet but shall venture nothing but my thanks for the instructions it gives me and my regret that it should have occasioned so unnecessarily a disturbance in your social and literary circle. So far as I understand the proceedings the memorialists[5] have great reason to be satisfied with yourself and others that they have been treated with so much delicacy before the publick. I have heard nothing by the way of another review and hope the dispute is amicably arranged; for though the establishment of another might call forth new talents I have some doubt whether, as a means of influencing publick sentiment through the country and giving a general impulse, as much would be accomplished just now by two rivals as by a combined support of that already so extensively circulated.

I have received within a few weeks Adelung's *Mithridates*,[6] Creuzer's *Symbolik*[7] and both works of Schoell.[8] His work on Greek Literature as you have undoubtedly learned has become wholly remodelled and instead of two volumes on Sacred and Profane has eight volumes on profane literature alone and from what I have seen of it am very glad of the change. The work of Schoell is all that I have yet received on your order. This by the way which you marked in your order at thirty sous a volume Cummings and Hilliard have charged to me for the Greek \$1.53 and the Latin \$1.30 a volume first cost and have added separate charges for duties, average changes and commissions bringing the whole cost of the two works to \$22.09. This I mention not by way of complaint but as evidence that our booksellers make us pay extravagant prices for our books from France and Germany without so large a tax to the importers. Besides I think their bills require explanation as the face of them leads us to suppose that we pay them only commissions. It would give me the greatest pleasure to have more frequent intercourse with you and shall not again delay so long to acknowledge your favours and assure you of respect with which I am etc. yours

J. Marsh

P.S. I have requested Cummings and Hilliard to refer to you for the editor of the last and best edition of Pindar in two volumes 8vo.[9] I could not recollect his name.

1. George Ticknor, *Remarks on Changes Lately Proposed or Adopted in Harvard University* (Boston, 1825).
2. Contrary to Marsh's understanding of events in Cambridge, Ticknor's success in reforming Harvard was limited to measures taken in his own department of modern languages.
3. Friedrich Wilhelm von Thiersch, *Griechische Grammatick, vorzuglich des homerischen Dialects . . .* Zweyte vielvermehrte . . . Auflage (Leipzig, 1818).
4. Marsh here refers to the Round Hill School in Northampton, Massachusetts, founded in 1823 by George Bancroft (1800–91), often justly called the "Father of American History," and Joseph Green Cogswell (1786–1871), who with Ticknor had all received their doctorates at Göttingen.
5. Objecting to Ticknor's proposal that resident Har-

vard faculty members not be appointed to the Corporation, Andrews Norton, Edward Everett and nine other members of the faculty presented a "Memorial" to the Corporation in 1824 in which they maintained their eligibility for the Corporation and deplored the erosion of their autonomy.
6. Johann Christoph Adelung, *Mithridates oder allgemeine Sprachenkunde mit dem Vater Unser als Sprachprobe in bey nah funf hundert Sprachen und Mundarten. . . .* mit wichtigen Beytragen zweyer grossen Sprachforscher forgesetzt von D. Johann Severin Vater (Berlin, 1817).
7. Georg Friedrich Creuzer, *Symbolik und Mythologie der alten Volker, besonders der Griechen* (Leipzig and Darmstadt, 1823).
8. Maxmillian Samson Friedrich Schoell, *Histoire de la Litterature Grecque profane, depuis son origine jusq'a la litterature grecque en occident*, 8 vols. (Paris, 1823–25). The two volumes on sacred and profane literature were published in 1813.
9. *Pindari Carmina et Fragmentu . . .* An annotated critical edition by C. D. Beckius, 2 vols. (Leipzig, 1811).

From Charles Hodge
Ms: UVM

Princeton
April 28, 1826

My dear Sir,

I feel indebted to you for your kind letter of the twenty-second. I have not had an opportunity of reading Herder's Briefe das Studium Theologie betreffend,[1] of which Staeudlin[2] speaks very favourably. I should prefer I think his direction for a three years course of study, or his Geist der hebraischen Poesie.[3] Perhaps the latter would be a useful work and more in accordance with the object of the Repertory.[4] Either however would be very gladly received, you can therefore follow your inclination or convenience on the subject, or take any thing else which you have deemed appropriate. I shall in making my arrangements for the next number allow for the twenty or so pages which you kindly promise. It is important the MS. should be in hand as soon as you can conveniently furnish it. If you should not be able to forward it to the General Assembly do not hesitate to inclose it to me by mail.

I have felt very much the force of your remarks as to the want of adaption of most of the German biblical writings to the state of things in this country and have therefore felt more at a loss for matter than I expected in contemplating the number of their productions. Your assistance in this business I shall highly prize.[5]

Will not your engagements permit your visiting this section of the country this spring. It would give me great pleasure to see you in Princeton. Whenever you may come this way I hope you will consider my house as your home. I feel much the need of the society of those who have cultivated the field which Providence has assigned me.

Very respectfully
Yours etc.
C. Hodge

1. Johann G. v. Herder, *Briefe, das Studium der Theologie . . .* (Frankfurt and Leipzig, 1790).
2. Karl Friedrich Staeudlin (1761–1826), German theologian at Göttingen (1790–1826).
3. Johann G. v. Herder, *Vom Geist der Ebraischen Poesie, Eine Anleitung fur die Liebhaber derselben, und der altesten Geschichte des menschlichen Geistes* (Dessau, 1782).
4. *The Biblical Repertory*, founded in 1825, was edited at various times by Hodge and the Alexanders and subsequently called *The Biblical Repertory* and *Princeton Review*, finally *The Princeton Review*.
5. Hodge went himself to Europe in 1826, staying there until 1828 to attend the lectures at Paris, Halle, and Berlin of De Sacy, Tholuck, Hengestenberg, and Neander.

From Charles Hodge
Ms: JMC

Princeton
July 22, 1826

My dear Sir

I ought perhaps long before this to have acknowledged the receipt of your communication for the Repertory,[1] for which I am much obliged to you.

I presume you mean to continue your translation which I shall be glad to insert as you may forward it. I would suggest however whether it be practicable to publish so extensive a work as that of Herder in this manner with sufficient expedition to render it interesting to the readers. I have observed that where the same work is continued from number to number in a periodical publication it becomes tiresome, merely because it takes away the novelty which all appear to expect in the complexion of each successive number. I have however no objection to your taking your own course—and printing

Herder—or any thing else you may wish to have inserted. I hope you will be able to send me a communication in season for the next Number. The sooner it is received the better.

Your communication amounts to twenty-six pages. I am therefore your debtor thirteen dollars, which I enclose.

Yours respectfully
C. Hodge

1. Marsh's translation of Herder's *The Spirit of Hebrew Poetry* was appearing serially in Hodge's *Biblical Repertory*, 2 (1826), 327–47, 506–45; 3, 429–44. Hodge attached a note to the second installment: "It is hardly necessary to remark, that in many of the speculations of the *Author*, neither the translator nor editor have any faith" (p. 545).

Educational Reformer 1826–1829

Marsh's Inaugural Address, delivered in October 1826 at Cottrill's Tavern in Montpelier and later published in Burlington, indicated the direction he planned to take in leading UVM out of a benighted Lockean and Scottish common-sense philosophical darkness into a clear spiritual vision of those "truths that wake to perish never." His curricular model was found in Coleridge, a debt to the English poet-philosopher acknowledged in surviving letters as well as the central ideas found in the proposal for reforms Marsh delivered to UVM's Board of Corporators on March 25, 1827.

Marsh conceived of the collegiate curriculum as an organic construct, each area of knowledge related in such a way that the student in his final year, especially through his philosophical studies, would achieve a comprehension of the meaning of nature and spirit, especially his own mind, which would allow him to enter the world a citizen and Christian prepared to meet the trials and difficulties the world presented as obstacles to both material and spiritual success. In Marsh's system, however, spiritual was more important than material success. With the death of his wife in 1828 and his father in 1829, spiritual consolations were necessary when worldly fortunes and happiness grew increasingly elusive.

From Ebenezer C. Tracy[1]
Ms: UVM

Bellows Falls, Vermont
December 24, 1826

My dear Marsh,

Your letter was most welcome not only as a token of your friendship but as indicating what I may hope for hereafter. I am indeed anxious on the subject of education in our State, and with your assistance shall not despair of bringing about something important within a year or two. The appointment of a Board of Education at the next Session of the Legislature may perhaps be secured, tho' it will require much writing to prepare the public mind for the organization of such a body with the requisite powers.[2] I supposed at one time that measures would be taken at the late session that would terminate in the accomplishment of this object. The plan was to have a committee appointed by the two houses to make inquiries on the subject of schools and report at the next session. This committee would have been so constituted as to secure an able report and it was hoped the formation of a Board. I suggested it to Mr. Hall,[3] of this place, and Wheeler[4] conversed with a number of the leading men at Montpelier. But I believe the members of the Council[5] were neglected, and therefore refused to concur in the resolution introduced into the House by Mr. Hall, and adopted then without opposition. I was in favor of appointing a committee of inquiry as a preliminary step because I supposed our wise legislators in general knew too little about the matter to adopt any more definite measures. Now, however, with the year before us we may, I should think, aim directly at obtaining the organization of a Board with good hope of success. But the subject must be kept constantly up, and be fully discussed, or no impression will be made on the mass of ignorance and worldliness that must be gained over to the cause before any thing can be done. I shall be glad to make it a very prominent subject of discussion through the year, and if you will begin, I think Torrey[6] and Wheeler will follow, and I know brother Joseph[7] will be glad to assist. Some of the Middlebury folks will say something, and I will "put in a word" from time to time as occasion may demand. If by such means any thing can be done towards securing for Vermont the blessings and the honor of presenting her common school system as a model to surrounding states, I shall rejoice in having established the Chronicle at whatever personal sacrifice. Pray write therefore as soon and as often as your duties will permit.[8]

It would indeed be pleasant to me to be near you, but I have not hope of it for the present. The jealousy of my Middlebury friends is very easily excited as I have already had experience. And I cannot live without their co-operation.

I have talked with our friend Chase[9] about the professorship. He is not disposed to favor any such attempt because your College is under the control of the state and therefore he thinks too much exposed to changes and because Episcopalians should take care of their own institutions. Perhaps you know that they are becoming more exclusive in their policy. Throughout this state they are anxious to do what they can to build up their College at Hartford, Connecticut.[10] They would be glad to have a professor at Burlington but it should be they think at the expense of *dissenters*. I must say that I am not pleased with the course pursued by that denomination. If they were as liberal as I once thought the great body of them I would not say a word, but they are assuming if I do not greatly mistake a higher tone, and after all that they may say I do not believe their policy congenial to our institutions or calculated to promote the best interests of Christianity. I am a Congregationalist, heart and soul.

I wait with some impatience for your address.[11] As for the Chronicle you will see that I do not make it just what I would. I am obliged to consult in some degree the taste of others. And then I have so much business to attend to that I cannot devote myself to the editorship as I wish. I hope an increased subscription will enable me ere long to procure assistance in the business part of the concern, and to take some other measures for its improvement.

Yours truly
E. C. Tracy

1. Ebenezer Carter Tracy (1796–1867), Dartmouth Class of 1819, Andover 1823, in 1826 was editor of *The Vermont Chronicle*, a weekly newspaper which had been originally established under the direction of the General Convention of the Congregational Churches of Vermont.

Marsh had moved back to Vermont in October to assume the presidency of UVM.

2. In 1827 the State of Vermont created a Board of Commissioners on Common Schools, though by 1828 the Board reported that there was little hope of it becoming effectual. An authentic Board of Education was not established until 1856 when Calvin Pease, then president of UVM, served as one of the three members appointed by the Governor.

3. C. F. Hall, an active citizen of Bellows Falls, would eventually help to establish the first Congregational church in that Connecticut River Valley town in 1850.

4. John Wheeler (1798–1862), Dartmouth Class of 1816 and Andover 1819, was pastor of the Congregational Church in Windsor, Vermont (1821–33), before succeeding Marsh

as president of UVM.
5. The Governor's Council was abolished by a Constitutional Convention in 1836 and replaced by a Senate.
6. Joseph Torrey (1797–1867), Dartmouth Class of 1816 and Andover 1819, was pastor of the Congregational Church in Royalton, Vermont, in 1826. Marsh persuaded him in 1827 to join the faculty at UVM as professor of Latin and Greek. He succeeded Marsh as professor of moral and intellectual philosophy (1842–67) and served as president from 1862 to 1866.
7. Joseph Tracy (1794–1874), Dartmouth Class of 1814, served as pastor at West Fairlee, Vermont, until 1829, then at Hartford, Vermont. Like his brother Ebenezer, Joseph Tracy at various times edited *The Vermont Chronicle* and *The Boston Recorder*.
8. Marsh wrote a series of articles for *The Vermont Chronicle* on common school education using the pen-name Philopolis: "Popular Education," *The Vermont Chronicle*, 4: nos. 3, 4, 6, 8, 9, 11, 12, 14, 16 (January 16–April 17, 1829).
9. Carlton Chase (1794–1870), first Episcopal bishop of New Hampshire, Dartmouth Class of 1817 with Marsh, was rector of the Episcopal church of Bellows Falls, Vermont (1820–44).
10. Trinity College.
11. Marsh's *Inaugural Address* (Burlington, 1826).

To the Corporation of the University of Vermont
Ms: UVM

[Burlington]
[March 25, 1827][1]

In presenting to the Corporation their views on the subject of reform in our system of Collegiate instruction the Faculty do not think it necessary to occupy much time in preliminary remarks or in minute details. We merely observe that it seems to be very generally agreed among men of intelligence in the country that reform is necessary and our own convictions fully coincide with the prevailing sentiment. Speculation on the subject has for a considerable period occupied a large space in our Literary Journals and reforms have been projected and are going into effect in some very important institutions. Other institutions also designed to supply the deficiency of our Colleges are fast rising into popular favour and the time seems to have arrived for trying the merits of that system of instruction which has so long and so uniformly prevailed in the Colleges of this country. We have been the more forward to offer our thoughts on the subject at this early period from the consideration that if a reform be expedient on more general grounds the present circumstances of the institution render it desirable that it should take place immediately. But omitting other considerations of this sort we will proceed to give in as few words as possible our own reasons for wishing a reform and our views of the system which should be adopted.

1) The existing system as it is carried into effect in our Colleges is too limited and too inflexible to meet the wants of the public. In a community where the field of enterprise is so extensive and the pursuits of life so various as in ours and when the practical value of knowledge and intellectual improvement is so much felt as it now is among all classes of men it is not to be expected that all will be satisfied with the same unvarying system of instruction. Admitting even the principle as we are disposed to do that the business of education is not so much to impart a stock of knowledge as to prepare the mind for its reception still it must be admitted too that our best systems do not give a full development of all the capacities of the mind and while every system must be acknowledged to be but partial in its effect and no one course of preparatory discipline will fit the mind alike for all the various pursuits of life it is at least supposable that the previous discipline best suited to the minds of men in one profession may not be so for those of men in employments entirely diverse. The conclusion seems to be pretty well established that our Colleges must provide instruction better suited than the present system to cultivate the minds of young men designed for other employments than those of the learned professions or their instruction will be provided for by the establishment of other institutions.

2) We do not think the system at present pursued in our Colleges as practical and efficient as it should be, considered merely as a system of discipline and in relation to the purposes for which it is more specifically designed. Practically there is far too little of actual teaching and too much is left to depend on the text book. The scholar for the most part is required merely to exercise his talents in apprehending the ideas of others instead of having his mind brought in contact with those of his instructors and freely employing his own powers of thought and judgment in the various methods which a proper system of discipline would require. There

is not enough of free and familiar discussion and of the actual trial of the scholar's powers to give the habit of applying them with promptitude and effect in the business of life and to impart that practical knowledge of one's own resources which is so important.

3) From the manner in which scholars are classed and some other circumstances connected with it in the established system we think there are evils arising which ought to be remedied. In the usual application of the system students have little intercourse in the pursuit of their studies except with the members of their own class. The distinctions that are made and observed by students are all relative merely and concern only the members of the same class. Consequently the highest standard of scholarship which has any practical effect in awakening the attention of the student (especially as the intercourse of the instructors is not such as to give them any influence as examples for their pupils) is to be found in each class for its own members and that too under such circumstances as more frequently to awaken feelings of envy than of emulation. The consequence is that in most cases all the precepts of the instructor to the contrary notwithstanding the highest aim of the student is low and he fails to form any correct apprehension of the object which he ought to aim at and which alone could call into exercise the latent powers of his mind. True, other examples and other ideas of excellence may sometimes have their influence than such as would be obtained by merely comparing themselves among themselves but they are accidental and do not result from the system itself.

4) Both in the progress and in its termination the course in the established system has too much the appearance of a predetermined and established routine to have the proper effect upon his mind. In the practise of our Colleges a degree has been so seldom refused to a scholar who has resided at College the usual period that its attainment is looked upon as entirely a matter of course and all the methods by which the merits and attainments of students are designated are so indefinite and imperfect as to influence them ordinarily but little and many of them not at all to any useful purpose.

knowledge of himself. We awaken the latent principles of his being into conscious existence. But the question occurs whether this being the primary object we may not in accomplishing it at the same time promote a subordinate purpose and whether we may not while pursuing the primary object with equal success indulge our scholars in some variety in regard to the secondary. It is admitted for example that the critical study of language is useful as a mental discipline. The scholar who is aiming at professional life by studying Latin and Greek for this purpose acquires at the same time a valuable subsidiary of a practical kind in the business of his future life. Might not one who is aiming at a different employment accomplish the purposes of mental discipline equally well and attain a secondary object of practical benefit to him also by a critical study of German or another modern language? This example is offered merely for illustration and may be applied also to different departments of science and though we would be the last to narrow in any respect the circle of studies which are designed and calculated to accomplish the great ends of education we are disposed to think that more scope may safely be allowed in the choice of those particular studies which are to be used as the means of it. While we would encourage too every young man whose means will admit of it especially if he be of promising talents, by every motive in our power to carry forward the work of self development much farther than is effected by our best systems of public instruction we fear that some evils result to society from the idea of comparative imperfection attached to every thing short of the attainment of a degree. The evils we apprehend arise from the notion that in a College education as it is conducted there is something definite and perfect compared with which every thing short of it is of no value and that consequently where there is not a prospect of obtaining the whole and receiving a degree many young men are discouraged from attempting any thing for their own improvement. The proper system for a community like ours we think should hold out encouragement and furnish means for improvement to all just so far as they have the power to avail themselves of them and should give them praise according to their progress whether more or less. Its comparative perfection as to its form would consist not in the degree of cultivation which it ultimately secured but as remarked before in the rapidity and thoroughness of its effects upon all the subjects of its influence. As to perfection in attaining the end of education we all know that it is beyond the reach of human devices. In regard to that we are scholars not at College only but in the world. The schoolboy is only in a class below his instructor and the highest cultivation attained in this world but imperfectly reveals the mysteries of our moral being. If these remarks be well founded perhaps the account above given of the best system of education should be modified especially in relation to those who have but little time to spare from the practical duties of life by a more specific regard to its secondary objects though we could by no means admit that a mere preparation for the active employments of society is the highest aim of education or that its utility is to be measured by the degree of its subserviency to our worldly interests.

But to use language somewhat less abstract and to apply our principle we would say that in regard to morals and the formation of character that is not necessarily the best system which secures the most minute and strict observance of College rules or even the external requisitions of morality but that which most effectually unfolds and exercises correct principles of action in the mind of the individual scholar. The virtue which is practised from a love of it and from the dictate of a growing moral principle is of more value than that which proceeds from a fear of College censures. The one affords permanent security for the future character of the individual the other may leave him exposed to temptation which he has no means of resisting the moment he ceases to feel his accustomed restraints. Nearly the same remark may be applied to every department of intellectual cultivation. The mind whose powers by whatever course of study are thoroughly awakened and exercised in the proper manner is prepared to act with promptitude in every emergency and can readily acquire the particular knowledge necessary in the peculiar circumstances in which it may be placed. The scholar for example who has successfully cultivated his reasoning powers and accustomed himself to the independent exercise of his own judgment in the use of them will be able to reason correctly whether at the bar or in the Senate, but he who has merely learned Euclid without studying for himself and putting in practise the principles of reasoning may be lost the moment he traverses beyond the book and in the practical duties of life may show himself a dunce. So the scholar who has studied as he should do the principles of language whether in learning Greek and Latin or some of the modern languages may with little loss of time apply them to the acquisition of a particular language sufficiently for all the practical purposes without studying general principles has nearly the same labour to repeat in learning another. To develope and cherish then those great principles and to fix those habits of conduct which are to form the character of the student in his future intercourse with the world and to call into vigorous and habitual exercise those powers of judgment of reason and invention which are the elements of intellectual power and at the same time to cultivate the graces of taste and feeling with habits of promptitude in the use of all the powers of the mind while in doing all this we employ as instruments those departments of knowledge which will in themselves be of the most practical utility to the different classes of students under our care are the objects at which we would aim.

For accomplishing we hope somewhat more fully these objects though we are aware that the system both in theory and practise will still be far from anything like ideal perfection we propose the following modifications of the existing course to the consideration of the Board.

1) We propose to render the mode of government more entirely parental and to confine ourselves exclusively to the exertion of moral and social influence. Where these fail of producing the desired effect and of awakening a spirit of improvement instead of resorting to the infliction of penalties and disgrace for the purpose of coercion we would prefer simply to exclude the individual from the enjoyment of his privileges and if a minor return him to his parents or guardians.

2) Under such regulations as may be detailed in the laws of the University we would admit to the enjoyment of its privileges those whose necessities

or whose purposes of future employment would limit their studies to a part only of the general course with the view of extending such advantages for improvement as we can offer to a class of young men who now are discouraged from attempting even a partial education beyond the elements of knowledge. Such students might for the most part be associated in the same class and would in other respects be subject to the same regulations as those pursuing the general course of study.

3) While for obvious reasons we retain the important characteristic of our Colleges, the practise of conferring degrees in the arts, we would endeavour to render them, especially the first, an index of a definite degree of mental cultivation and of a fixed amount of scholarlike attainments. For this purpose we would prescribe as usual requisitions for entrance and a general course of such studies as are considered best fitted for the purposes of mental discipline and at the same time of practical utility and nearly corresponding in amount with the general requisitions for the first degree in our most respectable Colleges. Such a course we believe may be easily accomplished by scholars of ordinary talents in the usual period of four years and this feature of the established course we think may be retained consistently with the objects at which we are aiming since we do not confine all who enter to the pursuits of the general course and the attainment of a degree nor limit those who do pursue it to the studies which it includes.

4) In classing the students for the convenient and successful pursuit of their studies and for giving efficacy to their instruction during their residence at the University we propose to free ourselves from the restraints of the established system and arrange them on purely practical principles at least so far as our time and limited number of instructors will permit us to carry such a system into effect. In pursuing a particular department of study we would divide the students into such classes and sections as their previous qualifications and the rapidity of their progress seemed to demand and transfer them on examination from one section or class to another when circumstances rendered it necessary for the better prosecution of their studies. Those who in pursuing the prescribed course showed themselves

able and disposed to do more than to accomplish that to the satisfaction of the faculty should be encouraged and assisted to pursue other additional studies which they should have the privilege of selecting subject to the advice and discretion of the faculty.

5) We propose to have all designations of rank of scholarship proceed on the absolute instead of the relative merit of the student. Instead of giving appointments to a part of a class only according to their relative standing we would on a close examination designate the positive improvement and merit of each by appropriate marks which at the close of the annual examination should be published in the annual catalogue of the University. Those who on leaving the University wished and were qualified for any other public designation of scholarship than the usual degree whether lower or higher than that should on examination be entitled to receive a certificate to that effect with the College Seal. The exercises for public exhibitions and commencements might be provided for in a different and more eligible method by the laws of the University.

In presenting this plan as the result of our reflections we do not venture to flatter ourselves that it is the best that could be devised nor do we expect or even wish the Corporation to sanction it immediately. We feel it to be a measure in which the interests of the institution are very much concerned and are by no means anxious to hasten its adoption. Of the wisdom of the plan as a theory as well as of our ability to carry it into successful effect in practise we wish the Board to judge and are anxious only that reform if necessary should be effected in the manner most beneficial to the University and to the interests of education among us.

1. The date of this proposal to the Corporation of UVM is recorded in the Corporation's Minutes of the first meeting Marsh attended after his inauguration as president.

To the Corporation of UVM[1]
Ms: UVM

Burlington
August 5, 1828

The general method pursued both in the instruction and government of the University during the past year has been, so far as circumstances would permit, conformed to the system contemplated in the By laws adopted at the last annual meeting of the Corporation. Instruction has been given chiefly by recitation with the use of textbooks, retaining for the most part the usual division into four classes, but varying from it and subdividing the classes whenever circumstances require it. In the class of textbooks, we have made less improvements than we had hoped from the difficulty of procuring in season those which we had intended to use. In the use of textbooks we hope the results of examination will show that they have not been abused, but only used as subsidiary to a better understanding of the subject of which they treat. Lectures have been given in chemistry and natural philosophy and a course commenced in the History of Greek and Roman Literature. In the statement of the number of recitations which follows, the whole number attended by any one class, has been included as in some instances different classes have been heard in the same subject. In the Department of English Literature, exercises in public speaking have been exhibited once every four weeks, consisting of original productions from the upper classes, and selected pieces from the lower. Forensic discussions were, on the same occasions, exhibited by members of the higher classes. Besides the public exercises of this nature frequent lessons have been given in speaking during a great part of the year in the method of familiar drilling by a single instructor.

1. Recitations in Rhetoric, 20. Textbook, Jamieson and Campbell.
2. Department of Languages. Roman Antiquities, 14. Adam's *Roman Antiquities.*
   Greek and Latin Languages, 504. Livy, Horace, Tacitus, Cicero, and as other authors could not be procured in season, *Graeca Majora.*
   French Language, 126. Luizac, Fenelon.
   Whole number, 644.
3. Department of Mathematics and Physics.
   Geography, 16. Woodbridge.
   Algebra and Geometry, 217. Lacroix and Legendre. Arithmetic Geometry, Spherics and Topograph, 133. Euler and Bezout.
   Mechanics, Optic, Astronomy, 60. Biot,

Poisson, Whewell, etc.
Differential and Integral Calculus, 37. Bezout.
Philosophy of Natural History, 11. Smellie.
Whole number, 590.
Chemistry and Natural Philosophy, 84. Lectures with daily examinations.

4. Department of Political and Moral Philosophy.
Political Economy, 61.
Politics, 16.
Natural and Revealed Religion, 21.
Logic, 10. Metaphysics and Ethics, 65. Whole, 173.

The time alloted for recitation has been the morning before breakfast and time immediately preceding evening prayers, during most of the year two hours each. This time has not at all times been fully occupied, but in most instances, from one to two hours have been employed morning and evening. A class has been formed of such as chose to join it for Biblical exercise on the Sabbath attended by about one half of the whole number and also a small class in Spanish, both instructed by Professor Torrey. In carrying into effect the system of instruction and discipline adopted at the last annual meeting, we have thus far much reason to be satisfied with the results and anticipate with confidence still better success when circumstances and more experience shall put it in our power to give it a more full development in practice. Some few students have been received in the prosecution of a partial course of study and there is reason to suppose that many will avail themselves of the privileges thus offered.

James Marsh, President

1. This letter was also published in J. I. Lindsay, *Tradition Looks Forward. The University of Vermont: A History, 1791–1804* (Burlington, 1954), pp. 273–74.

To Joseph Torrey
Ms: UVM

Burlington
February 14, 1829

My dear Torrey

I received your letter three or four days ago and take the first leisure moment to write you an answer.

My thoughts and feelings were so much occupied when you left us and for a long time after with that event which seemed to have left me alone in the world that I could not pay that attention to your plans or avail myself of them for promoting the interests of the University to the extent that I should otherwise have done.[1] I am glad notwithstanding as we all are both for your sake and our own that you are enjoying the privileges and feeling the impulses of life and power *intensified* as they are in Paris. We hope to enjoy some of the pleasure and much of the benefit of the experience and knowledge which you are acquiring in the halls of the Sorbonne and breathing the "Spiritualism" of Cousin.[2] It is exceedingly gratifying by the way to us who had learned to distinguish and admire the "Romantic" and Madame de Staël to learn that her school is carrying all the world after them in the very spot where Richelieu and the Academy promulgated and enforced the laws which crushed Corneille and spoiled Racine.[3] But I can interest you more by talking about Burlington than about Paris. There are some things too in Burlington which you will rather hear from a neighbour of ours than from me and I shall therefore proceed at once to tell you what we have done and are doing for and in the University. In the first place then I succeeded in getting the charter so altered that the Corporation hold their seats permanently and fill vacancies themselves when they please with power to increase the present number or suffer it to diminish. This is a great gain as it is and would have been greater had not the legislature tacked on a "provided" they should have the power to change back again if they choose. In the next place we have a fine Medical building so far completed that a part of the lectures were given last fall by our own new lecturer, Dr. Lincoln,[4] a very enterprising, promising, and agreeable young man who promises to stay with us and will be a great acquisition on every account. He will take up his residence here. We had a Medical class of forty and the prospects for the future better still. The foundation of the *center building* is laid up to the brick work, the brick partly on the spot and the remainder purchased for proceeding in the Spring. The outside will be completed before commencement. Mr. Huntington[5] proves to be a very excellent instructor and a promising scholar and there is already a full understanding among us that he is to be permanently fixed here in connexion with the mathematical department. Allen[6] too does remarkably well so far, better than Foot[7] did and will very probably be retained in connexion with your department. Our number of students is the same as last year[8] but they are taking higher ground in scholarship and several are preparing for examination on an extensive course of study in your department[9] beyond the regular course. I should have mentioned too that we have a commission appointed by the Governor and Council to attend the annual examination and report to the Legislature.

I gave, myself, several lectures in the fall of a practical character and in the Spring shall continue them on subjects calculated to be practically useful to all the students such as employment of time, use of books, modes of study etc. I hope too to be able to prepare some few lectures on Metaphysics and must beg you to procure for me the lectures of Cousin[10] and other things which may be useful to me. During the winter we have been engaged in various matters which I hope may indirectly benefit the University. We have kept up with some help from others a series of essays in the papers here on the subject of intemperance which I hope is doing some good and I have myself written more or less for the Chronicle[11] about every week for eight or ten weeks. I am now engaged in a series of essays on Popular Education in which I am taking an extensive view of the subject in all its relations. Three numbers have appeared and I believe it is attracting some interest. I have just finished too an elaborate review of Professor Stuart's Commentary on Hebrews of about forty pages written for the Christian Spectator and at the request of its editors.[12] I have had the hardihood, while I compliment the Professor very highly, to differ from him very widely on some important points and to exhibit the general view of redemption which Coleridge has given in his "Aids to Reflection." I am convinced of its truth and have not considered much the consequences to myself of advancing it. I have, however, so guarded it that I think no exceptions can be taken by the theologians though it bears hard upon the followers of Dr. Owen.[13] Professor Benedict is giving lectures on Electricity to a crowded audience at Goulds Hotel[14] and we are preparing the way for getting up a Lyceum among the people of the town. We think with pretty good prospects of success. I hope by the way you will take such notes as will prepare you to give a course of lectures to the people of the town here such as shall interest and instruct them. We are going to make them more cultivated and thereby better friends to the University. Mr. Smith is still here but movements are in the progress which must terminate in his dismissal soon.[15] We hope it may be without the ruin of the church and society but they are in a bad condition.

As to money I am sorry to say I cannot tell you as definitely as I could wish what you are to depend upon. I have commenced a subscription of two thousand five hundred dollars for you to appropriate and hope to make it up during the remainder of the vacation. There were a few hundred dollars appropriated by the Board to such objects that have not yet been applied and I hope to send you at least three thousand dollars. Mr. Benedict is going to New York the last of March to raise a subscription for other objects and I hope we may be so successful as to have some to spare for this.

I wish in the meantime you have an eye to such objects [. . .][16] cannot so well be gotten or so cheap by order. We wish to furnish the rooms in the new buildings you recollect with *helps* particularly [. . .] departments for the use of all the students and you will probably [. . .] up various matters illustrative of the classics without much expense [. . .] same time such as could not be obtained by order. I think [. . .] means of advancing it between you may be making [. . .] opportunities offer to the amount of several hundred or [. . .] on our responsibility without hazard. I shall write you again [. . .] forward a handsome sum of money when Mr. Benedict goes to New York [. . .] shall devote myself chiefly to this business for the remainder of [. . . .] As to the appropriation of money we must leave it almost wholly to the judgment of yourself and Brother Wheeler.[17] You can judge as well as I can what will be most valuable in my department and know what we already have. I beg you to write often to give us information and impulse. See and converse with the literary and scientific men and philosophers, they are the true objects of interest as you need not be told, tell us their views of things as exhibited in conversation, their plans, their hopes of the future in regard to the condition of society and the cause of truth. You must go to England if it were only to see Coleridge. He is the true philosopher and his "Aids to Reflection" is better than any other of his works. I have studied it much of late, have used it much in reviewing Stuart, and have spoken of him in a note in terms which will seem extravagant to those who are not well acquainted with his worth.[18] I shall probably review his "Aids" in the same work soon and shall I think venture to write to him before you will see him.

Our family and Mr. Benedict's send their kindest affections and good wishes. Give mine also to Brother Wheeler if with you. That you may return safely increased in knowledge and enriched with divine grace and prepared for our Master's service is the prayer of

Yours
J.M.

1. Marsh here is referring to the death of his wife Lucia.
2. Victor Cousin (1792–1867), French philosopher, in reaction first against the sensualist philosophy of the eighteenth century, became first an exponent of the Scottish common sense school. After studying Kant, Jacobi, Fichte, Schelling, and Hegel which, in 1821, cost him his position as assistant to Professor Royer-Collard at Paris, Cousin published during the 1820s critical editions of Proclus, Descartes, and part of his translation of Plato.
3. Here Marsh refers to the debate and ultimate victory of Romantic esthetics over earlier seventeenth and eighteenth-century classicism in France.
4. Benjamin Lincoln, M.D. (1802–35), Bowdoin Class of 1823, was appointed to the medical faculty of UVM in 1829 as professor of anatomy and surgery.
5. George Russell Huntington (d. 1872), UVM Class of 1826, was professor of mathematics and civil engineering only from 1829 to 1832.
6. George Allen (1808–76), of Milton, Vermont, was a tutor at the University from 1828 to 1830. Allen was Marsh's close assistant in publishing *Aids to Reflection*. Ordained an Episcopal minister in 1837, he first taught theology at the Vermont Episcopal Institute, then languages and literature at Newark College, Delaware (1837–45), and finally, because of his sympathies with the Oxford Movement, Greek and Latin at the University of Pennsylvania. As one of John Henry Newman's more vocal American sympathizers, Allen's conversion to Roman

Catholicism in 1847 brought him social ostracism at Pennsylvania for a few years. After 1850, however, he resumed his prominent position at the University, holding the Greek chair until his death in 1876.
7. Solomon Foot (1802–66) had been a tutor at UVM in Marsh's first year as president. He subsequently became a lawyer, served in the Vermont legislature and, as a Whig and Republican, in the United States Senate (1850–66).
8. Only twenty-seven students are recorded as graduating from 1829 to 1832. Forty-three graduated from the medical department.
9. Torrey taught languages until Marsh's death in 1842; thereafter he gave the regular courses in philosophy.
10. The only work of Cousin surviving in Marsh's personal library, now in the Wilbur Collection at the Guy W. Bailey Library, UVM, is his *Elements of Psychology: included in a critical examination of Locke's essay on the human Understanding*, translated by Caleb Sprague Henry (Hartford, 1834). Inscribed on the first flyleaf: "Rev. James Marsh, D.D./with the respects of the author," meaning the translator, C. S. Henry.
11. *The Vermont Chronicle.*
12. See letter from John Mitchell, December 26, 1828, JMC.
13. John Owen (1616–1683), English Puritan, sought refuge at Charterhouse Yard, London, at the outbreak of the English Civil War. While there he wrote and published *A Display of Arminianism, being a Discovery of the old Pelagian Idol, Freewill, with the new Goddess Contingency* (1643). Close to Cromwell at various times, preaching sermons and serving as Cromwell's vice-chancellor at Oxford, Owen was still noted for a moderate attitude. He was also the author of *Exposition of the Epistle to the Hebrews.*
14. George Wyllys Benedict (1798–1871) joined the faculty of UVM in 1825 as lecturer in chemistry and professor of mathematics and natural philosophy. He single-handedly built its department of scientific studies, while serving as secretary and treasurer of the University.

Gould's Hotel stood on the site of the present Hotel Vermont in Burlington.
15. Reuben Smith, installed May 3, 1826, as pastor of the Congregational Church in Burlington, was succeeded by John K. Converse in 1832.
16. Here and below ellipsis indicates torn paper in the holograph.
17. Torrey purchased 7,000 volumes at an average price of $1.25 per volume on his trips to Europe. John Wheeler and Torrey made this trip together except for Wheeler's visit to England.
18. Mitchell or Taylor deleted Marsh's note of gratitude to Coleridge and inserted a final paragraph in an attempt to discount much of what Marsh said about the doctrine of Atonement.

Introducing Coleridge 1829–1833

With his first revisions of UVM's curriculum completed, Marsh then turned to a larger audience. Perhaps recalling the resistance to Coleridge that another American friend of the English poet, Richard Henry Dana, Sr., had met when Dana sought the editorship of the *North American Review* in 1819, Marsh attempted first to prepare an audience for Coleridge's *Aids to Reflection* by writing to prominent orthodox Presbyterian divines like Archibald Alexander at Princeton and his old mentor John Holt Rice at Hampden-Sydney. As the surviving letters show, this tactic was fruitless and unnecessary, for there was another ready-made audience waiting for Coleridge throughout the country. It included prominent men in Massachusetts like George Ripley and Ralph Waldo Emerson as well as little-known men as distant from New England at Thomas Porter Smith, "Mr. Presbyterian" of Paris, Kentucky.

Charles Hodge of Princeton Theological Seminary, who had published Marsh's translation of Herder's *Spirit of Hebrew Poetry* in 1826, and Leonard Woods, Sr., of Andover Seminary, would object to Marsh's introducing Coleridge to America, but their criticisms in the long run were ineffectual. As George Ripley admitted in 1837, *Aids to Reflection* with Marsh's notes and commentary soon became a basic document in the formation of American transcendentalism.

To Archibald Alexander[1]
Ms: Pennsylvania Historical Society

Burlington
March 7, 1829

Reverend and dear Sir,

If I do not mistake your views of practical and spiritual religion I trust you will agree with me in regard to the expediency or at least desirableness of an object which I am going to mention and for which I wish to ask the countenance and favor of yourself and colleagues. The object is to republish in this country and put into as extensive circulation as may be among our fellow christians a few volumes of Selections from the best practical works of the English Divines of the Seventeenth Century. From my first acquaintance with those works the object which I now have in view has seemed to me to be one of great importance and the more intimate my acquaintance with them becomes the more decidedly do they appear to me every way better fitted to make the religion of christians "inward" spiritual and instinct with spiritual life than the corresponding works in most general circulation among us. My plan is to publish about five volumes 8vo, the first to contain Howe's[2] "Blessedness of the Righteous" and Treatise on "Delighting in God" with a Sermon perhaps, the second probably parts of Leighton[3] and the other volumes treatises and sermons of the same purely practical character from Barrow,[4] Bates,[5] Riccaltoun[6] and such other writers of the same age as are best suited to the end proposed. In reference to the selection I shall be glad of the advice of yourself and others qualified to give it and have written to Dr. Rice to the same purpose. To avoid all imputation of unfaithfulness in regard to doctrinal views I propose to publish the text unaltered as far as I publish at all and if I leave out any part of a treatise it will be by omitting entire chapters. What few notes may be added will be for the explanation of terms and phrases that are no longer intelligible to common readers.

A very enterprising bookseller[7] here is ready to undertake publication and if we receive the countenance of those whose advice ought to be had in regard to a matter so nearly concerning the interests of religion we hope to have the first volume out in the course of the present season.

Will you have the goodness Sir to consult your Colleagues and write me on this subject as soon as may comport with your more important occupations?

I see with pleasure that your Son[8] is engaged as the editor of the Biblical Repertory and that Professor Hodge[9] is again contributing his labours to the work. Please give my regards to Mrs. Alexander and to the gentlemen with whom you are associated and permit me to subscribe myself with very sincere regard and with Christian affection.

Yours truly
Jas. Marsh.

1. The Virginian who had been instrumental with John Holt Rice in the early financing of Union Theological Seminary at Hampden-Sydney. From 1812 to 1851 Alexander held the first chair of theology at the Princeton Theological Seminary.
2. John Howe (1630–1705), was accused of having a "platonick tincture" because of his knowledge of Cudworth and lasting friendship with Henry More, prominent Cambridge Platonists. Cromwell made him his personal chaplain after hearing Howe deliver a two-hour sermon. During the three months of each year when Howe served as Cromwell's chaplain, Increase Mather substituted for him at his parish in Torrington. Howe was later a leading figure in the efforts to amalgamate Presbyterians and Congregationalists.
3. Robert Leighton (1611–84), archbishop of Glasgow and in some matters a latitudinarian, argued that religion did not consist in external matters of government or worship. Leighton also attempted to reconcile resolutioners and protestors, meanwhile advocating full religious toleration even for Roman Catholics, Quakers, and Baptists.
4. Isaac Barrow (1630–77), chaplain to Charles II and master of Trinity College, Cambridge, was also a mathematician considered second only to Newton by his contemporaries. While not himself a Cambridge Platonist, he still attempted like them to reconcile differences of opinion.
5. William Bates (1625–99), "silver tongued" Bates, took part in negotiations for the restoration of Charles II. He too engaged in efforts to reconcile nonconformists with the episcopacy.
6. Robert Riccaltoun (1691–1769), Scottish Presbyterian divine and friend of James Thomson the poet, among other things had published anonymously a conciliatory pamphlet on the "Marrow Controversy" entitled "A Sober Inquiry into the Grounds of the Present Differences in the Church of Scotland" (1723).
7. Marsh's brother-in-law, Chauncey Goodrich (1798–1858), would publish in the next two years the three books Marsh had in mind as he wrote to Alexander: Coleridge's *Aids to Reflection* (1829), based on the writings of Robert Leighton; *Select Practical Theology of the Seventeenth Century* (1830), containing John Howe's "The Blessedness of the Righteous" and "The Vanity of Man as Mortal," and Bates' "Discourses on the Four Last Things"; and, in 1831, Coleridge's *The Friend.*
8. Joseph Addison Alexander (1809–60) was also an instructor in biblical languages and literature at Princeton from 1834 to 1860 as well as sometime editor of *The Biblical Repertory*.
9. Charles Hodge himself professed to be a true believer

in the Calvinism of the seventeenth-century English Divines. His learning and ability as a writer made him a powerful figure in conservative Presbyterian circles.

To James Richards[1]
Ms: Pennsylvania Historical Society

Burlington
March 21, 1829

Reverend and dear Sir

I propose to publish as soon as arrangements can be made for that purpose a Selection of practical religious works from the best English divines of the seventeenth century with the view of recalling them to a more general circulation among our fellow christians and my object in writing you is to request your name and such an expression of your views and that of your colleagues as may serve to give the christian public confidence in the character of the work. I have written to the Professors of the Theological Schools at Andover, New Haven, Princeton, and Virginia for the same purpose and from what I know of the views of several of them anticipate their cordial cooperation. The work will be undertaken by Mr. Goodrich the bookseller in this place and published in part probably during the present year. My design is to go to the extent of five volumes 8vo and to publish the most valuable only of the practical works of the most eminent divines of that century. The first volume will contain the "Blessedness of the Righteous" and other treatises of John Howe. The Second probably Selections from Leighton and the other volumes from other authors of the same general character. These works are but little known among us and from my first acquaintance with them I have thought as I know many other individuals have that they would be acquisitions of great value to our churches. Will you have the goodness Sir to send me an answer at your earliest convenience and oblige yours

With the highest esteem
Jas. Marsh.

1. James Richards (1767–1843), Yale Class of 1793, was professor of theology at Auburn Theological Seminary (1823–43).

take place in England and Scotland, that important discussions on questions of general interest to literary men and christians, when started there, soon draw attention here and are followed up with similar results. The miscalled Baconian philosophy has been no less talked of here than there, with the same perverse application. The works of Locke were formerly much read and used as text books in our Colleges but of late have very generally given place to the Scotch writers; and Stewart, Campbell and Brown are now almost universally read as the standard authors on the subjects of which they treat.[3] In theology, the works of Edwards[4] have had, and still have, with a large portion of our thinking community, a very great influence; and we have had several *schemes* of doctrine formed out of his leading principles which have had each its day and its defenders. You will readily see the near affinity that exists between his philosophical views and those of Brown; and yet it happens that the Unitarians, while they reject Edwards and treat him with severity for his Calvinism, as it is here called, give currency to Brown for views that would seem to lead to what is most objectionable in the work on the Freedom of the Will. There has lately arisen some discussion among our most able orthodox divines which seems to me likely to shake the authority of Edwards among them; and I trust your "Aids to Reflection" is with a few exerting an influence that will help to place the lovers of truth and righteousness on better philosophical grounds.[5]

The German philosophers, Kant and his followers, are very little known in this country, and our young men who have visited Germany have paid little attention to that department of study while there. I cannot boast of being wiser than others in this respect, for though I have read a part of the works of Kant it was under many disadvantages, so that I am indebted to your own writings for the ability to understand what I have read of his works and am waiting with some impatience for that part of your works which will aid more directly in the study of those subjects of which he treats. The same views are generally entertained in this country as in Great Britain respecting German literature, and Stewart's History of Philosophy especially has had an extensive influence to deter students from the study of their philosophy.[6] Whether any change in this respect is to take place, remains to be seen. To me it seems a point of great importance to awaken among our scholars a taste for more manly and efficient mental discipline and to recall into use those old writers whose minds were formed by a higher standard. I am myself making efforts to get into circulation some of the practical works of the older English divines, both for the direct benefit which they will confer upon the religious community and because, in this country, the most practical and efficient mode of influencing the thinking world is to begin with those who think from principles and in earnest, in other words, with the religious community. It is with the same views that I am aiming to introduce some little knowledge of your own views through the medium of a religious journal[7] which circulates among the most intelligent and serious clergy and other christians. It is partly with a view to this that I venture to address you and to request the favor of an occasional correspondence with you. In the last number of the Journal alluded to, the "Christian Spectator" for March 1829, published at New Haven, Connecticut, I have a review of Professor Stuart's Commentary on Hebrews, in which I have given a view of the Atonement, or rather of Redemption, I believe nearly corresponding with yours and indeed have made free use of your language. In a note, I had also given you credit for it, but the note was omitted by the publishers and a few paragraphs of their own remarks added. If you should have the curiosity to see the use which I have made of your works, the journal can be found, I presume, at Millers' American Reading Room or at the office of the Christian Observer.[8] It has been my intention to write an article, or perhaps more than one, for the same journal on your "Aids to Reflection"; but my other duties will probably prevent it for the present. I shall send you with this an Address[9] delivered by me on coming to my present place in which also you will find free use made of your works; and I cannot resist the inclination also to refer you to an article on Ancient and Modern Poetry in the North American Review for July 1822, which I wrote while pursuing professional studies at Andover, Massachusetts. If you should impute to me some weakness in thus referring you to some few things which I have written, I can only say, that as you seemed, in your "Literary Life" to be gratified with the use made of your political essays in this country,[10] I have also a farther motive in the supposition that you might be gratified with knowing that your philosophical writings are not wholly neglected among us. But you will probably hear more of this from two friends of mine now on the continent of Europe who intend calling on you I believe when in England and both of whom are among the few in this country who have carefully studied your writing. Their names are Rev. J. Wheeler and Prof. J. Torrey. The latter is attached to the same College with myself. If, after reading the pieces to which I have referred, Sir, you should think the seed which you have been sowing beside all waters is likely to bring forth any valuable fruits in these ends of the earth, I beg that you will pardon my boldness and write as suits your convenience to one who would value nothing more highly than your advice and guidance in the pursuit of truth and the discharge of the great duty to which I am called, of imparting it to those who are hereafter to be men of power and influence in this great and growing republic. With sentiments of the highest esteem,[11]

Your very obedient
servant,
James Marsh

1. Torrey published an edited version of this letter in *Remains*, pp. 135–38, deleting the reference to himself and John Wheeler.

2. C. Wiley, no. 3 Wall st, had published the New York edition of *Biographia Literaria* in 1817.

3. Marsh's experiences at Dartmouth and Hampden-Sydney could well attest to the ascendancy of the "Scotch writers." In September 1824 the Board of Trustees of Hampden-Sydney College approved a revised course of studies for the senior class, winter session, to include Stewart's *Philosophy of the Mind*. At Dartmouth Marsh would have officially studied Locke, Edwards on the Will, Bishop Butler's *Analogy*, and Stewart.

Dugald Stewart (1753–1828), the Scottish philosopher, held the chair of moral philosophy at Edinburgh where he was a disciple of the "common sense" school. He wrote *Elements of the Philosophy of the Human Mind* (1792–1817), *Outline of Moral Philosophy* (1793), and *Philosophical Essays* (1810). George Campbell (1719–96), a Scottish divine, wrote *Dissertations on Miracles* (1762), a treatise directed against Hume, *Philosophy of Rhetoric* (1776), and *Lectures* on

Ecclesiastical History (1800). Thomas Brown (1778–1820) studied under Stewart at Edinburgh and later joined him as professor there.

4. Jonathan Edwards (1703–58) in his *Freedom of the Will* (1754) earned his place as the first great mind in American intellectual history. With his other treatises, *The Great Christian Doctrine of Original Sin Defended* (1758), *The Nature of True Virtue* (1756), and *Concerning the Ends for Which God Created the World* (1755) Edwards first formulated what came to be known as the New England Theology.

5. Apparently an allusion to the Taylorian Controversy. In 1828 Nathaniel Taylor (1786–1858) delivered a sermon in New Haven, entitled *Concio ad Clerum*, which rejected the theory of a *felix culpa* in an attempt to refute Unitarians. Taylor argued that man's nature is not itself sinful, nor is it in any way the cause of sinning. Attempting to provide a basis for a theory of the freedom of the will, he concluded that man's nature is only the occasion of his sinning. Joseph Harvey responded with *A Review of a Sermon* (Hartford, 1829), finding Taylor irrational and un-biblical. *The Quarterly Christian Spectator* supported Taylor, but the opposition strengthened to the point of founding, in 1833, the theological school at East Windsor, Connecticut. Bennett Tyler, formerly president of Dartmouth (1822–28) and an ardent conservative who considered himself in the tradition of Edwards and Timothy Dwight, in 1834 became president of the school, which later became the Hartford Theological Seminary.

6. In 1822, for example, Emerson had been delighted by Stewart's "beautiful and instructive abridgement of the thousand volumes of Locke, Liebnitz, Voltaire, Boyle, Kant and the rest" (*Journal*, I, November 1823, pp. 289–90).

7. *The Quarterly Christian Spectator*.

8. John Miller of Black Friars, known as "the American bookseller," was James Fenimore Cooper's English publisher. Little else is known about him. *The Christian Observer*, a religious magazine "conducted by members of the establishment Church" in London, was also published from 1800 to 1825 in Boston and New York. Zachary Macaulay, the historian's father, was editor.

9. Marsh's *Inaugural Address*.

10. "To have lived in vain must be a painful thought to any man, and especially so to him who has made literature his profession. I should rather condole, than be angry, with the minds which could attribute to no worthier feelings than those of vanity or self-love, the satisfaction which I acknowledge to have enjoyed from the republication of my political essays (either whole or as extracts) not only in many of our own provincial papers, but in the federal journals throughout America. I regarded it as some proof of my not having laboured altogether in vain, that from the articles written by me shortly before, and at the commencement of the late unhappy war with America, not only the sentiments were adopted, but in some instance, the very language, in several of the Massachusetts state-papers" (*Biographia Literaria* [Boston, 1834], pp. 129–30).

11. In recounting his visit to Coleridge in 1833, Emerson wrote in his notebook: "I asked if he had had any correspondence with Marsh [;] he said No for he had received his book and letter at a time when he was incapable of any effort & soon should send him some new books & asked if I had seen his Church & State" (*Journals and Miscellaneous Notebooks*, IV, 1832–34, p. 30). See below, letter of November 15, 1829.

From George Ticknor
Ms: UVM

Boston
April 14, 1829

My dear Sir,

I received several days since your interesting letter of the 30th ultimate and soon afterwards the pamphlet[1] to which it refers. I feel indebted to you for both of them and beg you to accept my thanks. The pamphlet seems to me able and sound. I have been acting for four years, in all the instructions given by our teachers in the Modern Languages, on the principles it contains and, I think, with entire success—at any rate with a success much beyond what I promised myself when I began. We divide and advance the sections without any regard to the division of classes or the distinction even between graduates and undergraduates. We give full liberty of choice what they will study and, indeed, whether they will study any modern language at all. And each section in each language is advanced according to its proficiency, no person being permitted to leave off studying a language until he has learnt it and undergone a real examination, which gives full proof of the fact to a committee of the Overseers who make the examination *themselves.* The young men here as with you have acquiesced fully in this system and have gone on with their studies with an alacrity not to be mistaken. Nor has it been slightly or imperfectly applied as a system. At a late examination of about thirty in French, members of three classes were found in the same section, some of whom had been studying the language above two years, others a year and a half, and so on, till in one case an individual had studied it only three months. There was very little difference between them in attainment—great difference, of course, in original talent and disposition; and the full concurrence and cooperation of the students has been the more remarkable because nothing of the same sort has been attempted in the other departments, and because the attempt on our part has been much discouraged by the other teachers. But, as I said before, it is successful; and it is already producing its effect on others.

I was very glad, also, to see your testimony bound to the ancient languages, to the benefit of reading whole works of authors and not extracts, etc., etc., indeed, I did not observe any portion of your statement to which I did not yield a glad and full assent.

I have talked with some of my friends concerning your library and its wants. Such claims are usually met with as much good will among us as any we receive. But it has been for the last year, not thought expedient to press any such claims in relation to some of our own institutions, which would be very glad to put them forward, if the times gave any fair prospect of success. I should be sorry to discourage any attempts likely to prevail and it is not possible to tell with certainty what may be the result in any given case, but, I confess, I should be unwilling to undertake any thing of the kind just now. Our rich men and particularly our capitalists are suffering very severely.

We are printing nothing, I believe, at Cambridge in usuria juventutis,[2] except a small volume in Italian containing the Aminta of Tasso, the Saul of Alfieri, and two or three other *entire* works of established authors.[3]

German philosophy I have not now time to read or time to write; but it will please you to know that Dr. Follen[4] of Cambridge is fully competent to excite and sustain an interest in it among us, and that it is very likely he will do so. Mr. Channing (Rev. Dr.)[5] is, also, inclined the same way.

With great respect
Yours very sincerely
Geo. Ticknor

Will you do me the favor to send me by mail four copies of Professor Benedict's Pamphlet.[6]

1. *An Exposition of the System of Instruction and Discipline Pursued in the University of Vermont* (Burlington: Chauncey Goodrich, 1829; revised 1831).

2. For the use of the young or students.

3. *Teatro Scelto Italiano.* Contente *l'Aminto* di Tasso, *l'Artaserse* di Metastasio, *la Griselda* di Goldoni, *La*

Merope di Maffei, e *il Saul* di Alfieri, publicato da Pietro Bachi, precettore nell' Universita Harvardiana (Hilliard and Brown, ca. 1830).

4. Charles Follen (1796–1840), liberal political refugee from Germany, had taught at the University of Jena, but fled to America in 1820, arriving in Boston in 1824. In 1825 Follen was appointed tutor at Harvard. Promoted to professor in 1831, he taught German language and law. While not completely sympathetic to Romantic ideas, Follen still made the literature available to his students. In 1835, his appointment was not renewed at Harvard because of his alleged unorthodoxy.

5. William Ellery Channing (1780–1842), the "great Unitarian," delivered the famous sermon in Baltimore (1819) at the ordination of Jared Sparks which first articulated the American Unitarian creed.

6. While the ideas for reforming UVM's curriculum were substantially formulated by Marsh, George Wyllys Benedict was given the task of writing them out for publication. Tradition, apparently beginning with Marsh himself, has credited the pamphlet to Benedict.

From John Holt Rice
Ms: UVM

Union Theological Seminary[1]
April 14, 1829

My dear Sir

I have felt badly that none of us answered the very interesting letter written by you just after your great bereavement.[2] I wish you to know the circumstances which prevented my writing. Your letter came to hand just as I was preparing a sermon to preach on a particular occasion. As soon as this preparation was made, I had to leave home and was laboriously engaged during a tour of six weeks. On my return, I had all the cares of the commencement of the session. By that time, your letter, in being handed about among the neighbors, was lost. I waited to recover it; and thus the thing was put off from time to time, until your second letter came to hand.

If you suppose that your friends here have lost their interest for you, or that they were deficient in sympathy, you mistake. I can testify that many wept much on hearing that you were left alone, and that your children had no mother. Many prayed and do still pray for you. Could you visit us once more, you would see many evidences of affectionate remembrance.

I have just received Number One Christian Spectator, New Series. I have read a part of *your* Review of Professor Stuart on Hebrews—(Guess how I found you out.) and thus far like it well. But this Number of the work as a whole greatly disappoints me. I understand that this religious Quarterly aims to take the same position in the Church with the Edinburgh and Quarterly[3] in the literary world. But *inter nos*, it will never do. Forty pages in the beginning, of metaphysical theology and a continuation threatened! I know not how it may do for New England; but assuredly a work of that sort never can be popular in the South.

I do most fully concur with you in opinion as to the importance of getting into circulation the writings of the great men who lived in the seventeenth century. And if you can succeed in your design, a benefit of incalculable value will be conferred on New England. The *theological taste* has been too long formed on the model of metaphysics. Systems and sermons are moulded into this form—Rhetoric is extinct—Eloquence, instead of being like the garden of Eden, bright in celestial light, and breathing the airs of heaven, is a very *Hortus Siccus*, with every flower labelled, and pasted on blank paper; the colours are all faded, the fragrance gone, and "behold all is very dry."

There must be a new model. But it will never be framed by our teachers of Sacred Rhetoric. Indeed I have no doubt but that they will impede the progress of Reformation. Something may be expected from an increased study of the Bible. If it were studied *right*, great improvements would of course follow. For the spirit of that inimitable composition cannot be breathed into a man, without an awakening of something in him corresponding to its sublimity, its pathos, its overpowering eloquence. The men whom we agree in admiring were made what they were, in a great degree, by the Bible. Instead of sitting down to study it, with a system of metaphysics to control their philology, they brought themselves to the sacred pages that they might feel the *vis fulmines*[4] and breathe the heavenly aura of divine truth. Convinced that it was an emanation from the eternal source of truth, they entirely gave themselves up to its influences, and were borne by it extra flammentia mania mundi.[5] How different the writers of the present day! But I need not stay to point out the contrast. You have especially marked the difference in regard to religious feeling. It is true that the present age requires action. But certainly religion is getting to be too much, in some places, an affair of business. It is becoming cold calculating. And should the present excitement wear off, I apprehend the Church will be left in a deplorably desolate and barren condition. I would wish indeed the activity of Christians to be increased a thousand fold, but I wish to see them borne on by that profound deep toned feeling which pervaded the inmost souls of such men as Leighton, Baxter, and Howe.

But as to the business part of your undertaking, I hardly know what opinion to give. I should think that you would do well to have a subscription sufficient to cover your expenses. Selections have generally sold badly. The prevailing taste is for other things. Such poetry as Mrs. Hemans[6] is more popular than Milton's. A souvenir, in polite literature, and a sermon of *cut and dry metaphysics*, or *cut and dry rhetoric* is all the rage.

I think that there have been several English Editions of Leighton.[7] His whole works then would scarcely do well. Howe, Baxter, etc. are too voluminous for general reading, and would afford very good opportunity for selection. Bishop Hopkins[8] is one of my favorites of the old school—I could wish you to take something from him. Jeremy Taylor has been republished in this country.[9] Some extracts from Thomas Browne's Religio Medici would furnish a choice morceau—nor would I neglect the "silver tongued Bates." Barrow has vast force, but not much feeling. He has no rhetoric.[10]

If these hasty hints should give you any pleasure, I shall be glad. Mrs. Rice unites with me in most affectionate remembrances, and best wishes for your health and usefulness.

Yours most truly
John H. Rice

Your Exposition[11] has just come to hand—thanks!

1. Union Theological Seminary, Hampden-Sydney, Virginia. This letter was also published in *Remains*, pp. 149–51.

2. Marsh's first wife, Lucia, had died of tuberculosis on August 18, 1828, after four

years of marriage. In 1830 he then married her sister, Laura, who also died of tuberculosis, August 17, 1838. They were both daughters of James Wheelock and granddaughters of Eleazer Wheelock, founder of Dartmouth College.
3. *The Edinburgh Review* and *The Quarterly Review* of London were the most important periodicals of the time.
4. The power or force of lightning.
5. To be carried on a wind out of the madness of the world.
6. Felicia Hemans (1793–1835), author of the schoolboy perennials "The Boy Stood on the Burning Deck" and "The Stately Homes of England."
7. The most recent collected English edition of Leighton had been Person's in 1825.
8. Ezekiel Hopkins (1634–90), bishop of Derry, a preacher of some reputation, published "A Treatise on the Vanity of the World" (1668). Josiah Pratt published an edition of his sermons and other writings in four volumes, London, 1809.
9. Reginald Heber's fifteen volume edition of Jeremy Taylor's *Whole Works* (London, 1820–22) was also published in Boston, 1822.
10. See above letter to Archibald Alexander, March 7, 1829, notes 4 and 5.
11. *An Exposition of the System of Instruction . . . in the University of Vermont* (1829).

To Joseph Torrey
Ms: UVM

Burlington
July 16, 1829

My dear Sir

I have delayed writing several weeks since I received yours from Rome with the hope of sending you the money which I had encouraged you to expect. I could not make up my mind to tell you that the case was hopeless though we had tried begging very faithfully in vain. We have at length resorted to an effort for borrowing on our own responsibility but so unprecedented is the pressure for money in all parts of the country that money cannot be hired for almost any purpose.[1] As a last resort we have authorized Mr. Goodrich[2] who is now on his way to Boston to engage some of the booksellers on the best terms he can procure to send you $1000 either in a bill of exchange or partly in that way and partly in an order on booksellers there so that you can select them on the spot and Professor Benedict and myself become responsible here with a reasonable term of credit. I think there can be little doubt of his making such an arrangement as he will meet gentlemen of the trade from all parts of the country.

We are extremely sorry that we could not send more and that this was not done earlier. But circumstances too numerous to mention have deferred and obstructed our efforts. We have requested Mr. Goodrich if he can make an arrangement which he thinks reasonable to send directly to you and I hope you may hear from him as soon as you receive this. If you do not I hope you will wait a few days and if you do not hear at all from him I know no other method we can take and can only hope you may not have embarrassed your own funds by making purchases and that you may return yourself with all the European philosophy in your head and patience at heart.[3] We shall however try every method still that offers any chance of success and if you have advanced money so as to be under the necessity of drawing upon your friends in order to return we will of course be responsible as far as our responsibility will go. We are not discouraged and are confident we shall be able to raise money for the College whenever it gets into the country again for at present almost every bank has stopped discounting and no money is to be found. In other respects our prospects are more encouraging and we have many reasons to believe that the College is gaining fast upon the confidence and good will of the public. Our prospect for a class this fall is good and among the rest we have two from Wheeling, Va., already here and shall probably have several more from that region drawn here by our peculiar system and the cheapness of living here. The centre building is two thirds up and we hope may have the roof on by commencement.[4] We shall appoint Huntington[5] Professor and begin to make more noise in the world by and by.

I am greatly obliged to you for your very interesting letter from the city of the pope and particularly gratified with the discovery that I have any resemblance to such a man as Professor Tholuck.[6] Would it were in something more than outward form. However if you have an opportunity after receiving this pray give my highest regards to him. I hope you will establish a correspondence with him and I shall perhaps beg the privilege of joining in hereafter. You say he is well acquainted with all the German systems of philosophy and I shall wait with much interest for your report of conversations with him on that subject. Is he acquainted with Coleridge's views? I don't know whether I mentioned to you that I was about republishing Coleridge's Aids to Reflection with a preliminary essay and illustrations of his views from his other works. It is now advertised and will be put to press in a few days. The essay however will not be printed till after the rest and is not yet written. I should be exceedingly glad of such aid you would give me if here in regard to it and if you come in October hope I may yet receive it. My object will be chiefly to point out the bearing of his metaphysical views on theology and the adaptation of the whole to the state of theology in this country. Warm disputes are growing up here which I think his views if understood would wholly supersede and I am anxious to lay hold of any thing that may give circulation and influence to the work. Pray bear it in mind and when in England I hope you will by all means see Coleridge and if you think it is not too presuming mention my name and what I am doing.[7] I ventured to write to him once but Mr. Benedict could not find in New York where to direct the letter and returned it.[8] If you have means to purchase any books for me hope you will get all he has published we have not now and if you think it would be well received tell him I should count it a great privilege to correspond with him occasionally. If you can tell me any thing which you think would be of use in regard to the work mentioned hope you will write at length as soon as may be. The review of Professor Stuart has been spoken of in the most flattering terms by many whose opinions I was most anxious to know in regard to the view of [. . .][9] advanced in it and which were those of Coleridge. Professor Stuart professed [. . .] comprehend it. I cannot now write the other sheet which you mentioned and indeed think we have a much better claim upon you for double letters than you have upon me. I think it is of importance to engage valuable correspondents in Europe after you return and that we may make it useful to the College as well as ourselves. I should like one in Germany one in France and one in England with reference particularly to metaphysics and theology and will leave the selection to you. It is not easy or perhaps desirable to engage men of talents in the discussion of subjects by letter but a wise and observing scholar can give much information respecting the progress and tendency of opinions and principles in that manner. Professor Tholuck's views of Coleridge and of the relation of his metaphysics to those of Germany for example I should value highly just now and wish you might find means to obtain them for me. If he is not acquainted with Coleridge you can of course promise him a good reward for the trouble of reading. If you buy books I am willing to leave the selection in my department to your own judgment. Some of the German commentaries on Plato with Cousin I should think would be very important and the great German originals whom you mention. I will try to write you again while you are in England though indeed I fear this may find you there. Our friends here are all well and waiting for your return from which we expect both pleasure and profit.

With great esteem
Yours truly
Jas. Marsh

1. Since the Panic of 1819 the credit policy of the Bank of the United States had been favorable to industrial development rather than mercantile interests. Burlington in the 1820s was basically a village of merchants and shippers who had less access to cash than did men in commercial centers like New York City.

2. Chauncey Goodrich (1798–1858), the Burlington publisher and bookseller.

3. However difficult finding funds may have been at this time, Torrey was able to purchase 7,000 books during the series of trips he made to Europe beginning in 1829.

4. The center portion of the building on the UVM campus today called the Old Mill.

5. George Russell Huntington (b. 1782), UVM Class of 1826, was professor of mathematics and civil engineering only until 1832.

6. Friedrich A. G. Tholuck (1799–1877), the German divine, was professor of theology at the University of Halle and, briefly in the late 1820s, chaplain to the Prussian envoy at Rome. An evangelical pietist influenced by the Moravian Brotherhood, Tholuck was highly devoted to his students and, also like Marsh, frail of health. He was one of Germany's most eloquent preachers, one of Europe's most influential theologians in the years 1825–75 and was better known in America than perhaps any other European theologian. Influenced by Schleiermacher, Neander, and Hegel, Tholuck also had extraordinary talent for languages, studying nineteen of them. He led a regeneration of German theology, directing its emphasis from rationalism to scripture and the literature of the Reformation. He was

always especially attached to Americans. See below letter of February 15, 1833 from Tholuck to Marsh.
7. Torrey never visited Coleridge; Wheeler did.
8. Marsh's letter of March 23, 1829, carried by George Wyllys Benedict to New York and addressed to Coleridge, care of William Pickering, the London publisher, never reached its destination. Later letters did, however, as Coleridge told Emerson in 1833. See above letter of March 23, 1829, note 10, and below, November 15, 1829.
9. The holograph is torn here and in the next line.

To George Ticknor
Ms: Dartmouth

Burlington
July 26, 1829

My dear Sir

Permit me to introduce to you Mr. George Allen a young gentleman of this place and at present employed as one of our tutors in College. An introduction to the Athenaeum and any other attention of that sort during his stay in Boston will confer an obligation upon your humble servant.[1] I will be obliged to you also if you will send me by him a a catalogue of the Athenaeum, if consistent with your rules, and the works that are contained in A. Schelling's "System des transcendentalen Idealismus" and Kant's "Vermischte Schriften."[2]

We have just arrived here a Son of Mr. Henry Gray[3] whom we shall endeavor to make a scholar and thereby obtain more young men from your neighborhood. With my best regards to Mrs. Ticknor.[4]

Yours respectfully
Jas. Marsh.

1. Allen's visit to Boston might have been principally to see Mary Hancock Withington, whom he would marry in 1831, Ralph Waldo Emerson officiating.
2. *System des transcendentalen Idealismus* (Tubingen, 1800). Immanuel Kant, *Vermischte Schriften*. Aechte und vollstandige Ausgabe. 4 Bde (Halle, Königsberg, 1799–1807).
3. The name Gray does not survive in any of UVM's records from these years. Henry Gray was a partner in the Boston publishing and bookselling house of Hilliard and Gray.
4. Van Wyck Brooks has vividly sketched where Ticknor received Allen: "Ticknor's great house at the head of Park Street, dominating the Common from Beacon Hill, soon became the symbol of his renown. There he kept

his famous library, the amplest private library in Boston, housed in the largest and most elegant room, approached through a marble hall by a marble stairway, about which the butler discreetly hovered. Over the mantel hung the Leslie portrait for which Sir Walter had sat at Abbotsford, and the walls of the stately apartment were covered with books, methodically arranged and richly bound. And there, with his air of the scholar-nobleman, gracious but somewhat marmoreal, like his hall and mantel, Ticknor dispensed his counsels to aspiring students" (*The Flowering of New England*, p. 103).

From Francis Wayland[1]
Ms: UVM

Brown University
October 20, 1829

My dear Sir

I am ashamed to say that I know very little of Coleridge, and that that little has been derived more from conversation than from reading. I dare not therefore promise to comply with your request until I have seen the work in question.[2] From what you say of it, I should presume that he had fallen upon a field prolific of the seeds of things, and one thus far but little cultivated. It has for some time seemed to me that there must be some radical error in our mode of exhibiting religion for two reasons. First. The portrait is so unlike the original and second the effects of the agent, the most powerful in the range of immaterial agents, are so little worthy of the thing itself. He who shall show where this error is and how it may be corrected will deserve a statue.

Suffer me to say then in answer to your letter, send me a copy of the work only you must let me pay for it. I will read it and let you know what it will be in my power to do. I dare not promise more, and beg that this correspondence will not prevent you from making any other arrangements for having the thing done. My time is so occupied in very many little things which render continuous effort extremely difficult that I can speak with certainty for but a very little time in advance.

We are doing what we can in college with small means and many embarrassments. Your pamphlet seemed to me by far the best thing on college education that I had seen. I believe you will succeed and oblige us all to follow you. We have not power at present but are striving to make it as fast as we can. But how can colleges prosper directed by men very good men to be sure but who know about every other thing except education. The man who first devised the present mode of governing colleges in this country has done us more injury than Benedict Arnold.

I am dear Sir
Yours truly
F. Wayland

1. Francis Wayland (1796–1865), Union College Class of 1813, was minister to the Baptist Church of Boston (1821–26) before assuming the presidency of Brown University (1827–55).
2. *Aids to Reflection.*

To Leonard Marsh
Ms: JMC

Burlington
October 23, 1829

My dear brother

I intended before this to write to you on various matters but in the first place to mention to you a new acquaintance of mine in New York to whom I gave a letter of introduction to you and with whom I wish you by all means to be acquainted. The gentleman is Mr. John Morgan[1] who has been here this fall a few weeks to visit Miss Dewey, a sister of Mrs. Benedict.[2] He left here after his last visit on Monday evening last after I had given him the authority of the laws of Vermont for taking Miss Dewey along with him and calling her Mrs. Morgan. They will live at No. 1 Market and corner of [Hannon] St. in a house with his sister. My special reason for wishing you to become acquainted with him is that he is a special fine fellow and specially interested in Coleridge and all such matters. I think you will be greatly pleased with him and that frequent intercourse with each other will be pleasant and useful to both. I must by all means add that you will find Mrs. Morgan one of the sweetest flowers of the mountain, delicate, refined and intelligent and I venture to assert that you will find few places in your big city where you can spend your leisure hours more agreeably this winter than at No. 1 Market St.

1829–1833 But then I wish you to go sometimes for the special purpose of discussing Coleridge and concocting something respecting him for the public. To be serious, the work[3] will be out in a few days and I am anxious to awaken the interest and to enlist the talents of all the young men of my acquaintance to receive at least something like justice for a work which according to my full and firm conviction is a work of more importance to the interest of religious truth than any that has for a long time if ever been published in this country.

I have various reasons to feel some solicitude about it and among others the prejudice which you know has existed against me at Andover and the fact that the work will do some violence to certain general prejudices of the religious public. I received a letter the other day from E. C. Tracy at Andover saying that he expected I should be "misunderstood and burnt for a heretic" and that certain influential men could not be persuaded that any good thing can come out of that Nazareth Burlington. Such things I confess thin my blood a little but I care nothing how it may affect me personally. I am anxious that the contents of the work which I hold to be of great value should not be excluded from the minds of men by a cruel prejudice created through the influence of a few men who are determined to have all the world think with their tools and according to their measure. I know too that there are young men enough in the country capable of understanding, appreciating and defending the truth against the authority of such men and I trust they will do it. What I want is that you and every such man should do his part as a lover of the truth to make the work known by discussion, by writing, etc. etc.

It will be out within three or four weeks in about 450 pages. Give my best regards to Maj. Howard and his family and let me hear from you soon. Laura and Emily send their love to you.

Jas. Marsh

P.S. Father we hear is a little more comfortable but I fear will never be essentially better.

If you reflect a little you will see that I have reason to be earnest about the reception of Coleridge and the defense of his doctrines.

1. John Morgan (1803–89), Williams College Class of 1826, worked as a printer and studied theology privately in New York City. After his ordination he accepted an appointment to the Lane Theological Seminary where, in a dispute between the trustees and students, he was forced to resign because he supported the student's desire to discuss slavery. He then went on to become professor of biblical literature at Oberlin College.

2. George Benedict was married to Eliza Dewey.

3. *Aids to Reflection.*

From Ebenezer C. Tracy[1]
Ms: UVM

Andover
October 28, 1829

My dear Marsh

I thank you for your ready answer to my tardy epistle, and am glad to find that you are doing so much in your edition of Coleridge. You will make, as I judge, the main pillars of his system so prominent that they cannot be overlooked or neglected, and if you can once get the attention of thinking men fixed on his distinction between the reason and the understanding you will have done enough to reward the labor of a life. As prominent a place as it holds in the writings of Coleridge, he seems to me far enough from making too much of it. Indeed I shall expect a favorable reception for that and the note on Paley's Morals[2] from some who will be disposed to cavil at other parts of the work.

I am willing to undertake a review of the book for the Christian Spectator or anything else. But I doubt whether they would admit into the Spectator just such an one as I should choose to write. The managers of that work[3] know that they are regarded with no little jealousy by very many clergymen who have influence over public opinion in different parts of the U.S. and I suspect will be a little careful about publishing any other heresies than their own. Your review, you remember, had to appear with a tail piece by Dr. Taylor. Perhaps, however, as I understand they requested your views of Coleridge at length, they would be willing to publish mine of you and Coleridge together. It is worth the while to consider, however, whether such a review as Bacon[4] would write would not do the work more good.

From what I know of Bacon I should think he would be highly pleased with so much of the work as to write a rather enthusiastic and *taking* review, and his manner, you know, is such as is apt to gain favor for what he thinks well of. From some of Coleridge's doctrines he would dissent; and perhaps from so many of them and so decidedly that he would be unwilling to risk any thing worth reading respecting the book. If you should think it worth the while, I will write to Bacon on the subject. Should I have an opportunity I will suggest the matter to Choate,[5] but I have had so little intercourse with him on such subjects that I could not write to him purposely to such advantage. I think I shall have an opportunity to mention the subject to Dr. Rice in a few weeks.

Among the contributors to the Spirit of the Pilgrims[6] I know of but one who professes to be at all acquainted with the merits of Coleridge, and have never learnt his views very particularly. It is Richard H. Dana.[7] He has spoken of Coleridge in very high terms as a poet and as a religious man. I think he would be glad to write a review, and would have influence enough with the editor to procure its insertion. I will endeavor to consult him on the subject.

It may be more difficult to call public attention to the work effectually, than we are apt to suppose. The Quarterlys avoid theological discussions, and it would be impossible to do your public justice in an article which would be obnoxious to exclusion on that account. Several of the most important topics of your notes furnish legitimate matter for a publication that professes neutrality in theological discussions; and an article treating them without any allusion to the purposes they are made to answer in the book, might be considered admissible. Our theological journals, on the contrary, are all party publication, and tacitly or avowedly pledged, each to its own public for the support of particular doctrines. The Literary Magazines—for there are works so called—are pretty much in the same predicament with the Reviews. It may be therefore that no part of the periodical press will readily be brought to admit a full statement and defence of Coleridge's startling doctrines. The opponents of Dr. Taylor in Connecticut complain that they are excluded from every religious publication in the state.

But, as I said before, a discussion of Paley's Morals can be brought before the public in some way and made to excite attention. So can the distinction between reason and the understanding, in connection with some important inferences from it. So can the agreement of Plato and Bacon, and a variety of other topics; and all these may be so managed as, without such offence at first as to blind man's eyes, finally to gain for the whole work due attention. I shall be glad to contribute anything in my power to such a result, and if you think best will prepare and offer a review for the Spectator.

There is a copy of the "Friend"[8] in the Rhetorical Library here, and I am told it is read a good deal by the students. The Aids to Reflection would therefore be apt to excite some interest here.

I am very much engaged for two or three weeks just now; after the middle of November I shall have time to study Coleridge.

Yours truly
E.C. Tracy

1. Ebenezer Carter Tracy (1796–1862) was also a native of Hartford, Vermont, and a graduate of Dartmouth, Class of 1819. From 1826 to 1828 he was editor of *The Vermont Chronicle* and from 1830 to 1833 editor of *The Journal of Humanity* at Andover.
2. "Dr. Paley tells us in his Nat. Theology, that only 'contrivance,' a power obviously and confessedly belonging to brutes, is necessary to constitute *personality*. His whole system both of theology and morals neither teaches, nor implies, the existence of any specific difference either between the understanding and reason, or between nature and will. It does not imply the existence of any power in man, which does not obviously belong in a greater or less degree to irrational animals" (*Aids*, p. xl).
3. Nathaniel Taylor and John Mitchell.
4. Leonard Bacon (1802–81), Yale Class of 1820, Andover 1823, was minister to the First Church of New Haven (1825–66) and professor of theology, American church history, and church polity at Yale Divinity School (1866–81). In theological matters, and on political issues, as founder and editor of the free-soil *Independent*, Bacon was a reconciler and independent. Writing to Marsh in 1840 he described his position on the questions debated in the Taylorian Controversy as "rather that of an *Eclectic*. I regard the questions actually disputed as much less important than the liberty of disputing."
5. Rufus Choate (1799–1859), Dartmouth Class of 1819.
6. *The Spirit of the Pilgrims* was the successor to *The Panoplist*, which had been founded in 1805 by Jedidiah Morse, and ran from January 1828 to December 1833, edited first by Enoch Pond

and then George Cheever in its last year. Lyman Beecher was a frequent contributor.

7. Richard Henry Dana (1787–1879), lawyer and briefly editor of *The North American Review*, from which he resigned in a dispute over his editorial prejudices for Romantic poetry, subsequently became a close friend of Marsh. One son, Edmund, was in UVM's Class of 1839; another, Richard Henry Dana, Jr., was author of *Two Years Before the Mast*.

8. Samuel Taylor Coleridge, *The Friend: A Series of Essays to Aid in the Formation of Fixed Principles in Politics, Morals, and Religion*, with a brief preface by Marsh, was published in 1831 by Chauncey Goodrich in Burlington.

From Rufus Choate
Text: Brown, pp. 42–43

Salem, Massachusetts
November 14, 1829

My dear Sir

I thought it due to the respect and love I bear you, and to the kindness and delicacy of the terms in which you make it, to give your suggestion one week's consideration before trusting myself to act upon it. The result is that I feel it wholly impossible for me to execute this duty of friendship and literature in a manner worthy of the book or its editor, or of the elevated and important purposes at which you aim in this high enterprise. I know you believe me to be *willing* to do every thing in such circumstances which the relation we sustain to each other gives a right to expect, and it is with very real regret that I feel myself unable adequately to do this great thing. My habits have become almost exclusively professional, and my time, I don't very well know how, seems to be just about as completely engrossed by the cases of business as if, like Henry Brougham, I was habitually arguing my five causes a day.[1] But there are obstacles in the way which lie deeper, such as the difficulty of gathering up the faculties which are now scattered over the barren technicalities and frivolous controversies of my profession, and concentrating them finally upon a great moral and philosophical conception, like this of yours, worthily to write, edit, or review such a book. Though I never saw it I may say so. One should sit whole weeks and months, still, alone, in a study, with the Apollo Belvedere in marble to look upon, and Plato, Cicero, Bacon, Milton, and "all those" to converse with. I could no more raise myself into the mood for this achievement than I could make a better epic poem than the Iliad. But I rejoice that you have taken this matter in hand, and I firmly believe you will produce a glorious book most nobly edited. The employment of preparing it must be elevating and salutary, and I sincerely hope its general public success may be brilliant beyond the hopes of literary ambition. I shall buy the book, though I dare not undertake to review it.

I had no suspicion that the Orthodoxy of Andover "looked askance" at you or yours, and I suspect the matter has been overstated to you. But it may be so, since very much narrowness of mind and very great soundness of faith do sometimes go together, and the Professors have all a sort of strange horror of speculation, however regulated by a general orthodox belief, and a sincere love of truth and of man. But "*nitor in adversum*" says Burke, "is the motto for a man like me."[2] I should no more stop to consider how a volume of matured and brilliant thoughts would be received at Andover, than how it would be received by the Pope or President Jackson. "*Tu ne cede malis, sed contra audentior ito.*"[3] such was George Canning's self-exhortation, when he went forth morning and evening to fight the great battles of liberty and emancipation with the armed and mailed champions of old abuse, error, and political orthodoxy, and a thrilling and sustaining scripture it is.[4]

And now I shall insist upon your being perfectly satisfied with my declining this honor. If a more specific reason were necessary. I might add the principal term of our S. J. C.[5] is now here, has been for a fortnight, and will be till the last of December. Then I have to go to Boston for our winter's session. Nay, before that is over, I hope the country will ring from side to side with the fame of your book.

With best regards and wishes, and Mrs. Choate's respects,

I am yours affectionately,
R. Choate

1. Henry Brougham (1778–1868), despite his prominence in English political life during and after the Regency and despite his prolific writing for *The Edinburgh Review* in its early years (eighty articles in the magazine's first twenty numbers were written by Brougham), was hardly as

complimentary a comparison to himself as Choate seemed to think. Brougham was deficient in tact, apt to treat juries with impatience, and "seemed to think more of displaying his own powers than of getting verdicts for his clients" (*DNB*, 1360).
2. I strive against opposition. Edmund Burke (1729–1797), the English statesman.
3. Yield not to misfortunes, but confront them all the more bravely.
4. George Canning (1770–1827), English minister of foreign affairs (1822–27) and Prime Minister in 1827, advocate of Catholic emancipation and Greek independence, was the first foreign minister to have his nation recognize the free states of Spanish America. Canning asserted British independence from the Holy Alliance. Choate, whose principal accomplishments were as an advocate, here makes a good choice for comparison to himself. Canning was a remarkable parliamentary orator.
5. Supreme Judicial Council of the State of Massachusetts.

To Leonard Marsh
Ms: JMC

Hartford, Vermont
November 15, 1829

My dear brother

I am here according to your wishes and happy in being able to add something as I hope to the comfort and consolation of our dear and dying father. I came here the day before yesterday and found him much as I had expected from the letters of the girls though he has been more comfortable since I came than the early part of the week. His appetite is pretty good at present and he is quite fond of oysters of which I brought a few. We shall be able to get more now. But he is still much tried with pain in his back and hips, coughs and raises large quantities of matter and is extremely emaciated. I fear he cannot survive many days though perhaps he may several weeks. I shall stay with him for the present but shall probably see Dr. Twitchell[1] at Hanover in two or three days and he can perhaps judge better with regard to the progress of the disorder. The original disorder does not seem to me indeed to make any progress as he is little troubled with pain in the part immediately affected but his fever and cough must wear out his remaining strength fast. His mind seems quite composed and resigned to the will of God though he expresses less clear and animated views of the great objects of our faith and hope and love than I could wish to see him. I converse with him freely and am anxious to see his thoughts wholly fixed and intent on heaven and his heart there before he is called to possess his inheritance.

He seems much gratified at having us round him and we are all here now but Roswell and yourself. Mr. Goodrich[2] came last evening and will go on tomorrow but I think Arabella will stay and go when I do. It is difficult for me to be absent so long though I have now accomplished what I had to do with the work of Coleridge and you will see it in the New York bookstores in a few days. I wrote you a long letter a few weeks ago about it but I fear you have not received it as you did not mention any of the topics of it to Mr. Goodrich. I think you will find even my parts of the volume worth looking at. I must repeat in a word what I wrote before, that I expect the work will be not a little misapprehended and abused and I want you to do what you can to counteract the prejudices that may be raised. E.C. Tracy wrote me from Andover that he feared I should be burned alive for heresy and that the great men there were determined to believe that no good thing can come from that "Nazareth" Burlington. However, you will see I have managed to use Professor Stuart's authority for the doctrine that will be more obnoxious to prejudice as he is the author of a letter to the editors of the Christian Spectator which I have quoted and we shall see what will come of it.[3] At all events I think it will be acknowledged that I have spoken "out" and spoken freely —if not wisely. . . .

I see too by the papers that Rev. Benjamin Rice[4] of Petersburg, Virginia and a brother of Dr. Rice is about coming to New York as pastor of Pearl St. Church and hope you will not fail to call on him and introduce yourself with my respects. It will be introduction enough to tell them that you call by my request and you will find them glad to see you and they will make you perfectly at home in two minutes. Mrs. Rice is a sister of Dr. Alexander of Princeton and well worthy of her brother. I suppose they are coming about this time and presume that Dr. Rice will be there with them. If he is, wish you to see him, and shall probably have a package of books for Virginia containing one for him with a letter which I have written to him, sent to your care in New York. If so and he should be in the city, wish you to hand his to him there. At all events you will know where the books are and can see that he receives a copy.

There seems to be no chance yet to sell our property here and I am surprised you think of trusting Boyd[5] with so large a purchase as they say you mean in your letter to Arabella. But we must do the best we can—I find I was mistaken about Boyd's purchase but however he will not buy.

Mother thinks that father's pain is only relieved by the opium which is administered and it probably is so. There seems to be no ground to hope that we can do more than relieve him in such ways and prepare his mind as fast as possible for the solemn event that is coming so rapidly and so surely, and will come to all. He seems entirely patient and resigned but I hope may have more of the divine presence and more actual foretaste of heaven before he leaves us. Pray for him and for us all, my dear brother, and let us strengthen each other to every good work and word, doing with our might whatever we may find to do in our brief and hasty pilgrimage, that we may be the better prepared for that glorious rest which awaits the faithful.

With much love to all, your affectionate brother

Jas. Marsh

December 4, 1829

Pray write me soon and let me hear of your health and how you like my friends Mr. Morgan and his lady[6] and Coleridge. Mr. Goodrich has sent two dozen copies to C.'s publisher in London[7] and I enclosed one to Coleridge with a long letter. Those which I spoke to you of for Dr. Rice etc are sent in another way.

Give my love to Mr. and Mrs. Howard[8] and family.

Your affectionate brother

Jas. Marsh

1. Dr. Amos Twitchell (1781–1850), Dartmouth Class of 1802, practiced in Keene, New Hampshire, and was the most prominent physician in New Hampshire, and probably Vermont, in the second quarter of the nineteenth century.

2. Chauncey Goodrich, the Burlington publisher, had married Arabella Marsh. Leonard was studying medicine in New York City. Roswell had settled his law practice in Steubenville, Ohio.

3. Stuart found, on "reflection," that perhaps the

seem to me scriptural and excellent. And I have fewer objections to make to his doctrinal opinions than I supposed I should have when I read your Preface. And this fact leads me to think either that you have somehow misapprehended the prevailing sentiments of the orthodox in New England, or else that I differ from them more than I am aware.

As to many things which Coleridge asserts on the philosophy of religion, (if I am so happy as to understand him) I hold the same; though it would seem that both you and he regard those things as at war with what the Calvinists believe. But in some of these cases he appears to me to have adopted a mode of thinking and writing which makes plain things obscure and easy things difficult. I am able, if I mistake not, to take some doctrines which he holds forth, or rather covers up, with hard, abstruse, and almost unintelligible phraseology, and to express them in language which shall carry them to the mind of every enlightened Christian and philosopher with perfect clearness. Now I acknowledge it is a good thing to make men *think*, yea, and to *compel* them to it, if that is necessary. But it would be a serious question whether this can be most effectually done by investing moral and philosophical subjects in obscurity, or, by covering them with light. For myself, I wish as little of abstruseness and unintelligibleness in books as may be. I am conscious of too much of this in regard to many, if not most subjects, as they lie in my own mind; and I am always glad to find myself relieved by luminous thoughts and luminous language in others.

Coleridge appears to have a deep-toned piety, and very elevated views of the duty and happiness of communion with God. Nevertheless, I think his piety would shine more brightly, and would conduce more to advance the conversion of sinners and the welfare of Christ's Kingdom, if a less proportion of his thoughts were occupied with the abstruse things of religion, and if he had more of what distinguished Baxter, and Brainerd,[2] and Leighton too; more of a subdued, contrite, meek temper, so that he should say less and think of the reproaches which have been cast upon him. The philosophy of religion is, after all, worth but little. What can it do towards saving the world? What can it do for a Christian, when death draws near? What had the

Apostles to do with it? Or the martyrs? And yet it is this which appears to be the prominent object of contemplation with our Author. On this he appears to lay out his principal zeal. And here my beloved friend, let me say, that if the peculiarities of his metaphysical and religious opinions should ever take hold on the attention and feelings of ministers and students in general, and even of Presidents and Professors, as you seem to think desirable, I should look for consequences unutterably gloomy and dreadful. Even supposing him right, and supposing that in *him* a habit of thinking so metaphysical and abstract can consist with fervent piety and seek to do good; I doubt whether this would be the case with one in a hundred.

But in my apprehension, some of our Author's views of the doctrines of religion are not correct, perhaps I should do better to say, they are defective. *Most* that he advances on the Atonement meets my views. But he falls short, I think, of the plain doctrine of the Scriptures in regard to the relation of Christ's sufferings to the sins of men. Nor am I satisfied with his remarks as to Edward's doctrine of necessity, which I believe, in a general view, to be as demonstrable, as any proposition in Geometry. I should like very much to converse with you freely on that subject, and on some others. I don't quite understand what our author means by *free* will, what he sometimes, if I recollect right, makes essential to every moral agent, and sometimes peculiar to the Christian. So far as my recollection goes, his views at large on the influence of the divine Spirit appeared to me radically right, and his modifications of the doctrine exceedingly important. I should consider his chief error as to Christianity to be a defective view of the doctrine of redemption; and the chief source of error, a *philosophical* exegesis instead of *philological*.

Thus I have opened my heart freely, and filled my sheets and yet I have only said a little of what I should love to say, if I had time. The Lord bless you my dear friend and brother, in your great work, and bless the important institution over which you preside.

I should be glad to send you what I have published on Baptism,[3] had I an opportunity. Give my love to Mr. Torrey if he is with you.

I am yours with the sincerest affection and esteem
L. Woods

I have lately had a letter from Dr. Rice. He is well and prosperous.

1. Leonard Woods, Sr., (1774–1854), first professor of theology at Andover Theological Seminary (1808–46), was a moderate Calvinist and mediated disputes between Hopkinsians and Old Calvinists.

2. David Brainerd (1718–47), friend of Jonathan Edwards and missionary to the Indians of New Jersey, Pennsylvania, and western Massachusetts after 1742, caused a furor at Yale by his disparaging remarks about the piety of Tutor Whittlesey and the rector of the College. He was consequently expelled and went into the mission field, eventually residing with Edwards in western Massachusetts. His association with Edwards led first to the posthumous publication of his Journal (1746) and Edwards' life of Brainerd (1749).

3. *Lectures on Infant Baptism*, 2nd. ed. (Andover, 1829).

To Samuel Taylor Coleridge
Ms: UVM

University of Vermont
February 24, 1830

Dear and honoured Sir

I would not venture to trouble you with another letter before receiving an answer to my former one did not the circumstances which I shall mention seem to make it my duty to do so. Since I wrote before I have had the pleasure of learning something of your plans from my friend Mr. Wheeler of this state who enjoyed an interview with you. He tells me that you informed him you should publish soon another edition of "Aids to Reflection" with important alterations and it will probably be a matter of interest to the publisher here to be acquainted with the state of it. The edition of fifteen hundred published in November is so far sold and the work is engaging so much attention as to make it probable another edition may be called for in the course of the year. If so it would seem desirable by all means to publish from your second edition and I hope you will put it in our power to do so.[1] Any suggestions from you with regard to the additions which I have made to the volume and with reference to another edition here I should esteem a great favor. Especially would I be obliged to you if you could put it in my power to correct the typographical errors in the Letters republished from Blackwoods Magazine.[2]

The reception of the work among clergy and literary men has been so far as I have yet had the means of learning, very nearly what I anticipated. Most persons however who were not previously prepared for it would be unable in so short a time to form clear views of its character and tendency and we find that while they seem convinced of the great importance of it they are much bewildered by contemplating its principles solely in their relation to the systems to which their minds are accustomed. Some of the leading men among our speculative theologians of the older class will never comprehend its true character[3] while the most enterprising of the younger class are studying it with great ardour and admiration.

I have enjoyed the opportunity of reading within a few days a work of Professor Tholuck of Halle v. d. Sunde und Versohner[4] in which I find many striking coincidences with your own views and as he is known in this country as an orthodox and eminent divine I have thought I might make a profitable use of some parts of it in the next edition of the "Aids." My friend and colleague here Professor Torrey who has been more conversant with your writings than almost any one in this country and who has spent some time in habits of intimacy with Professor Tholuck during the past year tells me that his views coincide in most important points with yours and from the place which he now holds among the learned men of Germany I supposed the fact might be gratifying to you. I ought perhaps to have presumed that you were informed by a less circuitous method.

Mr. Wheeler expresses himself in strong terms in regard to the pleasure and profit which he enjoyed in his interviews with you and interested me much by his account of your conversation on several topics especially the Trinity on which I am anxious with many others to see your views at large.[5] It is a subject of great interest in New England and though the subject has been much discussed here little or no progress has been made in the development of it. Your philosophical principles and your mode of treating that subject seem to me likely to have more influence by far than any thing which has been published here. Dr. Channing[6] whom you know is considered I believe the leading advocate of Unitarianism and though a fine writer and possessing a mind of high order is not considered by those who are capable of judging I believe as a very profound philosopher or a very logical reasoner. His knowledge of German metaphysics is derived from secondary sources and confessedly superficial. I had the pleasure of conversing with him for the first time a few weeks ago and ought perhaps to take this opportunity to give you his explanation of remarks made by him respecting his interview with youself and which Mr. Wheeler I think told me had come to your knowledge. He told me that in letters to Mr. Allston[7] you expressed much gratification at the interview and a high opinion of him, that he in speaking of it observed you could not have heard much of him as he conversed little but left the conversation to you, that however he intended to express no *dissatisfaction* for indeed his object was to converse only so much as to direct your mind to the topics on which he wished to learn your views. He seemed chagrined that his language had been published in a gross and offensive form and seemed to suppose though he did not have it from me that you might have met with the account. He reads and advises his friends to read your writings and expressed much gratification that an edition of the Aids had been published here.

An early answer with regard to the publication of your next edition would be desirable. Mr. Goodrich would make an arrangement with your publisher[8] if he knew whom you employ as he will probably wish to procure a copy as soon as it is published.

With the highest regards
Jas. Marsh.

P.S. Mr. Goodrich requests that two copies may be sent to him by your publisher one to the C. and G. and H. Carvill, New York,[9] and one to the care of Hilliard Gray and Co. Boston.

1. Marsh's first American edition of *Aids*, published in November 1829, was from the first London edition; his second American edition used the second London edition. Shedd's edition (New York, 1853) used H. N. Coleridge's fourth edition with Marsh's "Preliminary Essay," though without most of Marsh's notes.

2. Coleridge, as he told

Emerson, failed to respond to Marsh's letters.
3. An allusion, doubtless, to Leonard Woods, Sr.; see his letter to Marsh, January 11, 1830.
4. See letter from Marsh to Torrey, July 16, 1829, note 6. Tholuck's treatise on sin and redemption was a seminal text in the development of Romantic theology.
5. During his tour of Europe with Torrey, John Wheeler managed to visit Coleridge briefly in late 1829 and was thus the only Vermont transcendentalist to see Coleridge plain. A journal of Wheeler's trip survived at Burlington until the 1950s but seems now to have been lost.
6. William Ellery Channing (1780–1842).
7. Washington Allston (1779–1843), the American artist and friend of Coleridge who painted his portrait.
8. While William Pickering and John Murray published much of Coleridge's work, especially Pickering from the late 1820s on, the first English edition of *Aids to Reflection* was published by Taylor and Hessey. The second edition of *Aids* was published in 1831 by Hurst and Chance.
9. C. and G. and H. Carvill were English successors to James Eastburn in New York City.

From William Allen[1]
Ms: JMC

Bowdoin College
June 17, 1830

My dear Sir,

By this opportunity I would say to you a few words, although I have but a moment's time, in which to write. Your remarks in the Introduction to Aids to Reflection are deemed by some rather heretical, and they even have been quoted, on the other side, as proofs, that there is a declension from the stiffness of former days. But on one great point, that of human *power*, so essentially connected with the sense of accountableness, I have for some years been inclined to adopt what I suppose are also your own views—and have occasionally given such instruction to the Senior Class: that is, have stated, that motives are not efficient causes, and therefore a volition is not accounted for by ascribing it to motives: a *determiner* must be found, and that determiner, unless some other Spirit, is our own Spirit. Our own mind is the originator: the cause. Here is power; and we would have no idea of power in God, unless we first found it in ourselves. The denial of this makes God the universal agent—and comes to Spinozism in fact—destroying the sense of responsibleness. We are all conscious of this power;

and reasoning cannot destroy this consciousness. Edwards[2] uses the term *cause* in a double sense.

Now, if the old notion of power is true, there is one thing, which we have to consider, and that is the method of reconciling it with our dependence on the divine Spirit, which being done, we shall have this great advantage in our doctrine, that, opposing nothing of old believed concerning the merciful agency of God, it casts away the doctrine, which if really embraced and carried out in just consequence must, agreeably to the argument of Dr. Priestley,[3] destroy the feeling of remorse, the reality of accountableness. But I have not time to enlarge. Let us search for truth.

With affectionate remembrance to Mrs. Marsh, I am, dear Sir,

Very respectfully.
Your sincere Friend,
Wm. Allen

1. William Allen (1784–1868), president of Bowdoin College (1819–31, 1833–38) and compiler of the first American biographical dictionary, had been president of the short-lived Dartmouth University and was married to Maria Wheelock (1788–1828), John Wheelock's daughter.

2. Jonathan Edwards.

3. Joseph Priestley (1733–1804), the English clergyman and chemist, among his earliest writings produced a theological treatise, *The Scripture Doctrine of Remission*, in which he constructs the argument of accountability referred to by Allen.

From Gulian C. Verplanck[1]
Ms: UVM

New York
October 14, 1830

Reverend Sir

As Columbia College has at the late commencement added your name to its list of honorary graduates you may perhaps read with some interest the discourse which you will receive with this letter delivered before the literary societies of that ancient and respectable institution.

Permit me at the same time that I request your acceptance of this pamphlet[2] to express to you the very great gratification which I have received from your preface and notes to your reprint of Coleridge.

and the results of our experience in as few words as possible. Facts are worth more than theories, however, especially when they are carefully observed with reference to the theories which they illustrate and indeed it is no less true that facts are food for nothing except as the exponents of theory or of permanent principles. Now in our case though the experiment has been made indeed on a small scale, that is with only about forty students, it has yet been made after much deliberation upon the principles adopted and with a distinct object in view. The results have been all that the circumstances permitted us to expect and such as fully to confirm our belief in the correctness of our general principles. We have no combinations or rebellions, no feelings of jealousy or of diversity of interest be-between the faculty and students and find the conduct of the idle and vicious as readily and as fully disapproved of by the rest of the students as by the members of the faculty themselves. We divide classes according to their progress so far as the interest of their studies seems to require it and the duties of the instructors will permit and as yet have found no dissatisfaction among the students on that account. Our simple principle is to keep every one employed and aid each in his progress as far as may be, and we find no evils growing out of it. Some accomplish three and four times as much as others and yet we do not find the poorer students disposed to cast the blame upon us, though several have left College who in a different system would probably have been retained. But we consider this as desirable on their account and their parents, if not on our own, as it would be we think unjust to them to permit them to be deceived and think it is useful for a young man to spend his time at College who cannot or will not learn. The pamphlet as you will perceive was written in haste and printed in a very cheap style but is such as the circumstances seemed to require as we had neither time nor money to make it what we wished. I send it to you Sir both on account of your connexion with the general Committee and because I do not recollect who was chairman of the Committee on the subject of College government and instruction. I have the impression it is one of your number in New York and will thank you, if it is, to hand it to him after making such other use of it yourself as you may wish. I send also other things with it as being necessary to explain the "Exposition" itself. I may probably have and I know that Mr. Woodbridge[4] and probably others will have, a wish to make their views known more fully to the same Committee or to the public in connexion with their report. The late meeting is every where so far as I can learn spoken of with much respect as an interesting assemblage, and now that the objects of it are more clearly defined I think we may anticipate from the next and future meetings results of much value to the cause of learning among us. I feel myself and know that many others have the same feeling that we are under obligations to your committee for their enterprise and liberality in bringing us together and for myself shall value the opportunity afforded of forming new and valuable acquaintances both among the gentlemen of the city and others as more than an equivalent of my time and troubles. With much respect and the best wishes for you and yours I remain your very obedient Servant

Jas. Marsh.

1. James MacFarlane Mathews (1785–1870), a Dutch Reformed clergyman, was the first chancellor of New York University.
2. A convention of clergymen and prominent educators had gathered in the City Council chamber in New York City to discuss the establishment of a university in the city of New York.
3. Henry Vethake (1792–1866) was professor of mathematics and philosophy at Princeton (1829–31) and then the newly opened New York University (1832–5).
4. William Channing Woodbridge (1794–1845), Yale Class of 1811, would establish *The American Annals of Education* in 1831.

From Charles Hodge
Ms: UVM

Princeton
November 22, 1830

My dear Sir

I am sorry that circumstances prevented my replying immediately to your letter of the fourth received by Mr. Fleming[1] last week. I feel indebted to you for the clearness with which you have expressed your apprehensions of the purport of Coleridge's theory on the Atonement though I am bound to state that my views on the subject remain substantially what they were before. You seem however to have misconceived in some measure what I intended to express in our conversations in New York. I am far from supposing that Coleridge "stands on the same footing with Socinianism"[2] in regard to that subject. I am well aware that all parts of his system are closely connected and that it is impossible that a doctrine so important as that of the atonement should in his mind be uninfluenced by the general principles of his religious philosophy which every one knows differs toto coelo from that of our Socinians and the German Rationalists. The idea which I meant to convey was this, that it seemed to me that there are but three radical views on the atonement, all others being modifications of one or the other of these. The first, which I presume is the one which the tribute of historical orthodoxy at least, is due, is that the atonement of Christ was intended to answer the necessity for the punishment of sin arising out of the perfections of the divine nature. The second that it was intended to produce an impression on the intelligent universe which should supercede the necessity of punishing transgressors by preventing the evils which would arise from gratuitous forgiveness; and thirdly that the death of Christ produced its effects by operating a subjective change in us. Now nothing appears more clear to me than that however Coleridge and Unitarians may differ, and differ I admit they do, as to the manner in which it produces this change yet they agree in this that the production of this change is its distinctive object and that it is in virtue of this change that our reconciliation to God takes place. You must be sensible that this is changing the whole system of the Gospels, as it has been commonly understood. That instead of the sinners depending on what Christ has done, as the ground of his acceptance, he is taught to look to himself, to a change wrought in his own heart, whether by "the law of nature" or by some incomprehensible and supernatural influence (as to this point) matters not, as the reason of his being pardoned and restored to God's favor. I need not of course take the trouble, in writing to you, to indicate the points of agreement between this and the old system especially as to the grand ultimate object and result of Christ's death viz. the sanctification of his people. I merely wish to convey the idea that I can not understand the "Aids to Reflection" in any other way than as rejecting the essential principle of the doctrine in question, in as much as it denies that the death of Xt is a satisfaction to Divine Justice either vindicatory or governmental, but teaches that it is only a means in common language to change the hearts of sinners.

Though my dear Sir, I feel so utterly unable to regard Coleridge otherwise than as having seriously departed from the truth as to this point I fully appreciate the force of your remarks as to the liability of the work and its American Editor being inconsiderately and unjustly condemned should the vague charge of Socianism be brought against it. Every feeling of my heart revolts at the idea of being in any measure instrumental in raising a thoughtless hue and cry against any thing or any person. But when a book has been sent out to the world its contents are the fair and proper subjects of candid examination. And if any one believes that they are erroneous, and injurious in their tendency, he is not only authorized but, bound to make it appear that they are so, if he has it in his power. I know that it is your object to cherish the love of truth and to promote the spirit of free investigation and that you desire nothing more, than that your own views and those of any work you publish should not be misapprehended or misrepresented. It is very doubtful indeed whether I shall attempt to prepare any paper on the subject of the Atonement, and I certainly should not say any thing in reference to yourself, even if I did. The subject is one of vital importance and I feel so little competent to do it justice and so little able to fathom the depths of German Philosophy that I am very loath to undertake such a task.[3] Still I think that it ought to be done. That some consistent [. . .][4] view of this subject is much needed in our country at this time and I confess [. . .] that the influence of Coleridge as [. . .] will not be favorable to the cause[. . .] this point at least.

Should I be led to write any thing [. . .] in which the views of Coleridge are referred [. . .] will endeavor to apprize you in [. . .] the ground taken that I may be [. . .] of doing any thing which better information [. . .] lead me to think an act of injustice. [. . .] I shall always be very glad to hear from you and am now

Yours with great respect
C. Hodge

1. Archibald Fleming (1800–75), a graduate of the University of Glasgow and UVM Class of 1828, attended Princeton Theological Seminary (1829–32) and during the 1830s and '40s was minister to numerous congregations in Vermont, New Hampshire, and New York. He also lectured on chemistry at UVM (1847–49).
2. Marsh had responded in a now lost letter to remarks Hodge had made about Coleridge at a meeting of educators and other clergymen in New York City convened to discuss and plan the establishment of New York University.
Faustus Socinus (1539–1604) argued that Luther and Calvin had not gone far enough in reforming the church. Socinus held that human reason was the only basis for Protestantism. In 1588 he disputed many of the central dogmas of the reformed church, e.g. redemption, Christ's divinity, and original sin. The German rationalists of the eighteenth century were accused of Socinianism for their emphasis on reason.
3. Although Hodge had studied in Germany in 1828, by 1839 and 1840 *The Biblical Repertory*, the journal published at Princeton with which Hodge had always been closely associated, would become vehemently anti-transcendentalist and anti-German. Joseph Alexander (1809–60) in 1839 called Emerson "an infidel and an atheist, who nevertheless makes esoteric sense of the new philosophy, of the new terms and phrases consecrated to a religious use." In 1840 he warned the magazine's readers against "German atheism, which the spirit of Darkness is employing ministers of the gospel to smuggle among us under false pretenses" [*Biblical Repertory*, 11 (1839), 97–98; 12 (1840), 71].
4. Brackets indicate a tear in the holograph.

To Leonard Marsh[1]
Ms: JMC

Burlington
February 26, 1831

My dear brother

I find it so difficult to get an answer from you that I am nearly discouraged about writing. However I must try once more and insist on such an answer at least as will let us know whether you are still in rerum natura or not. I received a few days ago a letter from the Carvills[2] with a bill of about twenty-five or thirty dollars. I wish you would see them and pay the $10 in your hands. I shall pay the rest soon. Have you seen the doings of our Literary Convention as published.[3] Wheeler wrote me they were published but did not say in what form and I have not learned. Pray send me a copy if one can be had immediately. A particular reason for wanting it is that we are about publishing a new edition of our pamphlet and may wish to say something with reference to the views exhibited in that convention. You have on the other page here a copy of our Course of study and will find if I hope sufficiently thorough. We are determined to take some measures to make our plans and their operation known to the public. The agents of Middlebury are so active that without some countervailing exertions they will get the ear of the public and the students. I happen to know of a single agent of theirs who since last commencement has persuaded three students to go there who had prepared and made up their minds to come here.[4] You must write something about us, our course of study etc etc.

By the way do you know who wrote an article about Coleridge copied in the New York Evening Post from an Oswego paper. Somebody sent me a copy from New York and Mr. Verplanck[5] who seems to be very friendly sent one from Washington. He conjectured it to be by a Mr. Bunner[6] as I read his writing, an old friend of his in the west of New York and once a member of Congress.

Mother is here for a few weeks and I hope you will write us before she returns. Daniel and Col. Pitkin are deep in the Amber concern.[7] What is the present elevation of your *Balloon*?[8] Does it go up or down. Pray write us all about it and when you can do no better come and see us.

Jas.

1. Leonard was still studying medicine with a Dr. Mott in New York City.
2. G., C. and H. Carvill, English successors to James Eastburn, the Broadway bookseller.
3. *Journal of the Proceedings of a Convention of Scientific and Literary Gentlemen, Held in the Common Council Chamber of the City of New York, October, 1830* (New York: Leavitt and Carvill, 1831). The meeting was held for the purpose of discussing proposals for establishing New York University.

4. UVM alumni records list only nineteen graduates, excluding medical graduates, from 1831 to 1834. Less than 150 students attended Middlebury College at any one time during the early 1830s.
5. Gulian Verplanck.
6. Probably Rudolph Bunner (1779–1837), an Adams democrat and the father of Henry Cuyler Bunner. The younger Bunner was editor of *Puck* (1877–96).
7. Their brother Daniel and a cousin, Thomas White Pitkin (1772–1861). Pitkin was the son of Rhoda Marsh, who was the elder Daniel Marsh's sister, and married Mary Bill, the daughter of Dorothy Marsh, another sister of the elder Daniel. Pitkin was a physician who earned the title of Colonel in the War of 1812. Pitkin's granddaughter, Caroline, married Louis Joseph Papineau, grandson of the Canadian Patriot leader. Daniel and Pitkin's efforts to find and market turpentine from Vermont's pine forests seem not to have been successful.
8. Leonard attempted various inventions, including a balloon and a water wheel device.

To Leonard Marsh
Ms: JMC

Burlington
April 17, 1831

My dear brother

I send you another line to tell you of a chance to send back again and beg you will not let it pass again if you can avoid it. This will be carried by Mr. Wood[1] of this place and he will stay either at Hayes' (The Franklin house) or at the new establishment of Howard and Lyon corner of Broad and Wall Streets. I send by him also a bundle of pamphlets which he will keep till you call for them.[2] They are directed to various persons and the best way to distribute them probably will be to put them in the Post Office. One to Professor Vethake at Princeton and one to Professor Adrain[3] at Philadelphia wish you would put in covers and direct them.

Wish you would look in the bookstores of Leavitt and Haven for Tholuck on Romans[4] and send it to me if you can find it and pay for it. Or you may show this and ask them to charge it to me. I want it as soon as may be and if it is not to be found ask Leavitt to get it for me.

We are all as usual here and hope to see you this Spring.

Jas Marsh

1. Rev. Nathan Wood (d. 1864).
2. Copies of the revised *Exposition of Instruction . . . in the University of Vermont.*
3. Henry Vethake (1792–1866), mathematician and philosopher, served as professor of mathematics at Columbia (1810–13), Rutgers (1813–17), Princeton (1817–21), Dickinson (1821–29), Princeton (1829–31), New York University (1832–35) and subsequently Washington College and the University of Pennsylvania.
Robert Adrain (1775–1843) was vice-provost of the University of Pennsylvania (1828–34) and, with Nathaniel Bowditch, one of the two most prominent American mathematicians.
4. Tholuck's *Commentary on Romans* (1825; Edinburgh trans. 1834–36) was one of the first fruits of the new Romantic theology.

From Alonzo Potter[1]
Ms: UVM

Schenectady, New York
August 18, 1831

Reverend and dear Sir

Will you pardon the liberty which, though a stranger, I take in asking of you the favour of a letter to Mr. Coleridge in England. Ill health compels me to resort to a voyage—and the "Aids to Reflection" which you have been the means of bringing before the American public have excited in me a sharp desire to see their author. The views which he presents which are so happily sustained in your introduction, are views many of which I have held some years, and I cannot but hope that their promulgation under such auspices, is destined, in this country at least, to effect a new era in Moral and Metaphysical Philosophy. Having it in contemplation to accept on my return, the chair of Moral Philosophy in Union College, to which I have been recently elected, I feel of course a peculiar interest in these views, and a desire to hear them developed from the lips of Mr. Coleridge himself. I am sensible that there is no gentleman in this country whose letters would be so likely to secure me the attention of Mr Coleridge,[2] and you will not be surprised therefore that I have felt emboldened to make the request with which this letter opens.

For the last five years I have been Rector of St. Paul's Church Boston, a station from which I retire now only from ill-health and a desire to do something towards placing Moral Science in this country upon a basis different from that on which it now stands.

What are my character and standing you may learn from any of the Episcopal Clergy of Vermont.

Should you feel warranted in acceding to my request, be pleased to enclose the letter to me at this place.

I am dear Sir with great respect

Yours faithfully
A. Potter

1. Alonzo Potter (1800–65) was rector of St. Paul's Church, Boston (1826–31), professor of philosophy at Union College (1831–45), and Episcopal bishop of Pennsylvania post-1845.
2. Potter seems not to have visited Coleridge.

Thomas P. Smith[1] to Chauncey Goodrich
Ms: JMC

Paris, Kentucky
January 27, 1832

Mr. Chauncey Goodrich
Dear Sir

About twelve months since I gave to a merchant of this place a memorandum to call at Towar and Hogans[2] and procure a copy of Select Practical Theology.[3] He procured me one, where I did not ask, nor did it occur to me that any mistake had happened until about the first of last month when I received a packet which on opening I found to be a copy sent by you to me in Philadelphia and then was sent to Mr. Kinnay of Troy.[4] I immediately wrote to Tower and Hogan who in reply say they know not how the accident occurred nor do I attach any other importance to it now than that it affords me an apology for my apparent neglect to pay you the sum and which to prevent all failures I herewith enclose to you.

I purchased when in Cincinnati in November last a copy of the Friend,[5] published by you, which has just been unpacked. How long before the Lay Sermons[6] will be out. Do send me a copy of them as soon as published.

And can you not, my dear Sir, procure for me by importation directly or indirectly, or otherwise, the whole of Coleridges works. I do not include the poems unless they contain some of his peculiarities. I am no poet. His Biography as published in America I had procured from a person who had never read it and who cared nothing for it.

The views of Coleridge on the Atonement are admirable and unanswerable. I would rejoice to see them in an American dress by such an one as the author of the prefatory remarks to Aids to Reflection—then they would be generally remarked upon, Reviewed and read—now no Reviewer is willing to Review Coleridge's work and few are willing to view for themselves. A Divine of some emminence in the west in a late Sermon on John 5 in one of his inferences argued the vast value of the Soul, because God would not give for a thing more than its value but he had given his son for the world, therefore the souls of the world were of equal value with the son of God. This you will probably say was stupendous theology—yet such views are prevalent here—and to say that paying a price as used by the Apostle was metaphor would lead to subject one almost to church censure.

Of Coleridge's views on Original Sin the Eucharist and Baptism I am not satisfied. He however says enough on the first to show the folly of the controversy between the Spectator and Biblical Repertory. On the second subject the Eucharist you can furnish me with any book on the subject such as President Marsh approves. I would feel under lasting obligations to you. On the subject of Baptism I think he is wrong; he however succeeds there in his main point.

I have been thinking that you can order them on from England, knowing better than I what Books to buy and where to apply to—the only difficulty is you may feel a little qualmish about trusting me—now to remove all doubts, say what sum I shall send you in advance by way of making you safe and I will do it. The Balance of the $5 after paying you what I owe, you will please use for my benefit in paying for such Book in whole or in part as will aid me in obtaining an insight in Coleridge's metaphysics. Hereafter you will please send Books to me, directed as formerly, with directions to deliver and receive pay for them when called for. I can send to Philadelphia for them twice a year and would prefer paying for them when received in Philadelphia. I trust I have opened my wants intelligently and that you will use your best exertions to supply them. Don't my dear Sir, answer me by declining the business, but as was said to me, go forward. Let me hear from you when convenient.

Respectfully
Tho. P. Smith

I was going to write but struck it out that I forgot that you were in the North and I in Kentucky—but you I suppose know the character of our folks.

1. Thomas Porter Smith (1793–1868), lawyer and county clerk of Bourbon County, Kentucky, was known as "Mr. Presbyterian" of northeastern Kentucky. See below, letter for November 14, 1834, from Smith to Marsh.
2. J. Towar and D. M. Hogan, printers and publishers in Pittsburgh, Pennsylvania.
3. *Select Practical Theology of the Seventeenth Century, Comprising the Best Practical Works of the Great English Divines, and other Congenial Authors of that Age.* Collected and arranged, with biographical sketches and occasional notes, by James Marsh, President of the University of Vermont. In five volumes. Volume 1. Containing "The Blessedness of the Righteous," and "The Vanity of Man as Mortal," by the Rev. John Howe, and "Discourses on the Four Last Things," by Dr. Wm. Bates (New York: G. C. & H. Carvill. Burlington: Chauncey Goodrich, 1830).
4. Unidentified.
5. Samuel Taylor Coleridge, *The Friend: A Series of Essays to Aid in the Formation of Fixed Principles in Politics, Morals, and Religion.* First American edition from the second London edition (Burlington: Chauncey Goodrich, 1831).
6. Samuel Taylor Coleridge, *The Statesman's Manual or The Bible the Best Guide to Political Skill and Foresight: A Lay Sermon, Addressed to the Higher Classes of Society* (Burlington: Chauncey Goodrich, 1832).

From Nathaniel S. Harris[1]
Ms: JMC

West Point, New York
April 9, 1832

Sir:

The relation in which you stand to the system of Philosophy, which promises to become "the American Philosophy," must excuse even a stranger for referring himself to you for information.

Will you do me the favor to indicate some work on the attributes, or indeed a body of Divinity,

a better philosophy in this country and particularly to make men perceive that there is still more in the depths of their own minds that is worth exploring, and which cannot be had cheap and handy in the works of the Scotch and English dealers in philosophy. Still there is a want of good text-books, of works in which that spirit of a better philosophy is carried into each of its special branches. And here the important question arises, which of the various disciplines which constitute the highest department of human knowledge, should be selected to begin the work of reformation. There are two on which I rest my hopes as the pioneers in philosophy. In a community which is deluged with superficial discussions on momentous questions which can be settled only by philosophic principles, I look upon Psychology and the history of Philosophy as the parents of a new race of thoughts and modes of reasoning. Those, therefore, who would dispose and prepare the public mind for the reception of philosophy in all its branches, who would lead men not only to use, but to understand their own reason, should lend the whole weight of their intellectual eminence to those two sciences. The one makes men acquainted with the ideas of others on the subject of philosophy, the other teaches them its realities in their own minds; the one leads their understandings abroad to become acquainted with the intellectual world without them, the other guides them home to its living springs within them. I am not acquainted with a thorough work or a good text-book on either of those sciences in English; and in German literature, rich as it is in valuable works in these departments, I know no one of which a mere translation would meet the wants of the community, though they furnish excellent materials. Thus, in the philosophy of the human mind, the Anthropology of Kant, and the Psychologies of Carus, Fries,[3] and others, would greatly aid an able compiler, but neither of them would of itself probably succeed in supplanting the genteel and palatable philosophy of Brown.[4] In the history of philosophy, an extract from Tenneman's great work,[5] considerably larger than his own synopsis of it, I should think would be the most suitable undertaking. A truly philosophical logic seems to me the third great desideratum; and it was with great pleasure that I heard from our mutual friend, Mr. Henry,[6] that you had actually announced one on the basis of Fries,[7] whose work I consider the best on that subject. Among the German works on logic, in your possession, you do not mention that of Schulze, (the author of Aenesidemus,)[8] which he used as a text-book in his lectures in Göttingen, and that of Jäsche,[9] compiled from the notes taken of Kant's lectures on logic. If these books should be of any service to you, I should be happy to lend them to you, and will send them in any way you may point out. There are many other topics on which I wish to communicate with you, particularly the plan of Mr. Henry to publish a philosophical journal, which seems to me a very desirable object. But I must conclude now, with the expression of my hope that this summer will not pass away without bringing me the pleasure of a personal acquaintance with you. At any rate, I earnestly hope for a frequent exchange of thought with you upon subjects of such deep interest to us both. With the highest esteem,

Your friend and servant,
Charles Follen

1. Charles Follen (1796–1840) was the first professor of German language and literature at Harvard (1825–35).

2. Follen's *Inaugural Discourse*, delivered September 3, 1831, attributed to German philosophy—the "science of sciences"—the great flowering of German literature and the phenomenal progress made by German scientists.

3. The first complete American translation of Kant's *Anthropology* was executed by Adolph E. Kroeger in W. T. Harris's *Journal of Speculative Philosophy* during the 1870s.

Carl Gustav Carus (1789–1869), German physician and philosopher at the University of Dresden, argued that ideas in experience unfold from an unorganized multiplicity to an organized and organic unity. Developing unity he called God. Not analogous to human intelligence, this developing unity is, however, the ground of being revealed through becoming. Carus called this theory "entheism." His book *Psyche: zur Entwicklungsgeschichte der Seele* was not published until 1846.

Jakob Friedrich Fries (1773–1843), German follower and elaborator of Kant, emphasized the analytic and methodological aspects of Kant's critical philosophy. Fries came from a Moravian Piestistic background and thus stressed the importance of "pure feeling" as a manifestation of "the infinite in the finite." One of his earliest publications, in Erhard Schmid's *Psychologische Magazine* 3 (1789), was entitled "Über das Verhältniss der empirischen Psychologie zur Metaphysik."

4. Thomas Brown (1778–1820), the Scottish metaphysician, argued in *Cause and Effect* (1804) that Hume's skepticism was not compatible with religion.
5. Wilhelm Gottlieb Tennemann's *Geschichte der Philosophie*, 11 vols. (Leipzig, 1798–1819), was translated into French by Cousin (1839) and Italian by Romagnosi and Poli (1832). B. B. Edwards and Edward Parks of Andover Theological Seminary also translated Tennemann's *System der Platonischen Philosophie* (1839).
6. Caleb Sprague Henry (1804–84), Dartmouth Class of 1825, Andover 1829, was minister to Congregational churches in Greenfield, Massachusetts, and West Hartford, Connecticut, until converting to the Episcopal Church in 1835. Ordained in 1836, he was appointed professor of intellectual philosophy at New York University (1838–52), gave courses in *belles-lettres* and history, and was the founding editor of *The New York Review* (1837–40).
7. Fries's *Wissen, Glaube und Ahndung* (Jena, 1805) was a popular exposition of his three-fold approach to reality. Marsh owned a copy of the book. Fries's chief work before 1832 was the three-volume *Neue Kritik der Vernunt* (Heidelberg, 1806–7), an attempt to correct and restate the Kantian critiques of speculative and practical reason. His *Ethik* (1818) argued for political equality and individual liberty.
   Marsh's translation of Fries was never published. A ms. text of lectures survives, however, with an inscription on the front cover indicating that it is based on a translation of Fries's *Logic*.
8. Gottlob Ernst Schultze, *Aenesidemus* . . . (1792). In 1831 Schultze had just published his fifth edition of *Grundsatze der allgemeinen Logik* (Göttingen).
9. Gottlob Benjamin Jäsche's *Immanuel Kant's Logik. Ein Handbuch zu Vorlesungen* seems not to have been generally available until 1866 when J. H. von Kirchmann published it in his *Philosophie Bibliothek*.

From C. S. Henry
Ms: JMC

Cambridge,
Massachusetts
May 15, 1832

My dear Sir,

I thank you very heartily for your letter, particularly for the information that you are about to publish a book on Logic. I shall eagerly await its appearance, and hope it may do much towards introducing a better and more precise language in philosophy. It occurred to me however, that, as the work must probably involve the results of psychological analysis, and also metaphysical principles, unknown or unrecognized in this country, it would not be quite easy to secure for its terms, distinctions, and forms a just appreciation. You might indeed do something in the way of a glossary, exercising the right formally conceded to every writer of employing such language as seems to him best, provided he precisely defines the sense in which he means to be taken. But you would *wish* certainly, to obtain something more than this *toleration*. You wish to effect a revolution in the Science. You do not wish to make changes *arbitrarily*; you would like that the validity, importance, grounds and extent, of the changes you make should be intelligently appreciated. It has therefore been a question with me whether we should not have to begin with psychology and the History of Philosophy. However, with so imperfect a notion of what precisely you mean to do in your work, it is not worth while to make suggestions which may be quite irrelevant. I only wish you the utmost success. Sure I am that your labors will *deserve* to be valued.

In regard to the projected Periodical. The more I cast about, the less sanguine I confess I am in respect to the practicability of doing much in that way. This comes in my mind, not so much from any intrinsic difficulties in the plan, or from the state of Philosophical and religious parties, as from the impossibility of finding any individual or number of persons, *rich enough*, and at the same time with enough of *interest* in the object, to take the pecuniary risk, and allow a fair experiment to be made. If I were rich enough I would certainly have a work set agoing, and I do believe that in the long run it would prosper. I do not think the difficulties stated in your letter are by any means insurmountable. Some of the objections you mention seem to me valid only on the supposition that the projected work must necessarily announce itself as the organ of a new sect or party in Philosophy and Religion, and take an attitude controversial and hostile to all existing parties. Probably I must have failed in giving a distinct notion of such a work as I would wish to see. In the first place, the work should not explain itself either wholly or mainly (and not at all explicitly) as a Philosophical and Theological Work. Again. It need not be *controversial*. It need not and it ought not to have a polemic, hostile, irritating character. Probably I explained myself imperfectly on this point; certainly I gave my judgment, *to you*, on the existing state of opinions with a sharpness and positiveness that, *in such* a *work*, would be polemic, and dogmatical and exceedingly unwise. Nor, farther, should I ever think of engaging in the vain attempt to *popularize* philosophy: to bring down the subjects of higher speculation from the region where they belong and where they are the property of those who have the gift of philosophic insight and the power of higher speculation. Contrary to all this, the work should seek to secure reputation, influence and authority on *general grounds*, rather than be considered as devoted to any special system or sect. It should endeavor to be superior to any existing work for sound learning and able writing. It should embrace all the general subjects of Learning, Literature, History, etc, presenting comprehensive views and able discussions. Only these subjects may be treated in a spirit and tone harmonizing with a better philosophy, and at the same time without any such formal and systematic, still less controversial, exposition of it, as would create suspicion or provoke hostility.

Now *in connection* with this *general* mode of conducting the work, every thing should be done, which may be done *wisely* and with prudent regard to the existing prejudices and parties, to *advance* the *great cause which we have at heart*. And I can think of several ways in which it seems to me much might be done, to which your objections would not apply, or in which the difficulties might be greatly avoided. In the *first place*, there are many subjects in psychology, metaphysics, and morals, which a prudent regard to the existing state of things would not forbid to be investigated in the way of calm discussion, and in which great and universal *principles* might be developed and unfolded, not negatively and controversially, but positively; in which the inquiry conducted above and aloof from the conflicts of particular parties, may set forth a *principle* whose *light* shall, of itself in thinking men, explode many an error and controversy without our taking the trouble to direct a special polemic against it, or to set wrongheaded champions right, who are squabbling together in mutual blindness of the great *principle* which would reveal to them all how idly they were combatting. As subjects of this kind, I might instance the question of materialism—the doctrine of Life—the principles of causality—the ground of moral obligation, etc.

In the *next place, Historical Exposition.* "The powers that be" cannot, with any grace, object to lucid and impartial exhibition of opinions which as matters of history, have been held. And it seems to me that much may be done in this way in regard to Philosophy and Theology to remove prejudice of one's conception, and to enlighten and emancipate thinking minds. Your own reflection will suggest what I would say on this point if I had time and room.

I have thus given some hints as to what might be done for Philosophy and Theology scientifically considered and without attempting too much to render it *popular*.

Then, as to the more popular portion of the work, there would be room to effect much by endeavoring to set forth in the most favorable light those *practical and spiritual* views and sentiments in which we are at one with all true Christians, and which at the same time are not otherwise seen so well in all their feelings and richness (e.g. doctrine of Holy Spirit, new-birth, divine indwelling, etc.) as by us who hold them as fruits and growth of a better philosophy. We might set forth these practical truths, these glorious *facts*, with unction, and show their harmony with the gospel and with man's wants.

Finally, I wish to see a work in which honor shall be given to whom honor is due; in which such writing as *you* and others have produced and may produce shall receive honorable and respectful mention in those thousand allusions, references and quotations which might perpetually have place in a general work where the writers appreciate and value such labors. If this was done in any present publication of weight and credit, one great source of my dissatisfaction would be removed. But the men and the works, which are respectfully named, or alluded to, or quoted, or given as authority, in our periodicals, are *not those* who deserve it most: while the men and the works which *we* think most of, are either passed in silence or named invidiously. Now I believe the influence of a work, in this respect, which should on general grounds acquire reputation and weight, would be immense in promoting the cause of truth and right.

As to answering these ends in any desirable degree by using the present periodicals, I believe you will be disappointed. Mr. Robinson[1] "does not wish what Tholuck does." On the contrary he is not only entirely without an affectionate interest in those subjects, but considers Tholuck's interest in them as "one of his weak sides." In general he has no respect, and even not a little contempt, for that whole style of thinking. This Leonard Wood told me—and Mr. Stuart (who exercises great influence over the character of that work) openly sneers at Tholuck's "Mysticism" and is waxing bitter against "Coleridgism".[2] Mr. Cheever told me this morning that Stuart had rated Edwards soundly for publishing an article by Cheever in his Quarterly Register on the *Study of Greek* in which respectful reference to and quotations from Coleridge occur.[3]

I have troubled you again with remarks at this length, not because I have any present expectation of proceeding in such a plan; but for your reflection and with a view to embrace any future occasion that should seem unquestionably favorable. Certainly I shall not wish to attempt anything of the kind without your fullest confidence and cooperation. It is barely possible that some such favorable conjuncture may arise in New York. I derive this impression from Mr. Cheever, who has recently returned from that city. Mr. Cheever is certainly a fine writer and a man of ability and tho I am sorry that of late he has been led a little into Taylorism, yet I am persuaded he will work his way out. With his respect for Coleridge, and his love of the old writers, he must soon see the narrow and shallow dogmatism of Taylor.[4] Dr. Mathews, the Chancellor of the New University[5] expressed himself strongly desirous to have a Review in New York and connected with the University. And perhaps in time something may come out of this. From seeing Mr. Cheever this morning, it occurs to me to trouble you still farther, in a matter of my own personal concern.

From the suggestion of Mr. Cheever and another person, I learn that Dr. Mathews has had some thought of putting me in nomination for a Professorship of Greek in the University. Now were I independent in circumstances and able to support myself in my present course, I should not for a moment entertain the thought of taking such a situation. But as I need to do something for a living, it occurs to me that the duties of such a place would lie in line of my pursuits, in part at least, and I should perform them con amore. As subsidiary in part to my fixed plan of learning and appreciating all the extant ideas in philosophy, and also with a heartfelt love for that glorious language in which Plato thought and wrote as no man ever thought and wrote, I have for ten years had a firm determination to *know all Greek*, toward which I have never ceased to make more or less progress. So that I feel as if I could discharge the duties of such a place. The suggestion therefore has struck my mind so favorably that I am not only willing to entertain an application, should one (as was mentioned it probably would be) be made, but am desirous of doing something to secure it.

Now therefore I should take it most gratefully if, from any kindness to me, or from any reliance you might place on my representations, or from any impression you may have of my zeal and ardour in the cause of good learning, and of my general ability, and attainments, you could say anything to Dr. Mathews or any of the Council, that might further this object, provided you should be applied to by him or them, or even if you could make a proper occasion to do so. I know I am taking a great liberty: but I do feel that the course of my studies, and my attainments have been such, that, ardent as I am and willing to work and work hard as I am, I should not in the issue, were a proper arena afforded, disappoint the recommendation of any one whose kindness might incline him to aid me in obtaining a chance to live and work and do.

With my special regards to Mr. Torrey—and begging the favor of a line from you if anything shall be said to you on this matter, I am dear Sir respectfully and affectionately yours,

C. S. Henry

P.S. I learn with great pleasure from Mr. Tracy[6] that you and Mr. Torrey are about a translation of

Tholuck's Romans.[7] I think it cannot fail to be acceptable and do good. I think of publishing in the course of the year a translation of Heinroth's Anthropologie and also an original Essay on the Doctrine of Cause and Effect: as to the principle of causality in its origin, against Locke and the Sensualism generally and specially against Hume and Brown. I shall wish to submit it to you before publication and to *dedicate* it to you, if you will let me.[8] I think it not unlikely that I may visit you in the month of June, or during the summer. I shall be rejoiced to hear from you as soon as your engagements will permit.

1. Edward Robinson (1794–1863) was the editor of *The American Biblical Repository* at this time.
2. On Moses Stuart's attitudes toward Tholuck see below, letter of February 15, 1833; and toward Coleridge see above, letter of July 16, 1829, note 6.
3. George B. Cheever (1807–90) remained a staunch defender of Coleridge's and Marsh's religious transcendentalism. In a eulogy on Marsh, Cheever, quoting Coleridge's *Biographia Literaria*, berated the corruption of the meaning of "Transcendentalism" which turned it into flights of lawless speculation. Cheever's "Study of Greek Literature" appeared in *The Quarterly Register*, 4, p. 273ff.
4. Nathaniel Taylor.
5. James MacFarlane Mathews (1785–1870), a divine of the Dutch Reformed Church and first chancellor of New York University.
6. Ebenezer Tracy was simultaneously editor of *The Journal of Humanity*, published at Andover, and *The Boston Recorder*.
7. Torrey and Marsh's translation of Tholuck's *Commentary on Romans* was announced in *The Biblical Repository* but was in fact never published.
8. C. S. Henry did not translate Johann C. F. A. Heinroth's *Lehrbuch der Anthropologie* (Leipzig, 1822) nor dedicate his translation of Cousin to Marsh; however, he did include notes on Locke in his translation of Cousin.

From Leonard Woods, Jr.
Ms: JMC

Andover
June 21, 1832

My dear Sir:

I received yours of the 13th just a day or two since and immediately procured from Mr. Robinson the loan of his copy of Tholuck's Dogmatik. The copy which I have in my hands belongs to Professor Yates of Union College[1] and is not exactly at my disposal, or I would have sent that. Besides the "Wissenschaft Dogmatik" to which I alluded in my letter to you, Mr. Robinson has also Tholuck's "Kirchlich-biblische Dogmatik."[2] Thinking that this also might be useful to you, I have procured the loan of them both. I shall go to Boston before the close of the month, and will leave them with Crocker and Brewster[3] directed to you. As to the business of the periodical respecting which I wrote you sometime since, it is suspended for a time, with the hope, though it is not a very definite one, that the Spirit of the Pilgrims, at the end of the present year, may take a shape, which will partially at least, answer the ends we have in view. The fact that there is such a wide defection from some of the fundamental articles of the Evangelical creed, and that so many are carried away with every kind of doctrine seems to prove that these articles have not been held on their proper basis, and that they must be more deeply grounded, before the stability of faith which is desirable, can be attained.

With sincere regards for yourself, and your fellow workers in the cause of truth, I am, dear Sir,

Yours etc.
Leonard Woods, Jr.

P.S. My Father wishes to be affectionately remembered to you—I thank you, for your favorable mention of the Preface to Knapp.[4] Since this letter was commenced, I have heard that Mr. Robinson has had another of the epileptic fits, which he has had so frequently during the past year. Although no immediate danger is apprehended from them, their frequent recurence produced a good deal of alarm.

1. Andrew Yates (d. 1844), Yale Class of 1794, was professor of moral philosophy at Union College (1797–1835).
2. Edward Robinson brought back and circulated a number of sets of lecture notes which he had taken while studying under Tholuck at Halle, including the lectures on "Kirchlich-biblische Dogmatik."
3. Boston publishers specializing in religious books.
4. Woods translated G.C. Knapp, *Lectures on Christian Theology* (1831–33).

1829–1833 From Richard H. Dana
Ms: JMC

Cambridge,
Massachusetts
July 14, 1832

Respected and Dear Sir,

Mr. Shattuck,[1] who hands you the letter of introduction from me, is a young man, not only of great delicacy of manners, but of great moral purity. You will find his attainments very respectable for one of his age—about 19. His father[2] is the best friend I have on earth; and I shall feel very grateful to you for any attentions you may show the son.

Mr. Shattuck has been educated entirely under Unitarian influences; but from one or two conversations which I have held with him lately, it is evident that he feels there is something essentially defective in the system—if it may be honoured with the name of system. I should judge, also, that his prejudices against evangelical religion, if not wholly at an end, were fast giving way, and that to acknowledge its truth he needed only to be taken out of the circle of Unitarian influence for a while, and to be brought acquainted with some intelligent christians who would converse freely and kindly with him upon it. Upon learning that he was to reside in Burlington for a time, I immediately determined to write you, under the conviction that you would take an interest in his spiritual welfare. Should he be brought to see the truth, and to receive it into the heart, he may be, in turn, the means of bringing others to it. Aside from the clergy, there have been no men so blessed in their efforts in this respect as some pious physicians in Boston. May he shortly be of their number! Any gentlemen whose society you may think would be agreeable and useful to him, you would oblige me by introducing him to.

Mr. Leonard Woods[3] was with me a day or two since. He desired me to let you know that the MSS. which you requested him to lend you, were left with Crocker and Brewster,[4] to be sent in their next package: he left the papers with them a day too late to be sent by their last.

Mr. Woods does not act as editor of the Spirit of the Pilgrims at present. Mr. Pond[5] still furnishes articles, and controls it. Mr. Woods merely superintends the press. At the close of the year, if the skirmishing here should not grow into a pitched battle, and the work be seized by one of the hostile parties, it may be made what we wish to make it. If it is to take a controversial form, Mr. Woods would decline acting as editor, but if the plan proposed by some of us can be adopted, he will undertake it. The more I see of Woods the better I like the character of his mind. His insight into the shallowness of the New Haven scheme[6] and his feelings as a son may lead him to think more favourably of the opposite system than it deserves: but I am well satisfied that his mind does not rest there; and when I remarked to him, that our divines must become familiar with a deeper and more spiritual philosophy before they could have a true theology, he assented to it fully and agreed with me as to the good that had been done by your republishing Coleridge. The interest he takes in all that relates to Tholuck speaks the same of him—(I know nothing of Tholuck except through my own language). Upon the whole, I do not know of any man who could come into the editorship of our Periodical, to the furtherance of our views, with less of suspicion and opposition, than Mr. Woods.

I do not suppose that any thing more could be *immediately* done than to infuse the spirit of a more inward philosophy, influencing theology and all our views of man, nature, literature and the arts: the spirit of this philosophy, I would say, may be breathed into these, and quicken them with a new life, though its form may not yet be set out before the public drest in all its appropriate terms. You may, however, depend upon it, Sir, that there are more minds,—particularly among the young—opening to the warmth and light of this philosophy, than you have been ready to believe. Was not the sale of the Aids to Reflection an indication of this? And, with Mr. Henry[7]—who is well acquainted with the Unitarians here—I am clear in it, that it is the true way of reaching the cultivated class among *them.* If we can convert the Spirit of the Pilgrims into such a work as we propose, it will help greatly to this end. But it would be rash in us to attempt it, unless we can be assured of your aid and that of your friends, who are blessed with a greater share of the intuitive faculty that seems to have fallen to the lot of many here. I trust you will all help on so good an undertaking. As to myself, my constitution is so broken by repeated attacks of sickness that I shall be able to do very little, if any thing. Indeed, I cannot reasonably expect to survive many more returns of my complaint. But should I live, I am no philosopher by education, and no more of one, by nature, than that which is necessarily contained in the essence of the little poetry God saw fit to infuse into my soul, may have made me.

When are we to have your System of Logic? Though not a regularly trained logician, I have a secret assurance that it will interest me. I wish that with the Lay Sermons we were to have Coleridge's work on Church and State[8]—I forget its title, though I have looked over the book. Should a difference of views upon the main point, be a reason for not publishing such a work from such a man? Had you foreseen how well "The Aids" would go off, you would, no doubt, have published it in such a form as that it might have been the first of a series of Volumes. I do not know how the "Friend" has sold, but *well* or *ill*, it would have sold *better* had not your publisher imposed upon you and the public an edition which is a disgrace to the press. The paper is absolutely wretched, and the price high enough for a thoroughly well printed work. I take the liberty of mentioning this to you, Sir, for I have heard it generally complained of. I believe that publisher is held to be quite sharp enough in his line of business. I hope that before long, you will feel it safe to publish a uniform and full edition of Coleridge's prose with an analysis. Such a work should undoubtedly have a wide influence upon the minds of our literary men. I suppose that, at present, you are too much engaged upon Romans, which I am glad to learn you do not intend to hurry in consequence of Professor Stuart being engaged upon the same. How widely different the two works will be! We owe a great deal to Professor Stuart. He certainly waked up our clergy to the importance of learning. But he is far from being a safe leader. He frequently advances particulars in exegesis in opposition to his main principle, and which, if carried out, would go nearly the length of the Rationalists. He is led into this by his vanity, which affects novelty and independence. He has an ardent, but dry mind, and turns with a most self-complacent contempt from that which is too deep for his sensuous philosophy. His reputation has suffered of late, I should think, from his writing hastily, and upon any thing and every thing and from an increasing diffusiveness. Yet, with all these faults, we have not a more important man among us, or a more open and kind one, I believe.

My acquaintance with you, Sir, hardly justifies the length of this letter, but I hope you will pardon it in me.

with great respect
Dear Sir yours
Richd. H. Dana

1. George C. Shattuck (1813–93), subsequently a prominent Boston physician and philanthropist like his father, after completing one year of medical study at Harvard (1831–32), visited Burlington, apparently to study medicine with Benjamin Lincoln, M.D. (1802–1835) of UVM's medical department.
2. George Shattuck, M.D. (1783–1854), Dartmouth Class of 1803 and a prominent Boston physician.
3. Leonard Woods, Jr.
4. The Boston publishers of mainly religious and educational texts.
5. Enoch Pond (1791–1882) was professor at Bangor Theological Seminary.
6. The revisions of the doctrine of Atonement proposed by Nathaniel Taylor.
7. C. S. Henry.
8. Samuel Taylor Coleridge, *On the Constitution of Church and State* (London, 1830).

To Richard Henry Dana
Text: Wells, pp. 160–162

Burlington
August 21, 1832

My dear Sir

I received your letter by Mr. Shattuck and am obliged to you for it as well as for the introduction of the young man. I have been much prepossessed by his very modest and amiable appearance and Dr. Lincoln tells me he has engaged in his studies with much zeal and success. Dr. Lincoln is himself a great enthusiast in his pursuits and as Mr. Shattuck spends most of his time with him and enjoys every advantage of books and private intercourse, I presume he will make fine progress in his professional studies. I shall do what I can with regard to the wishes which you express and hope he may lose nothing by coming here of any good impressions which he has received. But we have as you know a Unitarian Society here and as Dr. Lincoln attends that meeting he will of course go there also and I fear will not in general be much more favorably situated with reference in his religious interest than he was with you. Dr. Lincoln is not indeed a Unitarian but it is because he is too acute, too fearless, and too ingenuous to stop at Unitarianism. He takes that view which Tholuck (in his theology) says we must necessarily admit if, trusting to our own understanding and reasoning, consequently we seek to comprehend God, the universe and our moral nature and that is Pantheism. He, however, sees that there is more in Coleridge's Metaphysics than can be disposed of in the common philosophy and theology of the day and I hope has moral purity, power of reflection and strength of reason enough yet to find in himself the principles of a higher system. I mention this not I hope to his prejudice for indeed I love and admire the man for his perfect simplicity and frankness in the confession of these opinions as in everything else, but because he interests me much as belonging to a class which I fear is not small among us especially among those engaged in physiological inquiries. How can it be otherwise indeed when thinking young men are led to believe that Paley's arguments are the strong ground of our conviction of theism and that such philosophy as Brown's is the best which Christian divines and professors can put in their hands as a guide in solving the highest problems with which such minds are occupied. I have hoped as you do that reflecting Unitarians would find in a higher and spiritual philosophy an antidote to their prejudices against orthodoxy and still hope it will be so with many who would otherwise become Unitarians if not with those who are already so. I am not indeed acquainted with many but so far as I can judge from what I have known of the reception of Coleridge I fear we have not much to expect from those who are already committed. The characteristic arrogance and pride of understanding which seems every where to belong to them seems to me in its relation to speculative truth the very firstborn of that lie in the heart, the denial of which as the originant and universal spring of moral evil I have learned to look upon as the basis of their whole system. The Unitarian clergyman[1] here says with reference to Coleridge's works he shall not believe the water is deep because it is muddy. Is there not much of the same spirit in the disciples of Dr. Taylor? They seem to me to place the same confidence in their own understanding and in the same way to mistake a shallow system, which they have learned to comprehend, as containing all that is to be comprehended, while in fact it contains only their own notions. Indeed I see not how it essentially differs from Unitariansim in regard to that which I consider the most inward principle of both their view of moral evil in man, since, according to Dr. T's views, in the language of Gale's Court of the Gentiles, "the last differential reason, whereby grace is different from nature, must be resolved into nature, and natural free will would, from this hypothesis, be of itself and nextly flexible to spiritual good."[2] Thus the true doctrine of an evil heart of unbelief is denied and the whole system of theology falls into contradictions. But the truth is no one who adopts that view has philosophy enough to comprehend its bearing, I fear, or perhaps I should say I hope it is so and that only a little more insight into first principles is necessary to induce its abandonment. Such men as Mr. Cheever[3] I am sure cannot long adhere to it though Dr. Beecher[1] may do so.

I have been very glad to hear of the prospects with regard to the Spirit of the Pilgrims and to have my hopes confirmed of the proposed editor. He sees too clearly I am confident the need of higher ground for the maintenance of orthodox and spiritual views of religion ever to rest satisfied with his father's system as a whole.[5] We shall be glad and feel bound to send what aid we can here for promoting the success of such a work but we have laborious duties here and are already engaged in as many projects aside from our daily routine of duty as we shall be likely to accomplish at present. Besides I fear we are too much insulated to feel that sort of interest which prompts to write a frequent article for a journal. Professor Torrey has a very philosophical mind and is better read than I am, but it is very difficult to get any thing from his pen. For myself, though less modest and though I have at different times contemplated a variety of subjects on which I felt a wish to write, the truth is it costs me an effort to do so for which I have not ordinarily sufficient resolution, and in the absence of immediate necessity I find a thousand reasons for delay and so do little.

I expect to find Professor Stuart's Romans[6] considerably modified by his study of Tholuck's and am anxious to see it on that account. Yet I have no apprehension that it will be consistently and systematically conformed to it or in such a way as to supersede the demand for that work.

It will be several months before I can make out a System of Logic and I fear a thoroughly scientific system is hardly practicable without such novelties in terminology as would scandalise the "reading publick." Does Mr. Allston[7] correspond with Coleridge and can he have anything of his "Elements of Discourse." I do not anticipate in that a work suitable for a text book but am anxious to get it before making one especially on account of language. By the way I should be glad to learn from Mr. A. something authentic in regard to Coleridge's moral character and habits. You know the reports put in circulation and I am often asked about them. Though to a man of sense the inquiry is unimportant in its bearing on his writings yet the question is sneeringly asked in a New York paper whether such a man is to be looked to for remodelling the theology of Edwards.

I have rather supposed it would not be expedient at present to republish his tract on Church and State[8] but hope it may be found proper by and by to publish a uniform edition of the whole as you suggest.[9] And now my dear Sir after saying too much of my own notions and plans allow me to express the hope that your own pen will not be unemployed. I trust you may yet be spared to do much in what you consider your more appropriate sphere and even in those labours I need not tell you how intimately you are associated with the advocates of a living and spiritual philosophy. True poetry is truth ensouled and since Bryant[10] has ejected the muses to make room for "the whole hog" I know not where we are to look for such if not to you. The journal too must depend chiefly upon you and others in the vicinity. With great respect and esteem, yours very truly,

Jas. Marsh.

1. George G. Ingersoll (b. 1796), Harvard Class of 1815, was Unitarian minister in Burlington from 1822 to 1844.
2. Theopholis Gale, *The Court of the Gentiles, Part IV. Of Reformed Philosophie. Wherein Plato's Moral, and Metaphysic or Prime Philosophie is reduced to an useful Forme and Method* (London, 1677).
3. George B. Cheever.
4. Lyman Beecher (1775–1863), as pastor of the Hanover Street Church, Boston (1826–32), led a religious revival that extended through the six years he was in Boston. Always a controversial figure, the intensity of feelings evoked at the revival meetings in Hanover Street Church created a conservative reaction that compelled Beecher to leave Boston for Lane Seminary in Cincinnati.
5. Enoch Pond (1791–1882) was editor of *The Spirit of the Pilgrims* from 1828 to 1832. In its last year of publication, 1833, G. B. Cheever seems to have been editor. Beecher was frequently published in it. Marsh apparently is recounting a rumor to the effect that Leonard Woods, Jr., would be the new editor replacing Pond.
6. *Commentary on the Epistle of Paul to the Romans, with a Translation and Various Excursus* (Andover, 1832).
7. Washington Allston (1779–1843), the American artist and friend of Coleridge who painted the poet's portrait, was married to Dana's sister.
8. Coleridge's *On the Constitution of the Church and State*, which he started to write as an attempt to refute the parliamentary arguments for Catholic emancipation, became a treatise on social organicism.
9. William G. T. Shedd (1820–94), UVM Class of 1839, was the first American publisher of a uniform edition of Coleridge. His edition of 1853 was long-standard.
10. William Cullen Bryant (1794–1878). Marsh appears to be aware of how Bryant, though he had left the running of *The Evening Post* to Parke Godwin during the early 1830s in order to devote his time to purer forms of literature, never again was as productive as he had been in the years 1824–25 when he wrote "Rizpah," "Autumn Woods," and "Forest Hymn," some of his best poetry.

To Leonard Marsh
Ms: JMC

Burlington
December 18, 1832

My dear Brother

The draft which I sent you was not of the church here as you seemed to suppose but was one drawn

1829–1833 by the bishop[1] for his own use and is connected with a work which I hope he will publish during the winter on Gothic Architecture.[2] It was copied by laying the paper on and tracing it and though not very nicely done is sufficiently accurate I thought for your present purpose. The scale of feet was intended I take it to apply to all the dimensions—height, thickness of walls etc etc. His drawings are lithographed and he would have given me a copy but he has at present only one. His manuscripts too are with his goods froze up on the way but I hope he will get them soon and I will procure as soon as I can all the details you will want.

The church here is not at all correct in its style and has a cornice instead of battlements. The pulpit too is very different from what you want and would be of no use.[3] I am persuaded you will find it best to *build with brick*. The buttresses built of rough stone must cost much labour and the walls must be much thicker than will be necessary in brick. If you have a solid stone foundation brick will answer every purpose and you can carry up the tower of the same material. Here they have a wooden top to the tower. The battlement is quite a simple affair and cheaper I should think than a cornice. Another word—I would not put up the walls and finish it the same season. It will be seen to settle so as to crack and deface the plastering as this has done.

I must get you to send back Herder's Dialogues as I believe I must translate them myself and let Goodrich publish them immediately.[4] Our Tholuck is set aside for the present much to our disappointment by information that the author has announced a new edition with such alterations as spoil this. If it is put on board the stage at Banker's directed to Mr. Goodrich it will come safe and I wish you would send it then *by the first stage*. I have received and am reading Heinroth's Anthropologie. It contains many fine things and matter enough to think of. Cousin George P.[5] is sick again with a serious affection of the head and Lincoln[6] is much concerned about his symptoms. The pain in the head is intense with ringing in the ears, waking visions, etc.

Emily[7] has come safe and brought your letter with farther enquiries. The ornament above the

1829–1833 From N. Frank Cabell[1]
Ms: JMC

Bremo, Virginia
January 1833

Reverend and Dear Sir:

On looking to the signature, you will see a name, which has perhaps faded from your remembrance. But I take the liberty to recall it; from the not ungrateful recollection of the instruction which I formerly received, at your hands, when officially employed in our state, as well as from the hope that you will permit an interchange of sentiments on subjects which have now become of great interest to me; altho I made but a slight improvement of the opportunities which were once afforded me for this purpose.

To be explicit, my dear Sir, I was a member of a class, which recited to you in your department, while you remained in a literary institution of Virginia and who would wish you remembrance of that period of your life, to be in no respect otherwise than pleasing. Sure I am that I did not willingly contribute to make it different. It may not be ungrateful to you, my dear Sir, to be told, that it is to the influence—the abiding influence, of the literary advice received from you as well in our brief, private interviews as from your public lectures, that my mind chiefly owes its enlargement, direction, and in a great measure has taken its colouring.

It was from confidence in the opinions of my old professor that I was induced to take the step, which has for one of its results the infliction on you of this letter.

Shortly after it first issued from the press, I procured a copy of the "Aids to Reflection"—and set in right good earnest to compass its meaning if my faculties should enable me: When excited with all the patience of which I was master, and backed by a zeal for such studies, which had now become, (in my own eyes at least,) not contemptible. It was the first work of its great author to which I had had access. I subsequently procured his "Poems" complete, some occasional scraps of which I had before seen; and not long since was presented by a friend with "The Friend."

To return to the first: Well to it I set, much encouraged by the Preliminary dissertation: but had not advanced far when "Who is this that darkeneth counsel etc"[2] thought I to myself—but remembering my resolution, I persisted. A fortnight's close application sufficed for its first perusal. I could have mastered the "Principia"[3] sooner. And why not? My mind was a blotted sheet. Innumerable were the errors which I had to unlearn. I found that before I could catch the meaning of the true oracle, my ears must be stopped to the murmuring echoes of false syrens: Excuse this trifling. But to be literal and plain, my dear Sir, I must acknowledge my obligation to you. I had read the brutal article in the Edinburgh Review which had in a measure prepossessed me against the author.[4] I had read "false philosophy" until I was sick at heart. I believe I was earnestly desirous to get at the truth: but Scotch metaphysics and kindred stuff had poisoned its foundations. Book succeeded book, systems, as wave succeeds wave, and the first was uniformly effaced by the last. In the words of highest authority "I was ever learning and never coming to the knowledge of the truth"[5] because my first footsteps were ever on a quicksand. But here, altho I toiled up a steep ascent, whereas formerly I had run, I think I have reached a point where my prospect is in a measure cleared at last. I think I have found some of the seeds of verities at last. I acknowledge that vital importance of his main position and distinctions: and in the oft-repeated perusal which I have since given it my impressions have been confirmed. The theological controversies which are now shaking our church from one end of this empire to the other, can never I believe be terminated, but by acknowledging and referring to these or equivalent truths. But enough of what may seem impertinent, as it is most probably uninteresting to you and irrelevant to my present purpose.

My labor would have been lightened if I could have earlier met with "The Friend" and I had frequently thought of troubling yourself with some difficulties which remained on my mind; and I even now write you in the hope of obtaining information, which I know not where else to proceed so well. And if the leisure afforded by your official situation will permit, I would even venture to enquire whether you could not bestow a small portion of it in an occasional reply to Letters with which

—for alas! the *motives* are in the opposite scale—

We came on directly and found Bliss[2] quietly at work with his Hebrew, although then he had not been examined. I commenced with brother Fairchild[3]—the Hebrew under the instruction of Mr. Gregg,[4] who by the way tells me he was at Burlington last spring, at your house, probably when I was absent. In five weeks joined the class—Have read through the Christomathy—and am now reading the Bible—and should have been farther advanced but for the sickness of Professor Robinson,[5] occasioned, as perhaps you have heard, by a severe attack of the epilepsy. For a while his life was dispaired of—Is now able to attend upon his class, And is a noble instructor—considered by the class generally, I think, as the most able and philosophical instructor we have, as far as we have had opportunity to judge. By a new arrangement we come under Dr. Woods[6] three days in a month—in order to get a start in his department this year, so that we can attend to philological studies *some* during the whole course. The first three days we had introductory lectures, probably the same that he read to you—but gave us as a subject for a dissertation to be handed in at the commencement of the next month—The proof of the existence and moral perfections of God by the light of nature—Stated, as his question read, according to Paley, Clarke,[7] etc.—however remarked that he wished us to be perfectly independent in our investigations. The books to be read were all referred to—and the class to a man huddled to the library and drew them out—and left for *us* just what we wanted—Cudworth and More and Bates and Bretschneider[8] etc, which furnished us ample texts to preach Coleridge from. Well, the time arrived and we assembled before the *Seniour Professor* of the *first Theological Seminary* in the United States—to examine this *fundamental principle* or rather *foundation* of our religion. It was conducted in the manner of a recitation. And one of the class was called upon for his reasons for his belief in the existence of a God—and gave us the argument of Paley *revelation* and there was not the *least objection* to it. But when the Dr. came to prove the goodness of God, his *infinite benevolence* in the same way—a doubt came up. One of the class says, but we have evil in the world

—why must we not from this reasoning, conclude that there is therefore two Gods, etc—enough to give you a hint at the objection which was extended and discussed at some length. In such a way, however, as to make the matter noise and spread a *general doubt* over the whole subject and method of proof itself. And in such a way too, that the *class could not but see* it—could not—unless we can actually suppose men to follow the principles of their philosophy and therefore to have no knowledge except what can be acquired by the senses, as would seem to be the fact here—and of course no *ideas* strictly at all. At this *juncture*, however, this time of general doubt, I enquired—But—by this method of reasoning can we arrive at *certain* knowledge as to the goodness of God—his *infinite benevolence*. I was answered in the negative—but, sir, have we not perfect or *certain* knowledge upon this subject—To be sure—I was answered. And how then, I continued, did we obtain it. But was not answered directly. Still I could not believe that the general feeling was, that it was not from the light of nature or from reasoning in any way from effect to cause. I did not wish however to urge the matter too far at first, for we think it best to begin rather moderately and as it were, doubting some what, lest we throw the whole Seminary upon the defensive and so accomplish but little or nothing here in the effort to introduce Coleridge and sound principles of philosophy. Yes, introduce—for they hardly can be said to be here now—there is not a copy of the Aids to my knowledge in the Seminary except those *we* brought—*none* in the libraries, where there should be fifty copies and they would be read *now* if they were there—for there is a curiosity awake here to know what that author means or can say for himself who dares call in question the firm principles of Locke and Paley. We found *one* convert—a fine mind—a member of our class—Kaufman[9]—he caught at a hint I threw out at dinner table—called at my room, took Coleridge—renounced his heresies, which he says he never could believe and is now a great help to us. And *one other* kindred spirit is all we have met with since we left Vermont. His name is Homes—Henry Homes,[10] if I recollect rightly—from Boston, but now a Theological student at New Haven. He visited Andover during his vacation and pletely, and this will probably not be available for one and one-half years. I will leave it to your own judgment to decide whether or not it is advisable, under the circumstances, for you to publish your translation.

Right now I am working on the edition of a work on the Sermon on the Mount, which, I feel, would be more useful for your purpose.[3] In case you would like to translate this into English immediately, I am sending you the first sheets (the fourth and the seventh will be sent later) and will send the rest of them as soon as they are printed. Perhaps you will find the translation of this also fitting and proper.

What you tell me about your aspirations of stimulating the people of your country to profounder thinking has aroused my sincerest interest. Should you wish to send me an essay which contains the history of the study of English Philosophy since Locke, with special consideration and discussion of the principles before Coleridge, I should be very pleased and would translate it immediately into German and have it printed. Your dear friend Torrey, please greet him for me, once started such an Essay but still owes me the conclusion of it.

Professor Stuart's entire method seems to me to be rather barren and somewhat lifeless; I had written that once to Professor Robinson and he was so indelicate as to show it to Professor Stuart, who in turn exclaimed that I was a Mystic.

You may be assured of my sincerest respect and love. Unfortunately I cannot write you more this time.

Yours most sincerely devoted to you in the love of Christ.

Dr. A. Tholuck

1. F. A. G. Tholuck (1799–1877), the evangelical theologian at the University of Halle, was better known in America than any other German theologian of his time and was himself especially fond of Americans, Edward Robinson and Charles Hodge, among others, having studied with him. This letter has been translated by the editor.

2. *Auslegung des Briefes Pauli an die Römer*. 3te Auflage (Berlin, 1831).

3. *Philologisch-theologische Auslegung der Bergpredigt Christi nach Matthaus, zugleich en Beitrag zur Begrundung einer reinbiblischen Glaubens-und Sittenlehre* (Hamburg, 1833).

President Marsh Resigns 1833–1835

Marsh's revisions of the general curriculum at UVM gained attention and praise during the first three years of their application. But the school also needed money. With a student body of far less than one hundred men during Marsh's seven-year tenure as president, the college was frequently unable to pay its bills, including the president's salary. For professors like Joseph Torrey and George Wyllys Benedict, as well as John Wheeler, who succeeded Marsh as president in 1833, the occasional lack of a cash salary was not important because of their own independent wealth. The estate of Wheeler's father was the largest probated in New Hampshire until 1830. But Marsh, three times a father and in 1830 married to Laura Wheelock, his first wife's sister, received hardly anything from the estate of his own father Daniel Marsh, who had died in 1829, despite the large tract of land and handsome manor house Daniel had inherited from the grandfather Joseph Marsh, first lieutenant-governor of Vermont. Pressed by personal financial needs and weakened by the debilitating strains of tubercular lungs, Marsh's leadership of the University was so tenuous by 1833 that the Corporation suggested his resignation. As surviving letters suggest, the thought of resigning from an office that had become almost identified with the name of Marsh in only seven short years was embarassing, even insulting. Upon advice from members of his family, he sought a teaching position at Dartmouth, then Yale, but found nothing suitable. Given the reputation he had quickly earned as a liberal academic reformer drawn to German theological and philosophical thought, it is not surprising that neither school had room for him. Unsuccessful in these efforts, he redirected his attention to teaching philosophy. From surviving student notebooks, it appears that during the years 1834–40 he exerted a profound personal influence on many students at UVM. Unable to teach philosophy, psychology, and logic to the extent he had wished during his presidency, his resignation, then, allowed him to perform the task for which he was best suited.

of the institution; but on the other hand, I apprehend that it would be altogether disastrous.

The questions you have put to me will be my excuse for adding another remark, which, under other circumstances might appear indelicate. Our friends at Burlington urge a change in the presidency on the presumption that *public sentiment* requires it. But this presumption I conceive to be unfounded. What public sentiment in *Burlington* is, I will not attempt to decide;[5] but out of Burlington and thro the *state* generally, I believe it is decidedly in your *favour*. I will not say that your qualifications are *justly* appreciated, but I do say, without hesitancy, that the impression is extensive and is extending, that the present head of the University is an ornament to the state; and, that, if that institution is destined to rise and to achieve the noble end for which it was founded, it will be under his auspices.

But I must close. By the way, I have, since I saw you, had an interview with Brainerd[6] of *Randolph*. He says he shall enter six or eight next fall. He is himself favorably disposed towards us, but is rather within the jurisdiction of Dartmouth. May not a line from you to Mr. Nutting[7] be of use?

Yours truly
Worthington Smith

1. Worthington Smith (1795–1856), Williams College Class of 1816 and Andover 1819, was pastor of the Congregational Church of St. Albans, Vermont (1823–49), and then succeeded John Wheeler as president of UVM until 1855.
2. Edward Dorr Griffin (1770–1837), Yale Class of 1790, was president of Williams from 1821 to 1836.
3. Amherst College was founded in 1821.
4. Marsh was thirty-nine years old.
5. "Public sentiment" in Burlington seems to have been reflected in a letter from a group of Burlington citizens, including John Pomeroy, David Russell, and John Potwine, sent to the Corporation of UVM on June 17, 1833. Pomeroy and the rest had been applied to for contributions of money to a scholarship fund which the Corporation had recently established when they responded by saying that "those who are taxed have [a right] to be heard" on the topic of how their gifts were to be used. They required especially that the following steps be taken: 1—no religious sect would be preferred in appointments to the faculty; 2—the faculty must not proselytize students for conversion to any religious sect through promising

academic or other rewards; 3—the faculty should not preach at local churchs; 4—UVM's finances must be audited and the audit made public; 5—only interest from specifically invested funds should be used to finance scholarships.

The answer to this letter, written by Marsh on June 21, was prefaced with the assertion that "Knowledge to be efficient and powerful must take root in the heart and be controlled and directed by the principles of virtue." But those "principles of virtue" are not sectarian or in the "exclusive keeping of any order of Christians." In keeping with the original intentions of the Legislature of Vermont in its establishment of UVM, the letter continues, the college would continue to function on the following principles of conduct: 1—only men of the highest intelligence and scholarship would be appointed to the faculty. "That they ought to be religious men is too clear to be controverted," but no sect will be preferred. 2—The faculty "would neither countenance nor allow control or influence to be exercised over students with a view to their adoption of any peculiar creed." 3—On the question of supplying local pulpits, it would be "fastidious to say they [the faculty] should not supply a vacancy accidentally occasioned." In fact, "it might be politic and benefitial" to preach on public occasions in local pulpits and "thereby give an elevated character to the institution." 4—The $500 subscriptions to the scholarship fund, as well as all other college moneys, should be invested in the "most secure manner."

6. Asahel Brainerd (1771-1865).

7. Rufus Nutting, of Randolph, Vermont, was a schoolmaster succeeding his brother, William, at the school where Marsh had himself prepared for Dartmouth in 1812-13. Marsh had also arranged for the younger Nutting to replace him at Hampden-Sydney College in 1826, a position Nutting held for only one year.

To the Corporation of the University of Vermont

Ms: JMC

June 5, 1833

Gentlemen—

After mature deliberation, I have come to the conclusion to tender to you my resignation of the office, which I hold by your appointment. I do this, not from a disposition to desert the interests of this institution, or because I have any other specific object in view, but for the following reasons—

1—I do not consider myself as possessing all those qualifications, which, in the present state of this institution especially, the office requires, and hope that the corporation may

I have recently received several new books from Germany. Among them Twesten's Lectures on Dogmatics, Baumgarten—Creusius Dogmengeschicte, Nitzsch Christliche Lehre—and Schubert Geschichte Seele.[5] I have had them so short a time and what with the cares of settling, that I have not read them, except Twesten[6] which I think admirable. I expect also from a brief glance, that I shall find a rich treat in Schubert. It is more than eighteen months since I sent for these books, so that possibly you may have received them and know more about them than I do. If so I would be much obliged for your judgment of them.

Do you recollect a remark in Coleridge (Lay Sermons, Notes I think but I have not the means of ascertaining now) to this effect: Speaking of the grounding principle of Paley's Moral System, he says, its sophistry was first detected by Des Cartes—also exposed by Bishop Butler—*but* a new, and most original and *masterly refutation by the late William Hazlitt*.[7] To what work of Hazlitt does he refer? Two years ago I sent the quotation to *Rich*[8] of London, requesting him to find out and send me the work referred to—he wrote me that he *thought* it must be the Table Talk, would ascertain etc. That is the last I have heard from him, I have not been able to find any complete collection of Hazlitt's writings in this country; nor any person who could tell me the work alluded to by Coleridge. Can you tell me anything about it?

If you received the Heinroth and have made what use of it you wish, I would be glad to get it back again, as I have partly engaged to deliver a course of Lectures on Anthropology in the city the next Autumn; and the book contains a great many facts and references I should like to use. Do not send it immediately however unless you have done with it—send to my address, care of D. F. Robinson and Co., Hartford.[9] Phrenology is somewhat the hobby among several in Hartford, owing to a visit from Spurzheim[10] and lectures by a young physician Dr. Brigham.[11] I want in the course of my lectures if I should give them—to give a critical estimate of that pretended science. Pray tell me how you like Heinroth.

It would give me lively gratification to hear from you and of the progress you are making in your books. May God aid and prosper you in your noble enterprises in behalf of truth. Dr. Mathews[12] told me this spring, that the reason, the *sole* and *only* reason of my not being chosen last fall to their university, was narrowness of *funds* and discouraging prospects owing to disturbances by cholera, that they for that reason did not fill *either* of the chairs of the Literature of the Ancient Languages but nominally with Mr. Robinson[13] who would not come and *cost* them nothing, but their condition and prospects were such now, that by next Autumn, they would *offer me the place if I would take it*. I told him I would not take it—because my health was now restored so that I could return to my work of preaching—and that I felt under obligation to be employed in that work in preference to everything else, *unless* it should please God to open me a door to instruct and lecture in Intellectual and Moral Philosophy; for which I felt myself best qualified, that whenever he had any of that work for me to do; I would come—but meantime I was going to preaching. I have no belief however that they will have any such work to offer *me* to do. They stick to Brown and Locke.

Affectionately yours
C. S. Henry

P.S. My good friend, Dr. Cox[14] says Coleridge is a fool.

1. Johann C. F. A. Heinroth, *Lehrbuch der Anthropologie* (Leipzig, 1822).
2. New Measure Revivals had originally been devised and introduced by Charles Grandison Finney (1792–1875) and imitated by his followers, including Jedidiah Burchard in Vermont, during the mid-1830s. The central features of a New Measure Revival included an "Anxious Bench," which Finney described as "the appointment of some particular seat in the place of meeting (usually the front benches or pews) where the anxious may come and be addressed particularly and be made the subject of prayers and sometimes conversed with individually." Revival sessions were held over extended periods of time and called "Protracted Meetings." Like the Camp Meetings of the west, "Protracted Meetings" were accompanied by heavy emotional outpourings and vivid recitals of conversions among the attendants.

One of Finney's severest critics, John W. Nevins (1803–86), professor at Mercersburg Seminary, in 1840 called "Finneyism . . . Taylorism reduced to practice, the speculative heresy of New Haven actualized in common life. A low shallow department you have named, I have long been desirous of seeing filled, but I know that others are not now prepared to acquiesce in my opinion. Under these circumstances, it would be premature and probably fruitless to do anything with reference to Mr. M.[2] Should any such opening occur I will let you know of it.

You ask about the death of Henry Dwight.[3] He came from Boston in the month of June early and was soon afterwards taken with an intensely painful disease supposed at first by the physicians to be of a nervous description, but afterwards they confessed their ignorance of its nature. It was at first seated in one of his legs; and then his throat was attacked. On giving him a powerful antinervous medicine, he became deranged, and continued so for two or three days. After that he had less pain, a difficulty of breathing at times very distressing and extreme weakness. He died after eight weeks of suffering. He expected death for weeks and expressed such feelings and hopes, as a Christian would wish to have and see others possess. His resignation and patience under suffering were exemplary. During the last four or five weeks of his sickness, his bedside was watched by the young lady who was to be his wife, and she parted from him the evening of the night in which he died, not expecting that his end was so near.

I had learned that Tholuck's commentary on the Romans was about to be published at Burlington,[4] and did not know the cause of the delay. Dr. Heinroth's anthropology[5] I have never seen though I knew the author well in Leipzig. Tholuck's work on the Romans I have read or rather consulted a good deal and liked it much; his other works I am not familiar with. As my time has been occupied with my Greek studies lately, I have had no leisure for theological reading. I have occasionally looked into Twesten's Dogmatik,[6] a writer who ranks high with the orthodox of Germany, but I found his style such that I could not become master of his system without more study (and more knowledge of German philosophy perhaps) then I could command time for. I have lately been reading Hengstenberg's Christologie[7] in part, and though the book is not altogether satisfactory, it certainly makes out a strong argument for the new testament interpretation of the Messianitic prophecies in the old, and present a view of prophecy calculated to remove the distressing doubts that some have entertained concerning it.

I regret that a review has already appeared in part in the Christian Spectator of Stuart's Romans written by a young man of some learning here named Cowles.[8] I regret this the more, as its object, so far, is to show that Professor Stuart and Professor Taylor harmonize, and not to bring truth to light and [. . .][9] error. Mr. Stuart is going into the field of classical literature, ill-qualified I should think for the task which he proposes to himself, and we shall soon see the Phaeda edited with his notes.[10]

I hope we shall have the announced treatise on logic from your pen. I have heard nothing of the work except the bare statement of its being ready for publication; so I suppose it will not be long delayed. In closing allow me to express my pleasure in hearing from you and my hope that I may be again so favoured.

I am very sincerely yours
T.D. Woolsey

1. Theodore Dwight Woolsey (1801–89), Yale Class of 1820, studied theology at Princeton, Yale, Paris, Leipzig, Bonn, and Berlin, and in 1831 accepted the chair of Greek literature at Yale. In 1846 he became president of Yale, serving in that office until 1871.

2. It is difficult to say exactly who "Mr. M" was. Considering the strain on Marsh's relations with UVM, and his suggestion that Leonard inquire at New York University about a position for him there, "Mr. M" could very likely have been Marsh himself.

3. Henry Dwight (1797–1832), youngest son of Timothy Dwight, had studied at Andover with Marsh before going to Göttingen.

4. "We understand," B.B. Edwards said in *The Biblical Repository*, "that the gentlemen at Burlington are waiting for a new edition of Tholuck on Romans, before they commence their translation" [5(1835), 502].

5. Johann C.F.A. Heinroth, *Lehrbuch der Anthropologie* (Leipzig, 1822).

6. August D.C. Twesten (1789–1872) had been influenced by Schleiermacher some ten or more years before he wrote his *Vorlesungen über die Dogmatik der evangelisch-lutherische Kirche nach dem Kompendium des . . . W.M. De Wette*. 2 vols. (Hamburg, 1826–37). Twesten sought a middle way between the extremes of a return to old principles and the rationalism of his own time. He succeeded Schleiermacher at Berlin as professor of dogmatics in 1835 where he continued to seek a middle way between the modern Hegelians and the neo-legalisms of the conservatives.

have been written, and on which there will probably be written as many more—The Will. He is not at all a real metaphysician; but his mind is essentially a poetical one, and not of a high order, and therefore, necessarily philosophical, under the *poetic form*. How he has succeeded in this metaphysical form, it is not for me to say, having only run the article over some time ago, and not esteeming myself a competent judge. He said to me, that it might be all old matter, for ought he knew—that he wished some one to see it, who was familiar with the subject, and who would be frank eno' to say freely, what it was worth, or if good for nothing to say so—that this not being his particular walk, he should not be mortified, altho' what he had here written should turn out to be of no value. I know him well eno' to assure you that he may be taken at his word; and if you will be so obliging as to run it over when you have a leisure moment, and in a few lines to me to say just what you think of it, you will very much oblige both him and me. On one of the detached papers of notes, you will see a Prefatory Note, which he wishes should be first looked at. When you have a convenient and safe opportunity to return it, you can send it, directed to me, and to the care of Rev. B. B. Edwards,[1] or of Perkins, Marvin, and Co.,[2] No. 114 Washington Street, Boston. I know how much, sir, your time is taken up; and I would not have troubled you with this little matter, had I known of any other person whose opinion upon it I should hold to be conclusive. You must therefore pardon me in what I have done.

Coleridge is gone.[3] Comparing man with man, there is something rising to the awful in the sublime thought of such a mind opening upon eternity! What a feeling of the vast it gives one to think of such a mind expanding in the visual presence, as it were, of the Infinite. You have, no doubt seen the short notice of his death, at the end of that number of the London Quarterly Review which contained that discriminating and exceedingly beautiful Review of his poetry.[4] His death-bed was just such an one as I looked for such a man. His letter to his little godson was most touching.

You must by this time, Sir, be satisfied that what you have done to bring Coleridge into notice in this country, has not been in vain. Among the evangelical young men who have minds at all above the common run, I scarcely meet with one upon whom a good influence has not fallen from your labours. It operates as a new moving power in their minds—they see, feel and think like another order of beings—they now *see into themselves*. The deeps are moved, and must swallow up quick the brawling, shallow, rambling stream of Taylorism, and the artificial, formally cut canals of the other system. The Bible, only, a higher and a *purer nature* (if I may so express myself) will be applied to that which it was intended to meet, and to take into its own nature—to our *fallen natures*—the endeavour will at last be given over to apply its great principles of Love and Truth to a sort of mechanico-metaphysico automaton—dubbed man.

I wrote President Wheeler, last summer, about sending my son to your College.[5] As he could not be admitted into your or President Wheeler's family, and his eyes were in a very feeble state, I gave up my purpose at the time. He thinks his eyes are a little better; and is trying their strength cautiously upon Algebra. I have the hope that by next year he may be well eno' to, at least, make a trial with you. I trust, if you or President Wheeler should be able at that time to take him into one of your families, you will give him peace. You would find him giving the least possible trouble.

Are we not to see you this vacation?

For the sake of making one packet, I have taken the liberty to enclose a letter in answer to my appointment as an honorary member of the Phi Sigma Nu of your College; a few lines also to President Wheeler—tho' I have no great fancy for *poetising and orationing* on public days, from the interest I feel in your Institution, I should have held forth there had it been in my power.

When, Sir, shall you fulfill your engagements to Mr. B.B.Edwards? If we are not soon to see you bodily, I hope we are to mentally. I have written for him this Number. But illness prevented my doing as I wished, or correcting proofs even, into which have crept some errors.

With great regard, I am, dear Sir, yours

Richard H.Dana

and that by men of whom we most confidently hoped better things. I have placed such evidence as we have respecting the ultimate results of Burchardism before men in whose soundness we have been wont to confide, and they reply that there is conflicting testimony, or that the character of our population is such as to render safe here what would be dangerous in New York. I have tried to forewarn in this way those who had not come in contact with the man, and they have left me with apparently as deep a conviction as my own, of all the abominations and dangers of the system; but in a few weeks they have forgotten all and gone with the tides. Many of Burchard's admirers will acknowledge most of the faults that I can point out in his sayings and doings—and yet give him their whole influence. They will acknowledge that the testimony from Western New York, as a whole, is decidedly and strongly against his measures, and yet flatter themselves that somehow it will not be here as it has been and is there. I am utterly discouraged as to any attempt to influence the churches of this state through the press—by *direct* opposition to Burchardism, I mean. I have been trying experiments now for almost a year, and the result uniformly is, that men *will* burn their own fingers in this fire. This is the opinion, too, of Dr. Richards of Auburn, Dr. Tucker[3] of Troy, your brother Leonard, and many others who have seen the course of things and know how men are affected. Our conclusion therefore is, that the proposed measure would not effect its object, and would endanger the hold that we have on the public mind without any good in return.

I do not see that any better course is left us, than for the sound-hearted, each in his place and as he has opportunity in social intercourse, to expose the system and warn men against it; and especially to bring as much *truth* to bear on the churches, publicly and privately, as may be. If I thought open battle would really do any good, it would suit me better, incomparably, than such silence as we have been practicing. But all the experiments that have been tried here and all that I have been able to learn from judicious men at the west, lead to the belief that it would do more harm than good, *in the present state of things*. I look forward confidently to better times. Good men will see ere long the evil they are doing. For myself, *inter nos*, I have much less confidence in the character of the man, Burchard, than I once had, in fact, I have none at all.

I am glad to hear that our friends at the Northwest are so generally sound. They are likely to be tried. Perhaps Truair's[4] visit may turn out in good now.

I see nothing in the results of the meetings in this vicinity thus far to recommend similar experiments elsewhere.

Mr. Richards[5] will be at Burlington soon, and will show you some documents.

Let me hear from you often.

Yours truly, as ever,
E. C. Tracy

1. Marsh had approved the publication of a pamphlet which attempted to expose the unsound and, as the anti-Burchards saw it, theologically dangerous character of Jedidiah Burchard's revivals.
2. Josiah Hopkins (1786–1862), Yale Divinity School graduate (1808), had been pastor in Westford, Vermont, before going to Auburn Theological Seminary. Hopkins's letter contra-Burchard was published in the *Vermont Chronicle*, 11 (March 17, 1836), p. 42.
3. James Richards (1767–1843), professor of theology at Auburn Theological Seminary (1823–43). J. Ireland Tucker was rector of the Episcopal Church of the Holy Cross, Troy, New York.
4. In 1833 John Truair, formerly minister at Cambridge, Vermont, began to tour Vermont, stopping first at Fletcher, in an attempt to establish the "Union Church" throughout the state. Truair preached the abolition of "all covenants and creeds," calling for church organizations to be "blown away" and all Christians to come together and "see eye to eye." The "Union Church" at Fletcher was, according to the town historian, "as short lived as Jonah's gourd."
5. John Richards, pastor at Woodstock, Vermont, and subsequently at Dartmouth College. The "documents" were probably the "Preamble and Resolution" passed at a town meeting of Woodstock which condemned Burchard's new measures and Burchard himself as public nuisances. Cf. Russell Streeter, *Mirror of Calvinistic, Fanatical Revivals, or, Jedidiah Burchard & Co. During a Protracted Meeting of Twenty-six Days, in Woodstock, Vt. to which is added the "Preamble and Resolution" of the Town, Declaring Said Burchard a Nuisance to Society* (Woodstock: Russell Streeter, 1835).

surprised as I was, I was compelled to suppose, that his preaching and his measures must have some redeeming characteristics, which I had not learned, and in justice to you, and the very high regard, which I had ever had for your judgment in such matters, as well as for that of your highly respected colleagues, required that I should make farther enquiries, and review my opinions concerning the whole subject. From that time to this it has been almost daily the subject of thought and consideration among us. I have taken pains to learn all the important facts, as to the modes of proceeding at Montpelier and other places, and the results of experience as tested by the lapse of years in western New York, with the views of the leading clergy in that region, and from all these I found matter to confirm rather than weaken my convictions.

For the last ten days the system has been in operation here, after the church had, in accordance with his directions, been for weeks and even months in a process of preparation to give it its fullest effects. Mr. Burchard has been the sole preacher, and we have I suppose a fair exposition of the theory and practice of the system under our own eyes. I have not attended constantly, but have done so repeatedly, and have opportunities of learning minutely from day to day what is said and done. I trust, Sir, I have regarded it as a subject of solemn and prayerful interest, in its relation to the cause of truth, and the interests of evangelical religion among us, and have not been over hasty in forming my conclusion. I ought today too in justice to myself, in view of what I am well aware others may think, assert, if any one thing more than all others has given an interest to my studies for fifteen years, it was the paramount desire of apprehending and teaching aright the true principles of spiritual or evangelical religion, as distinguished from those systems which preclude the spiritual, as unitarianism or generally rationalism on the one hand, and fanatical counterfeits on the other. I will add that, all who know me are aware from my habitual language, that I regard, as the best practical exposition of spiritual religion the practical writings of Baxter, of Howe and Leighton, and the other congenial writers of the same age, and that I consider the Pilgrims Progress of Bunyan and the Life of David Brainerd,[2] as giving a fair and correct account of the work of the truth and Spirit of God upon the hearts of men, in what is termed religious experience. With these opportunities for a knowledge of facts, and with the most earnest and thoughtful application to the system of the principles implied above, and reluctant as I cannot but be, to differ on *such* a subject with men whom in every relation I so highly esteem, I am compelled to say that I cannot approve the system. Of the man I say nothing at present, but the system of operations, by which he seeks to promote revivals of religion, has a distinctive character, and must be judged by the *light of divine truth*, by its relation to the *established principles* of *religious experience*, and its bearing upon the *general interests* of the *church of God*. Now, my dear Sir, after all the consideration, which I am able to give it, I am prepared to declare my solemn conviction, that, as a system, and as here carried into effect, it cannot endure the test of examination in regards to either of these particulars. In trying it by the light of divine truth, I regard more especially the character of the doctrines, on which he relies, and which are most prominent in his sermons and other discourses. The general character of his preaching in this respect is indeed so marked by extreme crudity of conception, inconsistency and fallacy, that it may be difficult to say what his system as a whole is, and, my own conviction is, that he has no consistent views of divine truth. He pours forth with strange assurance the strangest crudities. But while he has swatches of various systems, and among the rest some of the naked and bald technicalities of Calvinism, (as that God has from all eternity elected certain persons in Burlington, and that he is the special messenger of God here to bring in his eternally elect. This he told me himself, and said he thought it pretty bold preaching), while he says such things I say now and then, nothing is plainer to my mind than that they are mere patches *stuck on*, and that the substance of his doctrinal views, so far as there is any thing systematic, is *Taylorism*.[3]

I have just heard him preach a sermon, which a neighboring minister, who professes to be a Taylorite, considers as distinctly in accordance with his views, and that too, in the points, which seem to me dangerous, and connected with his measures, almost inevitably leading the sinner to self-delusion. He takes a perfectly empirical and notional view of the *free-will*, and maintained through a considerable part of his sermon the perfect ability of the sinner to repent, and do all God required of him without any conditions or limitations. He has said indeed in other sermons, that no sinner ever repented without the influence of the holy spirit—but then he distinctly and repeatedly in my hearing has said—the only agency of the spirit in that regard is the presentation of motives. He ridiculed the notion, that God would require of the sinner any thing that he had not a natural ability to perfom.

Again he treated with ridicule in the same sermon those views of conviction of sins, which are necessarily involved in the sound Calvinistic doctrine on the other topic, and which are taught in the 7th chapter of Romans as well as in Christ's words—Come unto me ye that *labour* and are *heavy laden*. I might multiply statements of doctrine made in my hearing, which I am sure you could not approve, as either sound or safe, as well as specimens of his customary mode or argument by metaphor and comparison, where each comparison is only a nest of fallacies or sophisms. But as measures have been taken here to copy and publish his whole talk from his own mouth, I will not dwell on this part of the subject.[4] On paper his language will speak for itself, and if it is not found utterly inconsistent with sound theology, sound logic and common sense or even decency, then I must learn over again the first principles of all these matters.

I often find myself wondering, if it were possible, that Dr. Lord could patiently hear, and encourage the churches to expect substantial and permanent benefit from such exhibitions of ignorance, of contemptuous arrogance, and self-conceit, such scornful treatment of many things, that have at least been regarded by the greatest and best of men as sacred and solemn truths.

But not to dwell longer on this topic now, I beg to ask if Mr. Burchard's method of *getting up and conducting a revival* of religion, taken in connection with his leading doctrines, is not pregnant with the perils of self-delusion, and if it is at all consistent with the *established facts and principles of christian experience*. What is the practical use of such books as the Pilgrims Progress, of Edwards on the affections, and indeed of all our standard practical works, when they begin to reflect on their character and condition as sinners, they are to be sent to Mr. Burchard's anxious seats, and, according to his notions of the efficacy of particular faith in the prayers of the church, immediately prayed into the kingdom of God. Consider the mode in which ignorant and inexperienced persons are first literally dragged into those seats, taught to expect immediate conversion by a mere act of their own will, and the prayers of the church cooperating with his, consider the deceitfulness of the heart, the sophistical mode, (I cannot call it less) in which he illustrates the motives of the Gospel; and if multitudes are not deluded, it is not because the system does not directly tend to delusion. Mr. George Perkins Marsh said to him in conversation, "Your system is successful, you uniformly succeed in producing a revival, is not that of itself a proof, that it is a *merely natural process*???" I say it is unquestionable that the result can be explained from the natural causes put in operation, on psychological principles, without supposing any spiritual element in the whole process. Not that there may not be genuine conversions. So there may be in any circumstances, by the overruling influence of the Spirit of God.

I speak of the system, of its own proper tendencies, and of the *apparent* results. Where there is no cautionary and restraining influence, I only wonder the apparent conversions are not more numerous under the operation of such causes. But I maintain, that this is a case, in which enlightened Christians are bound to judge the effects from the causes, rather than the causes from the effects. If I find clusters of grapes on a thorn bush, I am not at once to conclude that the bush *produces* grapes. I am bound to suspect that they are *stuck on* and may prove only grapes of *wax*. Of the tendency to delusion, and of the actual delusion going along with it, one statement made by him in my hearing would seem to me to give ample proof to any enlightened mind. He had made the same statement at Woodstock, as my brother told me at the time. He was urging upon the church the importance of their praying in form, and manner, and time, literally and strictly according to his bidding, in order to give efficacy to his prayers in the anxious room. They must pray in small companies about town, six or eight in a place, *simultaneously* and coextensively with his labours, short prayers, once round, twice round, three times, till the two hours were spent. To prove by facts of experience, that this mode was efficacious, and a necessary condition of the result arrived at, he made the statement in question. In a city of ten or twelve thousand inhabitants in western New York,[5] in a meeting house which had a basement story, the church were praying in the room above, while he with the pastor were in the basement story with the anxious. At the first gush of prayer forty-seven were converted or gave their hearts to God. Like all his statements of this sort, it was stated as a *fact*, without doubt or qualification.

But what next—why these forty-seven it seemed were those on the *front seats* and he has repeatedly said and said too in conversation, that in his past experience *only those* were converted. He says there was one exception at Woodstock. There were others in the room, none of whom were affected. But he proceeded. These forty-seven were turned back into another room to have their names recorded, and another set called forward into the front seats. These were then prayed for, but it went, he said, *very hard*. None or few of them were converted, and the question arose what was the cause. Why, says the Pastor, go up stairs and see what the church are about. He went up, and found there a tall, gawky fellow from the country, showing himself off, or in other words speechifying. They put him down, and got the church upon their knees, prayed again, and salvation flowed like a river. So they continued, till after a time salvation stopped, and on going to look after the church again, behold, they had dispersed, and they concluded we may as well send home the rest of these anxious persons, they can get no good here.

This I heard with my own ears, as a *fact of experience*, from which to infer the duty of this church. He wanted the church to pray and labour to get sinners into the seats, and then by their prayers to secure their conversion. It is obviously the heart of his whole system of measures, and every thing undoubtedly depends upon his exciting in the church the kind of zeal, which such a doctrine inspires, and in sinners around them a feeling, which will bring them into the current. If it does not bear the brand of fanaticism indelibly stamped upon it, pray what constitutes fanaticism?

Connected with this, let me ask, does he not *misrepresent*, as he does many other things, and then turn into ridicule all the precautions, which a knowledge of the deceitfulness of the human heart has led the church to employ, in order *first* to prevent men from deluding themselves and in the *second* place to guard the church itself against being overrun with self deceived and worldly minded professors? He scoffed at them as absolute traditions, and says expressly that three days are long enough to find evidence of conversion.

The church here is entirely under his control, as we knew it would be, and the severest feelings cherished and expressed against all those who do not approve and float along in the current, as opposing the spirit of God, preventing the conversion of sinners, etc, and we of the College must suffer the penalty incurred nowadays by all, who venture to have a judgment of their own. My conscience will not permit me to see such bare faced quackery put in practice upon the sick and perishing souls of my fellow men, and either approve, or keep silence.

But the *important topic*, with which I cannot but regard yourself as deeply concerned, is the bearing of this system on the *general interests of the church*, and especially on the cause of evangelical religion among us. It seems to me so perfectly obvious on the very face of the system, that it tends, with direct and irresistible force, to do that for the church, which sheer jacobinical radicalism will do for the State, that I cannot look upon it but with dread, and the ejaculation—may God preserve his Church! Does it not tend to awaken in the church a spirit of fanatical self confidence in their own power? Does it not directly tend to depreciate the regular, and patient, and humble use of the ordinary means of grace, and the ordinary duties and charities of the Christian life? Does it not tend to settle the regular, and established institutions, and ministrations of the gospel? Does it not *set us afloat* upon a boundless sea of *novel and untried experiments*, and substitute the *shallowest empiricism* for all that has been regarded as fixed and established in the principles and practices of the church of God?

The chief argument, and almost the only one I have met with, in its defense, is grounded on the apparent and temporary results. Now I would ask, are we authorized to resort to the manifold devices of our own understandings in matters of this sort, and then judge according to the *appearance*, whether our devices are in accordance with truth? Are not those, who profess to be instructed and qualified to teach others the principles of religious truth, bound to try such systems of novel empiricism, and the spirit of those, who practice them, by a higher test —and surer criterion, than *such experience*, as he pleads for the efficacy of his measures? Is the truth and propriety of a method of religious instruction, and of measures for the promotion of the influence of the Gospel on the souls of men, to be determined *at all* by empirical results, in the sense in which he applies the argument? Must we not judge according to truth and righteousness, i.e. principles a priori, established in the unchanging verities of reason and the word of God? Did not Luther, Calvin, and the great English reformers, with Howe, Baxter and Edwards pursue this course, and is there any other safe course? I cannot believe there is, and have been astonished at the extent, to which the argument from experience has been urged in favour of these strange absurdities, and at the men, who have yielded to its force, or rather admitted it to have force. What wild fanaticism, let me ask, has appeared in the whole history of the church, that could not urge the same argument *for a time* with *apparent* force?

Where are we to stop in the career of experiment, if experience is admitted to have convincing force to justify such violations of all order, and of all the proprieties and decencies of religion, as I see passing every day with utter astonishment under my own eyes? Where is to be the limit of vulgarity and levity, of low and profane wit, and of histrionic grimace which may be supposed conducive to bring men within the sacred precincts of the house of God, and the hearing of *that gospel*, which in all its recorded words and deeds has not one iota of all this, but with *grave and solemn seriousness* commends itself to every man's *conscience* in the sight of God. Even supposing good may have resulted from the system in *particular cases* and under *peculiar restraints and limitations*, is it *safe* to commend to the confidence of the churches an ignorant, self-conceited, and reckless empiric, who is perpetually liable to be carried into greater extravagances, and outdo his own outdoings? I ask all these questions on the ground that, to a certain extent, good may have been occasioned by the system, and I say that, admitting this, there is enough in its obvious characteristics to seal its condemnation, and prove that it cannot be permanently and truly useful, or deserving of confidence.

But in *the next place*, I deny that experience is in its favour. Professor F.N.Benedict[6] of this college was at Rochester at the time, when Mr. Finney[7] kept up the same state of things, as we have here now, for nearly a year. He tells me, that the system was in all respects the same, and different only as the men differ in their personal peculiarities. The church, in which Mr. Finney laboured, had been formed by the excitable members from two other churches uniting. They kept the whole town in commotion, and a large school, which Mr. Benedict was teaching, was entirely broken up for months, a number of young men preparing for the ministry, and aided by the Education Society, were induced to leave their studies, and commence preaching at once, and all further prosecution of sound knowledge discouraged, as incompatible with the duty of Christians in this age. They numbered about 2,000 converts in the city, and talked of nothing less than the immediate approach of the millennium. That church a few months ago was nearly disorganized, and it was intended to sell the building to the Baptists, the fragments of the church going to those, out of which it was formed.

Professor Benedict's father was the pastor of a church in the suburbs of Rochester[8] of about 200 members, had had frequent revivals, and the church was in a flourishing, healthful state. This system was crowded in against the will of his father. It distressed and agitated him, and as his son believes was the occasion of his death. However, multitudes were added to the church, and *now* that church is literally disorganized, and there is no church there.

Professor Strong,[9] now in New Jersey, was, during that period at Hamilton College. He had been Professor Benedict's instructor in college. Professor Benedict says he told him a few months ago, at great length, of the utter dissolution occasioned among the churches of that region by the prevalence of this system of measures. Dr. Delamater,[10] whose eminent Christian character you well know, used to say, a few years ago, that a spirit of infidelity had been diffused through that region by the prevalence of these reckless experiments, that fifty years of faithful preaching would not remove. He would not even go to hear the preaching of Mr. Foot,[11] who was here at the time, and who, as I can testify, differed from Mr. Burchard only in his personal peculiarities.

Mr. Hopkins,[12] in addition to what he had already said, has recently written to his old parishioners in the vicinity of Middlebury, cautioning them against Mr. Burchard and expressing his utter astonishment at Mr. Merrill's course. Mr. Childs of Pittsford came up to Middlebury one day, told Mr. Merrill[13] he was preparing sorrows for himself, and went home. Rev. Mr. Parmalee,[14] a good old minister in this region, came here one day, and told Mr. Converse[15] in my hearing, that it was essentially fanatical, and did not differ from the system of Truair[16] who has been hatching a system of acknowledged fanatacism and making difficulty in Mr. P's vicinity.

Now in addition to all this, let me beg you, my dear Sir, as one having the higher interests and institutions of science and sound principles of religion at heart, to consider what must be the effect on these of countenancing and commending such men such measures. Their tendency is so palpably obvious, as not to need even the evidence of experience to prove it, and yet we have this evidence. At the Oberlin institute, where Mr. Finney is the leading man, and whose colleagues have a kindred spirit, they have submitted the question of the study of the classics and of the pure mathematics to the *decision of the students*, after reasons assigned pro and con by the Professors. As the result of this strange proceeding, as might have been expected, the students burned their classics, and are to be educated according to the most approved style of empiricism. Theology is to be learned empirically by reading Mr. Finney's empirical book, and following the big tent—to hear and learn by experience what is the most successful mode of converting the souls of men.[17]

Now, my Dear Sir, I ask with all deference, *where is this to end*, if such men as yourself and colleagues and Dr. Bates,[18] give commendatory letters, and accredit to our churches, such men as Mr. Finney, and, as all who know them both say, a far inferior man, Mr. Burchard. I say it with no unkind feelings, and I trust with no claim to very superior discrimination, but I must say, it is passing strange, how *such* a man, and *such* a system should have secured the confidence and approbation of enlightened and discerning men.

I must say, too, with Mr. Smith[19] of St. Albans in a letter of yesterday, that "Somebody besides Mr. Burchard must be responsible for these reckless experiments, and the community, returning to better views and wiser counsels, will hold some one responsible for this prostration of order, this sacrificing of the proprieties and decencies of religion, and substituting in the place of them levity, vulgarity, and I fear gross impiety. If twenty years will do away the evils produced in this state during the last ten months, and place truth and religion, order and decency in their former place, I shall be thankful. I look for a harvest of disorder and infidelity, and fanaticism from the seed that has been cast."

I trust, My dear Sir, you will not ascribe this letter and the earnestness, with which I express myself, to any other than the true motives, a sacred regard, as I hope, for the best interests of religious truth, and the souls of men. Circumstances here may make it necessary, or at least expedient, to publish something on this subject, and it may be thought best to put it in the form of a public letter to yourself, as the most prominent individual, who has made himself in any way responsible for this man and these measures. If you have any objections to that course, I beg you will let me know soon, as I would not willingly do anything of the kind against your wishes, and whatever I may do, I beg you will not consider it as implying any personal unkindness. With the highest regard, yours in the gospel of our common Lord.

J. Marsh

P.S. I am so full of this matter, and so many considerations crowd upon me, that I must add something to this already very long letter. Mr. G.P. Marsh tells me that on one occasion Mr. Burchard called all the people from the gallery and wished them *to sit in a body* when there happened to be but few, and remarked that we must avail ourselves of all the principles of our nature, obviously meaning in this case, that of sympathy. He afterwards asked him, whether he thought it justifiable to avail himself of that principle, of making men act upon each other, and *move in masses*. He said undoubtedly he might, and believed the spirit availed itself of such principles in our nature. He said afterwards in reference to a conversation which I had held with him on that point, that he believed the spirit operated just like natural causes, and that there was no distinction. Yet he publickly denies, that there is any excitement, or that he wishes for any. Another remark was made to me tonight by the same gentleman, which was obviously just, that there is no indication from his discourses, that his mind is at all imbued with the spirit, or stored with the language of Scripture. He and President Wheeler both heard him give it as his opinion publickly, that the way in which St. Peter knew that there were 3000 converted was by calling them to separate themselves into a particular place, and counting them off as he does. Many things as ridiculous as that will be found in his printed language, and yet it will be impossible to give the extravagant manner in which it is exhibited. Mr. Converse and the church here are completely at his bidding, and as to the reception of members, the established rules and guards entirely broken through.

I am writing this postscript Sunday evening, and I am sorry to say that today forty members have been received into the church without being propounded, some examined yesterday in the afternoon, some today at noon, and some it is said not at all. One of the Professors saw the examination yesterday as follows: Mr. Converse and the church were entirely set aside and Mr. Burchard took the whole into his own hands. He made a general talk to the candidates and then said that for himself he was perfectly satisfied with every one of them. But for the satisfaction of the church he would ask them a few leading questions and wished them, if they assented, each to nod his head. He then asked if they felt differently from what they did formerly, and read the bible with different views etc. and if they preferred going to meeting to going to shows and to balls, occupying in the whole of the examination not more than half an hour. A considerable number of them I know to be exceedingly ignorant, and from the nature of the case there can be no evidence. A number of the most intelligent members of the church are greatly scandalized by the proceeding and absented themselves from the communion today on that account and one intelligent woman, who at first concurred in the measures, has written for a dismission from the church. The church will immediately be in some trouble, and I know not what will come of it. I have read the above letter to G.P. Marsh and President Wheeler and asked them, if the language was stronger than the case justifies, and they say *not at all*. I have only room to add that Mrs. Burchard has the children as usual, and induced a collection of nearly a hundred to say, I believe every one of them, that they had given their hearts to God. How many of them will be taken into the church I know not. Mrs. Wheeler who was present said that there was but one face among them that showed any peculiar solemnity.

1. Nathan Lord (1792–1870), Bowdoin College Class of 1809 and Andover Seminary 1815, served as president of Dartmouth College from 1826 to 1863. His years in office were not among the more enlightened in Dartmouth's history. Lord was compelled to resign during the Civil War after being censured for defending slavery as a divinely ordained institution.

2. David Brainerd (1718–47) was one of the most brilliant members of Yale's Class of 1743. Expelled for impugning the piety of Tutor Whittlesey, Brainerd went to Pennsylvania and New Jersey as a missionary to the Indians, ultimately dying in the home of Jonathan Edwards who subsequently published Brainerd's *Journal* and a memoir of his life.

3. Nathaniel Taylor's revisions of the doctrine of redemption and atonement developed by 1834 into a school known as Taylorism and the debate over Taylor's teaching has since come to be

called the Great Taylorian Controversy.

4. Chauncey Goodrich had hired two undergraduates from UVM, C. Gamage Eastman and B. J. Tenney, to attend the protracted meetings in Burlington and Williston in order to copy down Burchard's sermons for a book-length publication of them. Russell Streeter's *Mirror of Calvinistic Fanatical Revivals* had cast Burchard in such a repulsive form and broadcast Woodstock's (or at least the town's fathers') low opinion of the revivalist, that Burchard, suspecting Marsh of plotting another stage in the campaign to defame him, first tried to buy off "Dr. Marsh's agents" and then allowed, in Williston, the church deacons to forcibly prohibit Eastman's note-taking and urged Joshua Bates to denounce Eastman and Tenney from the pulpit. Tenney recounted the series of encounters with Burchard and Deacon Avery in an Appendix to *Sermons, Addresses and Exhortations of Jedidiah Burchard*, ed. C. G. Eastman (Burlington, 1836).

5. Rochester, New York.

6. Farrand Northrop Benedict (1803–80), professor of civil engineering at UVM.

7. Charles Grandison Finney (1792–1875), the great revivalist of the Second Great Awakening.

8. Rev. Abner Benedict was pastor then in Mentz, New York.

9. Theodore Strong (1790–1869), Yale Class of 1812, taught mathematics and natural philosophy at Hamilton College (1816–27) and thereafter at Rutgers (1827–61), when he wrote to Farrand Benedict and recalled an episode during a revival at Hamilton while he was on the faculty there. Some of the students, refusing to attend classes in their adherence to the New Measures of the Second Great Awakening. stood up at one of the evening revival meetings and prayed for George Henry Davis, president of Hamilton, after a student characterized Davis as an "old grey headed sinner who was leading the students down to hell." Letter from Theodore Strong to F. N. Benedict, January 12, 1836, JMC at UVM.

10. Among the various Delamaters in the Dutch Reformed Church of New York and New Jersey, this one remains unidentified.

11. Joseph I. Foot (1796–1840), Union College Class of 1821, Andover 1824, was pastor at Salina (1831–35) and Cortland, New York (1835–37), and an itinerant revivalist like Burchard.

12. Josiah Hopkins (1786–1862) of Auburn Theological Seminary had been pastor in Westford, Vermont.

13. Thomas Merrill was pastor in Middlebury until 1842; Willard Childs (1796–1877), Yale Class of 1817, Andover 1820, was pastor at Benson, Pittsford and, after 1855, Castleton, Vermont.

14. Moses Parmelee (1788–1838) was pastor at various times in Pittsford, Londonderry, and Enosburg, Vermont.

15. John K. Converse was pastor of the Congregational church in Burlington.

16. John Truair was formerly minister in Cambridge, Vermont, but after 1833 was an itinerant preacher in the state, moving from town to town in an effort to form what he called the "Union Church" of all Christians.

17. Charles Grandison Finney's *Lectures on Revivals* was the handbook of itinerant New Measure evangelists. In 1835 Finney accepted the appointment to professor of theology at Oberlin College and in 1857 became its president.

18. Joshua Bates (1776–1853), president of Middlebury College.

19. Worthington Smith.

From George Allen
Ms: JMC

St. Albans, Vermont
March 21, 1836

Dear and Honored Sir

My wife is going to Burlington today, and I write this to make my excuses for not sending your MS. The truth is, I find it not of the most legible in your hand, and therefore presenting additional difficulties, and likewise too valuable to be read and then let go. I have therefore taken the liberty to begin to copy it—*simply* and *solely* for my own use. I should not presume to show it. Yet if even the copying it for myself should be unpleasant to you (as I grant it is unauthorized presumption upon your experienced kindness) I will stop. I am now going over Coleridge's works, slowly and I hope—thoughtfully and thoroughly. You dropt some hints in our last conversation on some points of pastoral duty, topics of sermons, theology, etc. which (if you were not now busied with the enlarged interest of religion at large) I should be begging you to expand in a letter. I hope I may trouble you—one of these days—with some such questions.

As I owe the awakening of my mind to the search after higher principles in literature, philosophy, and theology entirely to you,[1] I feel inclined to assert a *claim* upon you for further guidance and instruction. I have read the Rutland paper—and with unmingled satisfaction. I was a little inclined to make something out of your distinction of divine and human in the means of propagating Christianity, as being against your own views of Congregationalism, and necessarily moving you to inquire if these be not a form of Christian God too, (as well as the means of proding religious effort) which stands on a higher ground. But at this you will laugh. I have a dozen times tried to mature in my mind certain views of succession,[2] etc. which would meet some thing you said to me once on that subject. I should like (when I *have* thought it up) to submit them to you. As soon as I finish my copying (which will be in a day or two) I will take the first opportunity of sending your MS.

I remain, dear and
hond. Sir,
Most devotedly your
Friend,
Geo. Allen

1. George Allen had assisted Marsh in preparing *Aids to Reflection* for the press in 1829 when he was a tutor at UVM.

2. Allen apparently was exercised by the same questions that the Oxford Tractarians examined, especially, at this point, the question of Apostolic Succession. Like some of the Oxford group, Allen's evangelical Anglicanism led him, in 1847, after expressing strong sympathy for the Oxford Movement while on the faculties of Newark College in Delaware and the University of Pennsylvania, to convert to Roman Catholicism, an act which temporarily made him *persona non grata* with his colleagues at Penn.

From George Ripley[1]
Ms: UVM

Boston
February 23, 1837

My dear Sir

I venture to address you, though a stranger, with regard to a literary undertaking in which I feel sure of your interest and in which I should rejoice to receive your aid.

I propose to publish a series of translations from some of the most eminent French and German writers under the title of "Specimens of Foreign Standard Literature."[2] My aim in this work is chiefly to lay before our literary public some of the most celebrated writings in philosophy, history and theology which admit of naturalisation on American soil; and at the same time to accompany them with such productions of the lighter literature as shall create a popular interest in the publication. The principal writers from whom translations are to be given are Cousin, Jouffroy, Constant and Guizot in French, and Herder, Goethe, Schiller, Lessing, Jacobi, Fichte, Schelling, Richter, Menzel, Neander,

Schleiermacher and De Wette in German. I hope to secure as contributors to this series our most distinguished students of continental literature, and have already engaged the services of several on whom I place great reliance.

It would give me pleasure if you would consent to undertake the translation of such work in theology or philosophy as your taste may suggest, illustrated with an introduction and notes similar to your valuable commentaries on Coleridge. I mean to bring Twisten's "Dogmatik," into the series, though I don't know that you would fancy the translation of that, and for my own part, I should prefer some work of greater philosophical difficulty from your pen. I want, as far as possible, to give some idea of all parts of that enchanted circle in which the German mind has been revolving for the last seventy or eighty years.

This work is to be published as leisurely as possible, the aim being consummate finish and expressiveness in what is done, rather than abundance in what is attempted. But in case of moderate success, and with the exercise of the true German spirit, "ohne Hast, aber ohne Rast,"[3] I flatter myself that our scholars, combined for a few years, may do that for the great mother of our minds—for the genial literature, to whose influence our spirits owe so much—which our elder sister, Britain, has failed to effect.

It is proposed to issue the work in 12mo volumes of three hundred and fifty pages, three or four in a year, as circumstances permit. The publishers (Hilliard, Gray and Co. of this city) authorise me to offer the writers one half of the proceeds of each volume, namely, $200, on the sale of one thousand copies, and in that proportion on all sales after defraying the expenses of publication.

The two first volumes will go to press in October next, and should they meet with sufficient success to authorise the continuance of the work, the succeeding volumes will be commenced without delay.

I sincerely hope that you will unite with our friends in this matter, whom I can now count upon in almost every part of the United States, and believe me with great respect

Truly yours
Geo. Ripley

1. George Ripley (1802–80) was at this time still minister of Purchase Street Church, Boston.
2. Beginning publication in 1838 with the assistance of Frederic H. Hedge, Ripley's *Specimens of Foreign Standard Literature* brought translations of Cousin, Jouffroy, and Schleiermacher to many American readers for the first time and exerted a profound influence on the intellectual life of New England.
3. Goethe's personal motto: "Without haste, but without rest."

To David Read[1]
Ms: JMC

Burlington, Vermont
December 12, 1837

My dear Brother

I disagree with you about Canada affairs[2] and think it of moment enough to write a letter about. In the first place, taking things as they are or have been, we certainly have no ground of complaint against the constituted authorities of the Province. We are bound too as a community and as individuals to consider the government as the proper representative of the province so long as it is de facto the government. We are no more justified in encouraging and prompting revolution and disorder, certainly without knowing whether it be for good cause or not, than if the province were a thousand miles from us and we had no conceivable interest any way in the result. If we do it without regard to the interests of the people there and on the ground of a supposed interest of our own in a successful revolution, so much the worse and the more unprincipled is such interference. Looking no farther then, it seems to me an obvious duty to stand entirely aloof from the conflict instead of raising a hurra for the so-called patriots there and thus insulting the government which they are resisting. I confess the course of our petty newspapers in this region has looked to me quite singular and liable to very grave animadversion—nor does it seem particularly honourable that two pieces of the state artillery of Vermont, if the fact be as stated, have been taken by the royal forces in charge of the insurgents.[3]

But I take other ground, viz: that the Canadians as a people are utterly incapable of self-government—that there are at least ten chances to one their condition will be far worse in a state of independence than it now is—that the British Government has manifested and still manifests a readiness to do all that is reasonable to improve their condition and raise them to a capacity of self-government at a future day—and that if they take reins into their own hands before they are thus qualified, either the mass of the people will be quieted under a more despotic government of their own leaders or will be like the states of South America continually passing from anarchy to despotism or from despotism to anarchy, always in a broil and often embroiling their neighbours with them. With our knowledge of the hazards and difficulties of self-government even with a population like our own, is it any thing more or less than either the blind hallucination of fanaticism or the wicked and reckless ambition of a few leaders to blow the trumpet of political liberty and talk of our glorious revolution to the great mass of Canadian French nine tenths of whom can neither read nor write, who certainly have no strength of religious or even moral principle and whose very leaders with some talents and cultivation have so far as I have learned given no such proofs of serious and well grounded principles of action as furnish any guarantee for the sobriety and wisdom with which success in their enterprise should be employed. So far as the probable advantage of the people there is concerned, I confess I can see no reason to wish them success but far otherwise. Besides that I have no belief they will succeed and fear that by our ill-judged encouragement many more will be led into difficulty and ruin than otherwise would.

If we look at our own interest in the matter certainly nothing is clearer than this that the better government they have in Canada the more peaceful and prosperous they are among themselves and the more quiet and orderly in their intercourse, the better it will be for us. Now what considerate man would wish so far as our interests in these respects are concerned, to run the hazard of a change from what we have hitherto experienced to what we have a right to expect from the independent government of French Canadians? Does it become us, just now at least, to talk of the British government as one among the European despotisms when we all know that our own government for the last eight years has been more despotic and inflicted more wanton evil upon its subjects than any British sovereign could have done for many a year without losing his throne or his life.

I have no wish certainly to give up our own power of self-government and begin to hope from recent events that we may prove capable of shunning its *extreme* dangers, but I feel still as if we had gone to the very brink of anarchy and revolution and that only an all wise and overruling Providence could have given events the turn they have taken and saved us from the precipice. Now if we can barely live and must be subjected by the blindness and madness of party and the wickedness of self-interested demagogues every few years to such miserable and shameful misgovernment as we have experienced of late, what can be hoped for such an ignorant and [. . .][4] as the Canadians. As to having the continent cleared of European influence it seems to me a matter of perfect indifference to us who governs Canada so it be well governed and that it will be vastly easier to keep on good terms with Great Britain in regard to it than with such a government as they would be likely to have. Then there would be agitation about uniting them with which I would say—Good Lord deliver us—we have enough such now.

I am greatly obliged to you for James'[5] boots as well as for all your kindness to him and hope I may be able at some day to do as much for yours. The book which I gave Maria[6] I meant as a present to her.

With love to all yours
very truly
Jas. Marsh

A petition has gone from here to the Governor[7] to request him to issue his proclamation in regard to doings on the frontier.

1. David Read (1799–1881), a lawyer in St. Albans, Vermont, was married to Emily Marsh (1806–67).

2. The Canadian Rebellion of 1837–38, sometimes called the Patriots' War, was a complicated affair. Events leading up to the rebellion in Upper Canada, or Ontario as it was to be called after the implementation of the Durham Report, and Lower Canada, the present province of Quebec, in some respects paralleled the preface to the

American Revolution of 1776. A massacre in Montreal in 1832, demands presented to the Crown in the form of resolutions, non-importation agreements, and the Crown's refusal to allow a popularly elected legislature led, in Lower Canada by mid-1837, to the formation of *Les Fils de la liberté* and the wearing of the Phyrigian cap. Not far from the New York-Vermont -Canadian border, after an initial rebel victory at Saint-Denis, British regulars at Saint Charles routed the rebels in late-1837 and chased them into Vermont. President Martin Van Buren proclaimed American neutrality on January 5, 1838; but with the support of Vermonters, Patriot raids were staged against Canada from the vicinities of St. Albans and Swanton. One foray, led by two physicians from Quebec, Robert Nelson, who had received honorary M.A.'s from UVM in 1827 and Dartmouth in 1831, and Cyril Coté, a UVM medical graduate of 1832, was armed in Vermont, went into Canada and declared an independent republic, only to be routed again, chased back to Plattsburgh, New York, where Nelson, after being disarmed by American troops, declared a government in exile and organized a secret society of refugees and American sympathizers in New York and Vermont called *Les Frères Chasseurs* or Hunters' Lodges. Various newspapers advertised for members of the lodges under the guise of "Wolfhunts." The "hunt" took place in November 1838 when 3,000 men accompanied Nelson back into Quebec, only to be quickly dispersed or arrested by loyalist and British regulars at Napierville. Twelve men were executed.

3. Two cannon belonging to the artillery company of Vermont militia in Stowe somehow made their way into the hands of the Patriots. On December 6 a Patriot attack mounted in Vermont lost the cannon and flags sewn by the ladies of Swanton when they encountered forty loyalist militiamen near St. Armand, Quebec.

4. The holograph is torn here.

5. James Wheelock Marsh (1827–59), Marsh's second son, UVM Class of 1848, after teaching in Virginia and North Carolina, went to Hawaii as assistant to the minister of education, eventually became a member of the Hawaiian parliament, and published the first newspaper in the Hawaiian language.

6. Daughter of David and Emily Marsh Read.

7. Silah H. Jennison (1791–1849) was the sixteenth governor of Vermont.

To David Read
Ms: JMC

Burlington
January 6, 1838

My dear Brother

I certainly shall not complain of your treating my positions and arguments with as little respect as I do yours, though I believe I can see the fallacy of your objections to them. But there is little use in a discussion that looks directly and constantly at the change of one's opinions in a reference to a particular case when they have been made up and the feelings enlisted. The only way to arrive at truth is by the study of principles with no other reference to particular cases, than a perfectly disinterested one for illustration and example. International law has certainly its general principles which must be applied without fear or favour in order to come at the right in any particular case. The principles of neutrality are sometimes indeed difficult of application yet are tangible and clearly laid down, as well as those which prescribe the duties of one nation to the belligerent parties of another. Now I hold as *unquestionable positions* that we are to observe those general principles in *this case* and bona fide and that what our government cannot *rightfully* do no *individual* under that government can *rightfully* do. To say that *individuals* may do what the government cannot sanction, that we have a right to do as *individuals* what we are bound not to do as a *people* and nation is, according to my philosophy, "in direct contradiction to every sound principle of public morals," and sophistical upon the face of it.

I should have a great deal to say about your doctrine respecting the liberty of the press before we should fully understand each other on that subject. But I will only say here that you misunderstood me in supposing I had said that publications about Canada were punishable by our laws. What I said and still hold is that although *not* equally amenable with other overt acts, yet if *intended* to *have an effect in* Canada or to excite our population to take a more active part, they were equally wrong in a moral point of view and violations of good faith. I see not how a lawyer or a moralist can for a moment question such a proposition.

But I have said more than I intended on this subject and will only add an expression of grief at the extreme folly and heedlessness of our citizens at the West[1] and the disastrous consequences which are flowing from it. I should be almost mobbed if I were to say that in the affair of the steam-boat the wrong was on our side and the British justified by the law of nations in the measures of retaliation and prevention which they have taken and yet I could find authorities enough and reasons to boot for the assertion. But in reference to certain more general principles of politics will you read with care Coleridge's Friend from the 140th to the 194th page. If you will consult the principles there taught, I shall be prepared to look at the Canada question by new lights and perhaps come to different conclutions.[2] I have spoken to Mr. Shedd[3] in a way to learn that he has no wish to sell his place and I do not suppose that Blodget's[4] can be had at any reasonable price. I am not sure but Hyde[5] puts his place here high with a view to stimulate us to pay for mine and keep it. Perhaps if the question with him were what he would take for the whole he might be more reasonable. With love to all

Yours truly
J. Marsh

1. Rebel headquarters and the capital of Mackenzie's republican government of Upper Canada were established at Navy Island on the Canadian side of the Niagara River north of the Falls. The rebels were supplied from the New York side by a small steamer, the "Caroline," which docked at Schlosser, New York. While in Schlosser on the night of December 29, 1837, the "Caroline" was boarded and scuttled by a band of loyalists. An American, Durfee, was killed in the scuffle.

2. The main concern of these passages in *The Friend*, entitled "On the Principles of Political Philosophy," is to demonstrate the impracticability of Rousseau's *Du Contrat Social* and the failure of French physiocracy in the 1790s. In attempting to derive universal political principles from Reason, followers of Rousseau neglected to recognize that "universal principles, as far as they are principles and universals, necessarily suppose uniform and perfect subjects, which are to be found in the *Ideas* of pure Geometry and (I trust) in the *Realities* of Heaven, but never, never, in creatures of flesh and blood" (*The Friend*, Marsh's edition, p. 173).

3. Marshall Shedd (1786–1872), Dartmouth Class of 1817, was the father of W. G. T. Shedd, UVM Class of 1839. In 1837–38 he was pastor of the Congregational churches in Colchester and Essex, Vermont. David Read bought his home in Colchester and Marsh died in it in 1842.

4. Amos Blodget, attorney in Burlington.

5. Archibald Hyde, customs collector and dispenser of political patronage in Burlington for Cornelius Van Ness. Blodget and Hyde owned houses near Marsh's, which stood on the site of Billings Library, now the Student Union, at UVM.

1835–1838 From David Read
Ms: JMC

St. Albans, Vermont
January 8, 1838

My *dear Brother*

I supposed that our discussion had closed—but as yours of the 6th has been passed to me by the hand of Mr. James,[1] I regard it as a matter of courtesy to you, as well as pleasure to myself, to reply to it.

The position you take in your last, I consider just: in reference to the liberty of the press—it may be *morally* wrong, but not *legally* so. I drew the inference on reading your former letter that you held it to be legally wrong and punishable with *fine* and *imprisonment* to publish, with *intent* to have an effect in *Canada*. My inference may be wrong. I will quote your words— "If so do you mean to say it is *legally* right, i.e., not *punishable by our laws*, or that it is *morally* right?" A few lines after you add—"then again, though less likely to be punishable by *fine* and *imprisonment*, is not publishing with *intent* to render odious the legal authorities of the province, and to promote the interest of the insurgents, in a *legal* as well as *moral* sense, as effectually *aiding* and *abetting*, as any other mode of promoting the same end?"

With your views on this subject, as expressed in your last, we shall not probably differ—but a question (which I cannot look upon as yet without confidence in the position I took) remains unsettled between us—i.e. whether the acts of *Government* and *individuals* as such, are, in their relation to neutral rights, one and the same, or in other words, whether an individual *can* rightfully do what the Government under which he lives *can not*? Answer—if an *individual* should take his life in his hands, go into the territory of one of two belligerant nations, and join the army—it would be no breach of *international* law, or of *moral* law, (if war in any case is moral). If a nation should send an army into the territory of one of two belligerant nations to assist them, it would be both a violation of *international* law and of *moral law*. If General Van Rensselaer,[2] of his own free will, went to Navy Island, it was no breach of neutrality; otherwise if our Government sent him there. Contracts between nations have the

1835–1838 citizens can in no way be attoned for but by a surrender of McNab and his party to the laws of this country. "An injury" says Kent "to an individual member of a state is a just cause of war, if redress be refused" (p. 48). Because some of our citizens volunteer in service against the Royalists, or furnish arms and munitions of war to their enemies, I can not see wherein it furnishes ground for them to come into our territory and murder other of our innocent and inoffending citizens. I know of no *law of retaliation* that will extend to this length—no doubt they were provoked to the act by the conduct of our citizens, but they seized upon, comparatively, a trifling provocation for committing so unheard of and horrendous an outrage; instead of *retaliation* merely, they committed a *tenfold* aggression. I think McNab a hot headed Scotch-man and *no general*, or he would not have been caught in that thing. The Caroline must be looked upon as a *common carrier* merely and had a right under our existing treaties with Great Britain, to land in safety at Chippiway, even if she had munitions of war on board for the Patriots; but the goods themselves in such case would be liable to immediate seizure. If the Caroline had been fitting up at Schlosser in our port as a vessel of war, arming itself with cannon and for the known and acknowledged purpose of making an attack upon Chippiway (the enemy's shore) it would have furnished them with an apology for destroying the boat—but even then, it would have been another Copenhagen affair,[4] and a violation of the law of nations though unusitate rei[5] would have been their palliation. I have looked for authorities to justify the act, but can find none.

I have looked into the *Friend* and think it rather a hard tax that you have imposed upon me—it is much easier to *adopt* than to *criticise* the arguments of so learned and distinguished a man as Coleridge. I have room to say only a word, with regard to the moving doctrines of the revolution in France. Coleridge and Rousseau, I regard as both in the *right* and both in the *wrong*. Rousseau was in the *right* as to his abstract principles of Government—and Coleridge was in the *right* in contending that the natural imperfections of man unfit him and remained a lasting, at least an existing, obstacle against the enjoyment of those principles. Rousseau was *wrong* in advocating as practicable a form of Government which could only be applied to man and enjoyed by him, when divested of his corrupt and sinful nature—as if the people of France were so pure and elevated in their moral character, as that they were capable of individual self Government without any other supervisory power, than pure Reason. Coleridge was in the *wrong* in denying the justice of these principles when applied to Government after having so manfully contended for them as applicable to man—i.e. in not suffering "Expediency" to enter the thoughts of a man, but in adopting it as the proper basis for the Government of nations. He governs nations by the "understanding," but individuals by the "reason."[6] Do you not long to see the day when nations shall be governed by the *reason* too? When the doctrines which we now call Jacobinical may find in time to come a successful application to a higher and more elevated station of human perfectability? Can mankind be brought to that elevation? I fear—but is it proven to be impossible? I would like to say more on this subject if I had room.

(Will there be any harm in asking Hyde what he will take for the whole—if not, will you please do so?)

Very affectionately and
truly
D. Read

I have just had a letter from Roswell.[7] He is in the front rank of the Patriots.

1. Lewis James (1795–1874) was a physician in Swanton, Vermont.
2. Rensselaer Van Rensselaer (1802–50) was the son of Solomon Van Rensselaer of War of 1812 fame and had been once described as "a gin-sling, sottish looking genius of twenty-seven, but apparently much older from disease and dissipation."
3. Colonel Allan McNab (1798–1862) during the rebellion commanded "the men of Gore" and then the loyalist forces at the Niagara Frontier where he commissioned Andrew Drew, R.N., to seek and destroy the "Caroline," an episode which cost the life of one American.
4. In 1801 neutral Denmark had refused to comply with British restrictions on neutral navigation during the Napoleonic campaigns. Nelson and Hyde Parker led a British fleet into the roadsteads of Copenhagen and forced compliance with the British restrictions on Baltic traffic by defeating the Danish fleet on its own doorsteps.

5. An unusual circumstance.
6. Coleridge does not make the distinction as Read has it: "That Reason should be our guide and governor is an undeniable Truth, and all our notion of right and wrong is built thereon: for the whole moral nature of man originated and subsists in his Reason. From Reason alone can we derive the principles which our Understandings are to apply, the Ideal to which by means of our Understandings we should endeavor to approximate. This however gives no proof that Reason alone ought to govern and direct human beings, either as Individuals or as States. It ought not to do this, because it cannot" (p. 170). Sound government Coleridge found based on the maxim "*expedience* based on *experience* [original italics] and particular circumstances, which will vary in every different nation, and in the same nation at different times" (p. 173). The maxim is constructed out of the Understanding, not Reason.
7. Roswell Marsh (1793–1875) was practicing law in Steubenville, Ohio.

To David Read
Ms: JMC

Burlington
January 11, 1838

Now really Brother Read, I must beg you in earnest to get out of this slough of popular delusion before it becomes as it soon will a matter of reproach to every decent man who has been carried away with it. Recollect I said at the outset that in six months every man of sense would be ashamed of having any thing to do with it and I do not hesitate to reassert it. I do not mean ashamed of *motives* for I give many of those concerned credit for the best but of the foolish and intemperate excitement to which it would lead and of the vague and indiscriminating views of political principles on which it is based. Again in saying that the course pursued by the press and by public assemblies is against "public morals" it is not meant that individuals have acted immorally i.e. against conscience but that exciting the community to do what the laws of nations and the laws of the country forbid is unsettling the principles of public morals in that community. This brings me to the point in your last letter which I wish particularly to notice, the distinction between what the government may do and what individuals may do. It seemed to me that the principle I stated was so obvious as not to admit of dispute and yet it has been disputed and in fact the more I have thought of it the more I see that it must be relied upon almost wholly to justify the course which has been pursued. But just look at the reductio ad absurdum which the assumption of that distinction so easily admits. If one individual may go into Canada without violating the laws of neutrality and of this country then 100 nay 1000 or 100000. Thus our citizens might actually conquer all the British Provinces while the Governments are in a state of profound peace. It is only necessary to show the British Minister that the government has not sent them and it seems he has no right to complain. Does not the absurdity of the conclusion show the absurdity of the premise. But in fact the first principle of international law is that the government of a country is responsible for the conduct of its subjects towards foreign governments. It is not only bound to punish and compensate aggression when committed but to prevent aggression. Every such aggression is not indeed at once and at the outset to be construed as a violation of neutrality or of international obligations when promptly disavowed and *repressed*. But let our Government tell the British Minister that its citizens are not *under its control* and that it has either not the disposition or not the *requisite powers* for putting a stop to such goings on as those at Navy Island and rely upon it, he would take leave in twenty-four hours. If such is our relation to other nations we should at once be placed without the pale of the law of nations and be but a horde of outlaws at war with all nations. It may be that legal provision has not been made for effectually discharging our international duties in this respect, but if not it must be made without delay and such you will soon see is the doctrine held at Washington. The proceedings at Navy Island are just as much a violation of neutrality as the destruction of the boat at Schlosser. One is as easily disavowed by the government as the other and the outcry against the one in the same breath that hurras for the other is ridiculous if it were not worse than that.

One word more as to the responsibility of the press and here again I beg leave to refer you to a brief paper of Coleridge for principles from p. 55

to 66 of the Friend. The subject is admitted by him and is indeed especially under a government like our own of great practical difficulty.[1] But in reference to what I said on the subject I may still maintain as I certainly should do, that publishing *with intent* to produce effects in Canada against the British Government is both in a *legal* and *moral* sense an *act* and as much a violation of the spirit of international law as enlisting a soldier or sending ammunition. The difference in its amenability to law and punishment results from the difficulty of adequately defining and proving such an offence or if you please from the imperfection of our laws. As to our constitution having guaranteed an absolute freedom of the press from all legal responsibility, whether in its treatment of foreign governments or of our own, I hold to no such thing. I do hold that the course practically pursued in this country in respect to the press or in fact its practical irresponsibleness and consequent licentiousness is one of the greatest issues of the land and is tending more effectually than any thing else to loosen the foundations of all law and government to sweep away all reverence for truth and right, all respect for the lights of wisdom and the maxims of experience and all the "bulwarks of public decency and public opinion." "Political calumny" has already joined hands with private slander, and every principle, every feeling that binds the citizen to his country and the spirit to its Creator will be undermined—by the mere habit of hearing them reviled and scoffed at with impunity. It is such views of what is going on among us and not any special interest in or peculiar regard for her Majesty's Provinces in North America that makes me in earnest in this matter. The symptoms as symptoms are alarming and the courage that I had gathered from the result of late elections is more than neutralized in my own mind by seeing how excitable the community is and with how little heed and how little regard for law or duty we may be hurried into the most shameful excesses.

Here is General Brown[2] haranguing public assemblies, openly defying civil authority, advertising in the Middlebury paper for guns, knapsacks and cartouch boxes for a "great Wolf hunt" and giving out that in a few weeks he shall be on the line with a great military force and yet our very sapient district attorney can find nothing to do. Then on the other side, if a man opens his mouth about enforcing the insulted laws of his country, he is a tory and told that nothing but hanging is good enough for him.

As to your quotations from Kent, just turn from p. 117, which you referred to over to the *next page* —consider what had been going on for weeks in violation of what is laid down on that page[3] and that our government opposed no effectual interference, then read Mr. Adams' defence of Gen. Jackson's conduct in Florida[4] and you will be fully answered. Yet it is not probable the British Government will justify the destruction of the boat, nor will our Government justify the occupation of the island by its citizens and I trust prompt measures will be taken at Washington to wipe out the disgrace which it brings upon the country.

You do not admit the justness of Coleridge's distinction in regard to the implication of the law of reason to one's own acts and to constitutions of national Government. But do you not see that if you only admit as you do that the abstract principles of reason cannot be applied absolutely but must be modified by the character and condition of the particular people, you have in fact granted all that he asks and all that is necessary in reference to the case before. It must be determined not by mere abstract principles whether a revolution would be desirable for Canada but by a careful and thorough examination of the character of the people by the lights of past experience, by the exercise of that sound and deep political wisdom which few possess and which places the question entirely beyond the focus of vision in which objects present themselves to the eyes of a popular meeting at St. Albans or elsewhere.

I have seen a letter from Roswell to Mr. Goodrich but should not think from that that he was very zealous though he places it upon the wrong ground and without due consideration of the principles involved.

With much love to all
yours truly
J. Marsh—

1835–1838

1. In "Essay X," *The Friend*, Coleridge discusses the question of licensing book publication and the possible dangers inherent in unlicensed publication. His conclusion to the argument appears in the opening of "Essay XI": "a book should be as freely admitted into the world as any other birth; and if it prove a monster, who denies but that it may justly be burnt and sunk into the sea?" (p. 61). Unlicensed books, even though possibly libelous, and turnpike travellers, even though possibly highwaymen, must be treated equally: "Innocence is presumed in both cases." Coleridge, however, recognizes a difficulty in the highwaymen-libelous book analogy. With highwaymen, the law need only prove the fact and identify the offender. But libelous books present the problems of determining the kind and circumstances of criminality, problems which, like "the hues of a dove's neck, die away into each other, incapable of definition or outline" (p. 62). Even "the most meritorious work" could at some time be found to fall within the category of libel. Yet Coleridge argues that, in the case of "rank and unweeded press" which would degrade the manners and principles of a people and their "general tone of thought and conversation," his very love for literature would call for the interference of law as an "Ithureal spear, that might remove from the ear of the public" reptiles of "vain hopes, vain aims, inordinate desires" (p. 66).

2. T. S. Brown, the rebel leader, was active in Vermont throughout most of 1838.

3. "Every power is obliged to conform to these rules of the law of nations relative to postliminy, where the interests of neutrals are concerned. But in cases arising between its own subjects, or between them and those of her allies the principle may undergo such modification as policy dictates" ["Of the Law of Nations," *Kent's Commentary* (New York, 1826), p. 118].

4. In 1818 John Quincy Adams, then secretary of state, supported Andrew Jackson's war on the Seminoles and the execution of two British nationals in the course of Jackson's campaign on the ground that the Spanish authorities were incompetent to police Florida and thus Jackson's punishment of the Indians and Arbuthnot and Armbruster was justified.

In 1838 President Van Buren protested the sinking of the "Caroline" by Canadians, but in turn prosecuted Mackenzie and some of the American volunteers in Mackenzie's "army."

"Another Light Extinguished" 1838–1842

Few of Marsh's own letters survive from the last four years of his life. From extant correspondence it is clear, however, that he actively communicated with many people beyond the mountains surrounding the Champlain Valley and frequently travelled to Boston. He preached on one occasion to the patients at a hospital for the insane near Boston; and at other times sought money from the University's friends in Massachusetts. He moved in the circles of both the conservative Boston Brahmins, like Ticknor, and Utopian reformers and transcendentalists like George Ripley and the Channings. Marsh remained critical of both, however, always believing that the integration of head and heart, nature and spirit, was a difficult task demanding intellectual rigor and discipline as well as profound and imaginative depths of feeling. Continuing his studies in German philosophy, including Hegel, even after the death of his second wife and the breakup of his household once more, Marsh carried on the search for physical and spiritual unity that began at Dartmouth in 1815, grew during his first readings of Coleridge in 1818–19, and despite great physical and economic hardships sustained him throughout the last years of his life.

From George Ripley
Ms: JMC

Boston
February 23, 1838

My dear Sir

As I had nothing definite to suggest in reply to your letter of July last, I have delayed writing until this moment.

My purpose of issuing a series of translations[1] has been welcomed with great ardor by all sorts of persons; and, at present, there is a fair prospect that it may be accomplished to the extent of several volumes. It is not published by subscription, however; and of course nothing can be relied upon, with any certainty for the future.

I depend on Mr. Hedge[2] of Bangor for one or two volumes of Fichte, including an account of his life and philosophical career, with the translation of the "Bestimmung des Menschen," "das Wesen des Gelehrten" and perhaps the "Grundzuge."[3] He may perhaps fail in this, as his health is very precarious; and it gratifies me to think that in that case, you may feel disposed to take the work into your own hands.

"Ritter's Logik,"[4] I know only by description. Troxler in his excellent book,[5] I find, speaks well of it; and from all accounts I should judge that it would make a very valuable work in English. I am perfectly willing to take it on your recommendation; after the public shall have been somewhat prepared by a few works of a more popular character.

I have a great respect for Fries[6] as a philosophical writer. I think he is an admirable continuator of Kant; and that he has done much by his recognition of the class of truths which are independent of demonstration, and founded on immediate deduction from our inward nature, to redeem the system of Kant, from some of the principal allegations that lie against it. His method is unquestionably the correct one. How can we advance a step unless we take our start from psychological analysis? Fries is true to this as the needle to the North. He leaves the matter however in a too subjective state to satisfy my mind. He gives me the building, beautiful in its symmetrical proportions, shown upon by the clearest light of day, and opening magnificent perspectives into the vast Unknown beyond; but I want a deeper foundation. I am still standing on I know not what; I do not rise above the sphere of self; I have not legitimized the objective reality of my idea. As at present advised, I must think Cousin leaves Fries in the rear. They both travel on the same road. But I come to firm footing with the former, which I do not find with the latter. Has my admiration for Cousin led me to be unjust to Fries?

It did not occur to me that the "Wissen, Glaube und Ahndung"[7] would do to translate. It was written, if I remember, as Fries states in his Preface, to secure his claim to the ideas which he held as his own, while the larger work was in preparation. Of course, it is an outline so compact and rigid, that it did not seem likely to come within the reach of our readers. On second thoughts, however, I'm inclined to believe that a good book might be made of it, by additions and a sort of running commentary, prepared from his "Neue Kritik der Vernunft" and "Metaphysick."[8] I should be glad to see such a work from your hand.

I take the liberty to ask your acceptance of my first two volumes, which are just published. I have ventured to make some distinct references to your Edition of the "Aids to Reflection"; and also to exhibit a view of Coleridge in which I cannot hope for your sympathy.[9] However, I am sure that we are both laboring for the same object; and if you can make Coleridge instrumental in the restoration of a spiritual philosophy among our countrymen, I will a l'autre hand for Cousin. The work to be done here is of such immense importance and needs such clear heads, strong hands and earnest hearts that I am glad to cry All Hail to any brother-worker, wherever found within hearing distance. I look for much from your brave young men who I am told leave College with the seeds of a pure philosophy properly scattered over a good soil.

Leonard Woods[10] means to translate Twesten for my series. I want to have it made a truly catholic work if it goes on, representing all great ideas without reference to outside distinctions. I am sincerely grateful for the interest you have expressed in it thus far, and remain,

With great respect
Ever yours truly
Geo: Ripley

1. *Specimens of Foreign Standard Literature.*
2. Frederic Henry Hedge (1805–90) resided in Bangor, Maine, but had studied in Germany and with Emerson and Ripley was one of the organizers of the Transcendentalists Club.
3. Johann G. Fichte, *Die Bestimmung des Menschen . . .* (Berlin, 1800); *Ueber des Wesen des Gelehrten und seine Erscheinungen im Gebiete der Freiheit* (Berlin, 1806); *Die Grundzüge des gegenwärtigen Zeitalters. Dargestellt in Vorlesungen in Jahre 1804–5* (Berlin, 1806).
4. Neither *Abriss der philosophischen der Logik* (Berlin, 1824) nor *Vorlesungen zur Einleitung in die Logik* (Berlin, 1823), by August Heinrich Ritter appeared in *Specimens of Foreign Standard Literature.*
5. Ignaz Paul Vital Troxler,

Logik. Die Wissenschaft des Denkens und Kritik aller Erkenntniss, zum Selbstudium, . . . (Tubingen, 1829).
6. Jakob Friedrich Fries (1773–1843), professor of philosophy at the University of Jena and author of, among many titles, *Handbuch der Religions philosophie und philosophischen Aesthetik* (1832) and *System der Logik* (1837).
7. Fries's *Wissen, Glaube, and Ahndung* (Jena, 1805) was written for an audience of laymen, rather than professional theologians or philosophers.
8. Fries's *Neue oder anthropologische Kritik der Vernunft* was published in various editions from 1828 to 1831.
9. Ripley said in his Introductory Notice: "Coleridge cannot satisfy the mind whose primary want is that of philosophical clearness and precision. He is the inspired poet. . . ; but the practical architect, by whose skill the temple of faith is to be restored, cannot be looked for in him."
10. Leonard Woods, Jr. (1807–78), professor of biblical literature at Bangor Theological Seminary.

From James Gillman[1]
Text: *Remains*,
pp. 153–54.

Highgate
February 24, 1838

Dear Sir

Although your kind and sympathizing letter has remained unanswered, it gave me unfeigned satisfaction, as I felt it a mark of regard for myself and an affectionate testimony of love for the memory of one of the best of human beings. Sorrow and sickness have, ever since we lost him, followed so closely on each other that I have left many things undone which I yet never lost sight of; and among them was the assurance I owed you of my sense of the value of those feelings which induced you to address me. I am sorry I cannot give you any information respecting the writings Coleridge has left. But Mr. Henry Nelson Coleridge[2] intends himself the pleasure of forwarding the new works, entitled "Literary Remains,"[3] published since his death, by the Bishop of Vermont,[4] who has offered to convey any parcel to you. I am obliged by your introduction of that gentleman to me; we were highly pleased with his manly simplicity, and interesting appearance and manners. I beg your acceptance, my dear Sir, of the first volume of Coleridge's Life.[5] The second volume is not yet finished, but it will, I think, be the most interesting of the two as it will contain so many notes and memoranda of his own. How much I wish you could have known or even have seen him! I enclose the copy of an epitaph I wrote for a very humble tablet, which I put up in our church at Highgate; and also a copy of his will, which latter will no doubt interest you deeply; a copy too, of the last thing he wrote, ten days before he breathed his last and when in his bed and suffering greatly. I must now, my dear Sir, beg you to accept my cordial regard, and to rest assured of the sentiments of esteem with which I am

Yours faithfully,
James Gillman

1. James Gillman was the young surgeon who ventured to take in Coleridge in 1816 for a month at his home in Highgate in order to treat him for opium addiction; the relationship and residence at Highgate deepened and lasted for the remaining eighteen years of Coleridge's life.
2. Henry Nelson Coleridge (1798–1843), nephew and son-in-law of Samuel Taylor Coleridge, married Sara Coleridge in 1829 and was appointed Coleridge's literary executor, editing *Literary Remains*, *Aids to Reflection*, *Confessions of an Enquiring Spirit*, and *Table Talk*.
3. *The Literary Remains of Samuel Taylor Coleridge*. Collected and edited by Henry Nelson Coleridge (London, 1836–39).
4. John Henry Hopkins.
5. James Gillman, *The Life of Samuel Taylor Coleridge*, I (London, 1838).

From Richard H. Dana
Ms: UVM

Boston
February 24, 1838

Dear Sir,

From having been confined to the house since the first of October, except about three weeks at the close of November, I am, as you may well suppose, much reduced in strength. I have within a week or two renewed the Readings with my Class; but they exhaust me exceedingly. I am now better fitted to be abed than to be scribbling here. I can't, however, let Edmund[1] leave without sending a line by him. He is soon, I take it, to come into your branches of study. I am glad that it is so. He will enter them with a mind strongly prepossessed in favour of his instructor and with a thorough and wholesome respect for him. The importance of this state of mind to the pupil I have always been well aware of; and was gratified to see set forth as it is in that article of unusual tho't, in the last October Number of London Quarterly Review—The Universities[2]—an essay which I hope you will look at, if you have not already done so.

Altho' I am confined to the house, I hear a good deal of what is rife abroad, and amongst the rest, of the notions now in vogue with many of the educated class and with their followers. Mr. Emerson's lectures[3] seem to have taken the lead. Mr. Emerson is not, I understand, considered at all remarkable as a reasoner; but is distinguished rather, for throwing out striking detached thoughts, or perhaps, with more truth, thoughts strikingly exprest. They take the aphoristic form; and that, you know, almost always give an air of profoundness to whatever is so enunciated. He is, also, rich in illustrations. That he has systematized his thoughts is hardly possible. I cannot find that he is bottomed on any thing. The Infinite, and our higher Instincts were much, and, I should think, vaguely enough talked about; and in the last lecture but one (on Holiness) *abstraction* was the word. The *highest* Instinct, that which leads us to a conscious, supreme *Being* was put down as the product of the ignorance and weakness of man requiring an Object out of self, but from which the intellectual man freed himself through the process of abstraction. So instinct went quite by the boards. Abstraction, abstract qualities, were the all in all. How these exist primarily, and independently of some *Being*, absolutely, and not as attributes, he has never, that I can learn, attempted to explain, nor has he even alluded to this difficulty, I believe. But I am no metaphysician: it may be made clear perhaps with more ease than I am aware. A Unitarian lady told my daughter that in walking home with Mr. Emerson after the lecture, she said to him, I must have an object out of and above myself, which to look to, and on which I may depend. He replied, that if we would but look into ourselves, we should find *there* all we needed. His lecture on Holiness is held by many as equivalent to Atheism. An intelligent Unitarian clergyman, one of the more serious sort, told me that now and then there were expressions which had a somewhat different aspect, but that, take the lecture as a whole, he could make out of it nothing short of atheism. It is melancholy to think how many young men and females, quite *girls*, are running wild with these notions—at least, in their minds they are little more than notions. And these young people before long are to be fathers and mothers.

Edmund attended Mr. Emerson's course, and I think can give you some slight apprehension of the lectures. I think that what he has perceived of the spirit of unbelief in this community has been good for him. Brownson, of whom you have probably heard, a man who preaches "on his own hook" and is editor of the new Boston Quarterly Review,[4] is setting free the lower classes from the bondage of old religion. A gentleman told me that he heard him say, a few Sundays ago, that the great purpose of man was to aid and elevate his fellow-man and that he who did this was *a christian, though the denial of God were on his lips.* We have all forms of unbelief; and though I wish not to judge, I must say that others, lay and clergy, are covering over an infidelity not essentially short of this, with what they term *spiritual philosophy.* Here is, indeed, a sad state of things amongst us.

If you looked into Mr. Henry's[5] last New York Review, you probably saw in the article on Coleridge's Literary Remains, a statement by C. that in his public lectures, delivered several years before Schlegel's appeared, he had expressed the very views respecting Shakespeare which were afterwards published by Schlegel,[6] and that when he, Coleridge, in subsequent lectures read from his old notes, his auditors thought he had stolen from Schlegel. He refers to Hazlitt,[7] also, as supporting him, C's, priority. Mr. Allston[8] confirms this and tells me that he was dining at a Mr. Montagu's[9] in London and that when this very matter was spoken of, Hazlitt turned to him and said, Coleridge uttered these very things twenty (or many) years ago. The same thing may have occurred independently to both Coleridge's and Schlegel's minds; though it is more probable that Coleridge—who was always pouring forth from his full mind and who had dwelt so long on Shakespeare in his lectures—when he went to Germany imbued Schlegel with his thoughts on Shakespeare.[10]

I state this because I believe you had taken an impression unfavourable to Coleridge's claim. Mr. Allston is perfectly clear about it. Besides, dear Sir, I have for several years past had a yearning of heart towards Coleridge, which I have never felt towards any other man. Bitter indeed, have been his enemies over the dead. And the Unitarians here now seem to hate him and show a spirit of detraction whenever they can: they can't forgive so great a man for speaking of Unitarianism as he does.

President Wheeler has ordered Carlyle's French Revolution,[11] which my son takes in his trunk. The President may think that I am very unqualified in my censure of Carlyle. I have read none of Carlyle's reviews save the early one headed Characteristics;[12] but I have read his Sartor Resartus[13] all through and I have looked here and there into his Revolution. The former work is bad enough, in all conscience, in respect to style; but this last is the greatest outrage ever perpetrated on our Mother English. In what I have read of Carlyle I am completely at fault in finding the *originality* of the man; it is plain enough that he has been to others for his thoughts, though so stuffed out and bedizened, that common eyes may not discover them for old acquaintances. Yet, they certainly are no new race of intellectuals—as Mr. Allston said of his Marabeau.[14] I have met with few original thoughts, but with much original English; so may it be said of all I have read of him. He may delude many who are not thorough thinkers; indeed has already done so to very many here. And he is a dangerous writer for young men too fitted to captivate young men. Exaggeration, presumption, affected independence, and thoughts in a dress as meretricious as a harlot's. Those who are not disgusted at faults in him, and at his self-complacency, and at his egotism *egotized*, are in great danger of having much harm done them: for there certainly must be a demoralizing influence in him over those of the young to whom he is not an offence. I don't know of any *writer* who ever called up in me such a disgust at the *man*, as has this Carlyle. Yet they are mad after him here;

and *those* who are mad after him, and the *character* of their admiration, indicate the spirit of their God.

Richd. H. Dana

1. Edmund Trowbridge Dana, UVM Class of 1839.
2. The article was a review of William Whewell's *Principles of English University Education* (London, 1837) in *The Quarterly Review*, 59 (1837), 439–83.
3. Emerson delivered ten lectures on "Human Culture" at the Boston Masonic Temple in the winter of 1837–38.
4. Orestes Brownson (1803–76) published *The Boston Quarterly Review* from 1838 to 1842.
5. C. S. Henry.
6. "'I gave those lectures at the Royal Institution, before six or seven hundred auditors of rank and eminence, in the spring of the same year, in which Sir Humphry Davy, a fellow-lecturer, made his great revolutionary discoveries in chemistry. Even in detail the coincidences of Schlegel with my lectures was extraordinary, that all who at a later period heard the same words, taken by me from my notes of the lectures at the Royal Institution, concluded a borrowing on my part from Schlegel. . . . Mr. Hazlitt, I say, himself replied to an assertion of my plagiarism from Schlegel in these words; —That is a lie; for I myself heard the very same character of Hamlet from Coleridge before he went to Germany, and when he had neither read nor could read a page of German.' . . . Recorded by me, S. T. Coleridge, 7th Jan. 1819.—Vol. II [of the *Biographia Literaria*], p. 202, 203." Quoted in "Literary Remains of Coleridge," *New York Review*, 2 (1838), 107–8.
7. William Hazlitt (1778–1830), the English essayist, critic, and friend of Coleridge.
8. Washington Allston, the American painter, friend of Coleridge, and Dana's brother-in-law.
9. Basil Montagu (1770–1851), a friend of Coleridge since the 1780s, was a prominent London lawyer whose home at 25 Bedford Square was often the gathering place for London's literary society.
10. Approximately seventy pages of Chapter XII in Coleridge's *Biographia Literaria* are taken directly from Schelling, a debt which scholars have carefully documented along with Coleridge's other debts to Schlegel in his lectures on Shakespeare. See W. J. Bate, *Coleridge* (London, 1968), pp. 131–38, for a thorough and sympathetic discussion of the question of Coleridge's plagiarism.
11. The 1838 Boston edition of Carlyle's *French Revolution* survives in Marsh's library at UVM.
12. Carlyle's "Characteristics" was written in October 1831 and published in *The Edinburgh Review* (December, 1831).
13. *Sartor Resartus* was first published serially in *Fraser's Magazine* (1833–34). Its first book edition was published with Emerson's help in America, 1836.
14. "Mirabeau" was published in *The Westminster Review* (January, 1837).

To Richard Henry Dana
Ms: JMC

Burlington
March 8, 1838

My dear Sir

I am greatly obliged to you for your kind letter by Edmund and for your account of the current "notions" of the good people of Boston. If I had not done being surprised at anything in the way of shallowness in theory and of levity and foolish excitability in the corresponding movements of the day, I should I confess be greatly surprised at some things which you and your son tell me. From his accounts of Mr. Emerson's lectures they must contain with scarcely a decent disguise nothing less than an Epicurean Atheism dressed up in a style seducing and to many perhaps deceptive. I am curious to know whether the Spiritualists among the Unitarians are as a class tending the same way. Of this one might be confident a priori that they must either return under the guidance of an awakened conscience and the spirit of God to the whole "truth as it is in Jesus" or trusting in mere speculation rest in some form of Pantheism. It was natural to indulge the hope that in such a population as that of Boston the better tendency would prevail. But to become as a little child at the feet of Christ is not indeed the obvious way to the truth in their own understandings and I fear our Unitarian friends are getting farther from it in their recent speculations.

Tholuck holds as it seems to me with good reason and Coleridge essentially the same that the ultimate truths of Christianity and indeed all properly spiritual truths are not within the compass of speculative knowledge but are the objects of faith alone. Thus the personality of God cannot be proved by speculative reasoning yet conscience commands us to recognize his personal being. I have looked with a good deal of interest to the selections from Cousin which Mr. Ripley[1] has sent me to see if I could find any more light on this point than in what I had before seen of his works but confess I do not find it. His "substance" and "cause" do not necessarily involve the idea of a free personal agent and cannot therefore be the proper object of worship. Though he expressly denies the identity of his doctrine with that of Spinoza on p. 78,[2] yet I do not see how this previous statement differs essentially from it and compared with Coleridge's statement p. 61 of the *Table Talk*[3] it is identical with Spinoza and contradictory to the Christian idea. I must write to Mr. Ripley about this matter.

To write a good letter on metaphysics is not an easy matter because it is not easy to write on metaphysics at all.

J. Marsh

1. Better than eighty percent of Ripley's *Specimens of Foreign Standard Literature* consisted of translations from Cousin.

2. "I must remind [my adversaries] that the God of Spinoza and the Eleatics is a pure substance and not a cause. In the system of Spinoza, creation is impossible; in mine it is necessary." Victor Cousin, *Exposition of Eclecticism*, from *Specimens of Foreign Standard Literature* (Boston, 1838), I, p. 78.

3. "You may state the Pantheism of Spinosa, in contrast with the Hebrew or Christian scheme, shortly, as this:—
Spinosism
W – G = O; i.e. The World without God is an impossible idea.
G – W = O; i.e. God without the World is likewise.
Hebrew or Christian Scheme
W – G = O; i.e. The same as Spinosa's premise.
But G – W = G; i.e. God without the World is God the Self-subsistent."
Table Talk, *The Complete Works of Samuel Taylor Coleridge*, edited by W. G. T. Shedd (New York, 1853), VI, p. 280.

From Joseph Henry Green[1]
Ms: UVM

King's College, London
February 25, 1839

My dear Sir

Interested as I am in all that relates to the character of my lamented friend Coleridge and to the promulgation of those truths which it was the great aim of his life, even at the sacrifice of his worldly interests, to establish, I need not say how much gratification I have received in learning from one so well qualified as yourself to give an opinion that Coleridge's writings are appreciated and that with your aid they are forming for themselves a widening circle of admirers in the United States.

In reply to your inquiries respecting his works that remain to be published, I beg to acquaint you that he has left a considerable number of miscellaneous papers of the nature of which you will be enabled to form a judgment from the three posthumous volumes entitled, "Literary Remains," which have already appeared. No time will be lost in putting forth another volume. Much, however, will still remain for publication, including a variety of essays and detached observations on subjects of theology, biblical criticism, logic, natural science, etc., in connection with his philosophical views. dare not, however, promise any finished work, except a short though highly interesting one "On the Inspiration of the Scriptures." And I may add, that, beyond the design of getting these works through the press and of reprinting those which are out of print, no intention exists at present of publishing an uniform collection of his prose writings.

I presume, however, that your main inquiry relates to the work that was expected to contain the full development of his system of philosophy; but I regret to say that this, which would have been the crowning labor of his life, was not accomplished; nor can this unfortunate circumstance be a matter of surprise to those who are acquainted with the continual suffering from disease which embittered the latter part of this truly great man's life. I cannot doubt that the announcement of this desideratum will be no less a disappointment to Coleridge's transatlantic friends than to his admirers in England; but to none will the disappointment prove more grievous than to myself, as the task of supplying the deficiency devolves, by my dear friend's dying request, on my very inadequate powers. I am now, however, seriously at work in the humble hope of fulfilling this duty (as far as my means of accomplishing it permit) and I propose, in the first instance, to give a succinct and comprehensive statement of principles, such as will enable the readers of Coleridge's writings to see the connection of the thoughts under the guiding light of the unity of the ideas from which they flowed. In this attempt to set forth the principles of Mr. Coleridge's system, I am not without the hope of establishing them as the principles of philosophy itself and of showing that the various schemes which have been framed by the founders of the numerous philosophical schools and sects are not disparates or contraries, but merely partial views of one great truth and necessary steps and gradations in the evolution of the human mind in its inherent and necessary desire of philosophical truth. In closing this, I trust that I shall be enabled to rescue the all-important doctrine of ideas from the obloquy and scorn which a narrow and barren pseudo-philosophy of the senses has but too well succeeded in throwing upon a Method alone calculated to vitalize and realize human speculation and to give power and dignity to the mind. Nay! I do not despair of reconciling philosophy with religion and of showing that, whilst philosophy must consent to be her handmaid, religion may derive a reciprocal benefit, in the proof that religion is reason as the essential form of inward revelation. Whether my ability be equal to the task of giving an outward reality in distinct statement to Coleridge's high and ennobling speculations can be only known to the God of truth, to whom I pray for light and strength under the almost overwhelming sense of the difficulty of doing that which could be adequately done only by the Author. I remain, my dear Sir,

Yours, very sincerely,
Joseph Henry Green

1. Joseph Henry Green (1791–1863), a surgeon, was a friend of Coleridge, visiting him frequently at Highgate. Appointed to the chair of surgery, King's College, London, in 1830, Green gave an opening address for the winter session, 1832, on the function and duties of the professions of divinity, law, and medicine, based on Coleridge. Coleridge's will named Green and H. N. Coleridge his literary executors, giving Green the special function of disposing of Coleridge's library and publishing from mss. and marginalia an exposition of the system of Coleridge's philosophy, a task that consumed the remainder of Green's life.

From Henry Nelson Coleridge
Ms: UVM

10 Chester Place,
Regent's Park,
London
June 2, 1839

Dear Sir

The bishop of Vermont[1] having kindly offered to convey a small parcel to you, I gladly avail myself of the opportunity to beg your acceptance of the third and fourth volumes of the Literary Remains of Mr. Coleridge, published, by me, and also a copy of a new edition of the Aids to Reflection, in which you will see that I have reprinted your Essay. All Coleridge's works are now printed uniformly except the Biographia, and sold cheaply; and I hope to add the Biographia Literaria to the number within a twelvemonth.

With great respect believe me, dear Sir, yours very faithfully

Henry N. Coleridge

1. John Henry Hopkins.

From Swords, Stanford and Company[1]
Ms: JMC

New York
July 18, 1839

Reverend and Dear Sir

We have just received a new edition of Coleridge's "Aids to Reflection" published in London, to which is prefixed the Introductory Essay, furnished by you for the edition published in Burlington some years ago. We have resolved forthwith to republish this work, with the Essay aforesaid, provided we have your consent to do so, which we respectfully solicit. Not having within our reach a copy of the American edition, we are not able to ascertain if Mr. Goodrich took out a copy right for this portion of the work. If he did so we presume he would not object to allow us the liberty of using it, if it should secure your sanction.

Will you Reverend and Dear Sir oblige us by an early answer to this application?

Very Respectfully
We are Your Obedient
Servants
Swords, Stanford

1. Swords, Stanford and Company, the New York publishers, brought out John McVickar's edition of *Aids to Reflection* in 1839 with McVickar's preface, which was hostile to Coleridge, but without Marsh's "Preliminary Essay."

To Henry Nelson Coleridge
Ms: JMC

Burlington
January 20, 1840

Dear Sir:

I send you with this a copy of our edition of the *Aids to Reflection* just published here by Mr. Goodrich. It is as you will see simply a reprint of yours with nothing of what I had added to the edition of 1829 but the "essay" retained.[1] The first sheet containing the title page and advertisements was printed last and together with two or three of the last sheets while I was unavoidably absent. This may account for some errors in the printing which I should probably have corrected and in part also for the undue prominence of my name upon the title page. The publisher as he says thought it necessary thus to distinguish this from another edition published in New York[2] and purporting also to be a copy of yours. This fact of rival editions being simultaneously published will be gratifying to you as it certainly is to me, at least so far as this, that it proves the growing demand for the work among us. Nor should I have any cause to complain of the fact that others had sought to associate their own views with it as I had done but I think I have some cause to complain of the "reasons" which Professor McVickar assigns for rejecting one essay and inserting another in your edition. I should not trouble you with the mention of it however were it not understood that his edition is also published simultaneously by Pickering in London. I shall only express the hope that Mr. Coleridge's friends will not be persuaded by Professor McVickar that I have misrepresented his views or sought to pervert them to narrow and sectarian uses. A large portion of my most valued friends here are in fact episcopalians and if I have credit for anything it is for catholicity in regard to all such matters. It is no more than proper for me to say also that I was applied to by the New York publishers for the privilege of using my essay which I was obliged, tho reluctantly to decline, before the reasons were found for dropping it. I have not indeed seen a copy of the New York edition, the communications with New York being difficult at this season—only an outline of the "reasons" has been sent me. In looking at these again I think I ought to add that by "evangelical doctrines" could be understood in this country only those leading doctrines of spiritual religion which in Mr. Coleridge's works are opposed to Grotianism,[3] Unitarianism, etc. With these statements as to matters of fact I have no fear of suffering in your estimation by means of the "reasons" in question.

Arrangements will soon be made I think to republish the *Friend* here possibly with notes designed to render the great principles which it teaches more obvious in their application to our institutions and thus extend its practical influence.[4] The edition published here in 1831 is nearly exhausted.

I wrote you some months ago enclosing a note to Mr. Gillman and as I had waited in vain for a private conveyance sent it by mail, paying postage to New York. I shall send this with the volume accompanying it through the hands of the booksellers and endeavor to have it reach you free of charge.

Yours very respectfully
James Marsh

1. *Aids to Reflection* . . . with a Preliminary Essay by James Marsh, from the fourth London edition with the Author's last corrections, edited by Henry Nelson Coleridge (Burlington, 1840). Marsh's extensive notes in the edition of 1829 were not retained in the 1840 edition.

2. John McVickar's essay in his edition of *Aids* (New York, 1839) was less hospitable to Coleridge than Marsh's "Preliminary Essay."

3. In 1609 a theological dispute over the doctrine of free will and predestination developed in Holland between Jacob Arminius and Francis Gomarus, professor of theology at Leiden, which evolved into a quarrel between church and state. The States of Holland held that they had authority over the Calvinist churches in the country. Hugo Grotius (1583–1645), Dutch theologian, jurist, and "father of modern international law," was spokesman for the states' position, defending their authority over the churches in his *Ordinum pietas*. Church forces, led by Prince Maurice, arrested Grotius in 1618, but he escaped to Paris in the following year. Grotianism, like Socinianism, was a rationalistic religious profession, excluding the validity of grace and inward faith and relying, like Unitarianism, on proof-from-miracles arguments for the evidence of Christianity.

4. Samuel Taylor Coleridge, *The Friend: A Series of Essays to Aid in the Formation of Fixed Principles in Politics, Morals, and Religion*. First

American edition from second London edition (Burlington, 1831). No enlarged edition was ever published in Burlington.

From John H. Bates[1]
Ms: JMC

Colchester, Vermont
February 9, 1840

My Dear and Reverend Sir,

If a clear understanding of doctrinal points in religion may be considered of importance, I trust I shall need no other apology for sending to you for advice at this time. It is nearly five weeks since I was accepted as a member of the church here and should circumstances appear favorable, I was desirous of uniting by baptism next sabbath and with reference to that object, have been giving more particular attention to the "confession," which I suppose to be substantially the same here as adopted by most congregational churches. Being able to place entire confidence in the Bible, and feeling myself not only under absolute obligation to give my hearty consent to whatever doctrine may be truly contained therein, but also perfectly safe in so doing, though unable to comprehend it, the doctrine of "election" does not awaken such painful sensations in my mind now as formerly. Indeed according to my former notions of its meaning, I have had such an aversion to the doctrine as almost to preclude any consideration of it. That a part of the human race was chosen to everlasting life, while the remainder were elected to eternal death, according to the eternal design of the Creator, so as to preclude the supposition of any choice on the creature, and then to command *all* men to repent and believe, was a doctrine too hard for thought, and difficult to be understood; and if taken in its most literal sense, seemed calculated to produce apprehension if not dispair, in as much as impossibilities would be required of a part of mankind, or else involving the supposition of an unequal distribution of the rewards of obedience. And yet the doctrine of election or predestination seems to be a prominent one in the Bible. And at the same time man seems every where in the scriptures to be addressed as a free moral agent with the ability to choose and liberty to act according to the dictates of reason and conscience, which I would believe to be in accordance with the laws of God, which he is commanded to obey and threatened with punishment in case of disobedience. And here the chief difficulty lies in reconciling the two apparently contradictory doctrines. That "God governs all his creatures and all their actions according to his eternal design" and that too "in perfect accordance with the free moral agency and accountability of his creatures" is a doctrine the two parts of which separately considered seem capable of being understood, but when considered as a whole, it presents a difficulty which as yet has only been increased by reflection. How can it be made a *reasonable* doctrine? I find no difficulty in supposing that I may be mistaken as to its meaning or the meaning of the texts quoted in its support, but this can do but little towards satisfying my own mind at present.

If the importance of the subject should seem to justify an answer to this, I doubt not but much difficulty may be removed from my mind. In the mean time I remain yours,

With the highest regard,
J.H.Bates

1. John Hoskins Bates (1819–71), UVM Class of 1840, entered the ministry in 1851 after studying at Western Theological Seminary. He served the Presbyterian Church in Antrim, New Hampshire (1853–66).

To John H. Bates
Ms: JMC

Burlington
February 12, 1840

My dear Sir

Your difficulties are very natural and very common in relation to election and foreordination as usually stated in our formularies of faith. Nor indeed does it make much difference how the matter is stated or what formula you adopt if you look at the real ground of difficulty involved in every system which recognizes the two cardinal doctrines of a divine government and the free agency and accountability of man. Turn it as you will and state it as you may, for the human understanding the difficulty is still there and still *incomprehensible.* You cannot avoid it without adopting a system at war with *conscience* and with the essential conditions of our *moral* being. Hence we are driven to the position that the apparent contradiction arises from the Incommensurateness of our finite understandings and we only obey the dictates of our practical reason of conscience and the moral law when we assert, as in our confession of faith, that both doctrines are true. The application of the philosophical view of the subject and the mode of considering the subject of election in particular, are best stated in "The Aids to Reflection" p. 111 of the edition of 1829 and 177 of the new edition.[1] But as you may not have either by you, I will say in a word that each individual is concerned with the doctrine only as it is *practical* and of *immediate reference* to his *own character and condition.*

Believing then as you do, I suppose that *all* are not in the right path and that you were once in the broad way of the world, to what will you ascribe the change which as you humbly hope has taken you out of the worldly mass and authorized you to hope on the appointed grounds of hope that you are now at one with God? Can you ascribe it to any previous foresight or wisdom or goodness of your own? Does it result from any thing in your own nature or in your natural will that you are thus distinguished from the worshipers of idols, from the slaves of superstition, from unbelievers and your former unbelieving associates of every class, or will you ascribe it to the grace of God as alone making you to differ? And if you do this and find yourself constrained by your most cherished feelings as a Christian to do this, then do you not practically believe in the doctrine of election?

The difficulty which the nature of the subject necessarily involves, it must be confessed, is aggravated by some of the hard sayings of Calvin and his more zealous followers by urging unduly the points of doctrine which apparently conflict with each other and instead of suggesting the true ground of solution, requiring an explicit belief or assent of the understanding to doctrines which *for the understanding are* contradictory and irreconcilable. Whereas it is only by a consciousness more or less distinct that the truth transcends our understandings and in this consciousness, yielding to the authority of reason and our moral convictions, that we can receive these articles of faith in singleness of heart.

A similar contradiction is held forth and made still more abhorrent to all right moral feeling and right views of the divine character in the views which are sometimes exhibited of the limitation of the atonement and of predestination as connected with the universality of the terms in which the gospel is proffered to all. But this contradiction is not rendered explicit, at least in our confessions of faith and I need not dwell upon it.

I rejoice that you find yourself prepared to take your stand publicly as a disciple of Christ and trust that you will be enabled by divine grace to witness a good profession and spend a life of devotedness to his service.

The remarks which I have made seem to me to meet the difficulties which you suggest or at least to direct the mind to that way of considering them which may enable each one to resolve them so far as they have a practical importance.

With much and affectionate regard—
Yours truly
J. Marsh

1. In the portion of the *Aids* which Marsh refers to here, Coleridge saw the Redemption as a great constituent of faith. Taking original sin as the antecedent ground and occasion of Christianity, Coleridge viewed the Redemption as an edifice raised on that ground to act as a remedy to the disease of original sin. The reality of the doctrine of Election he found attributable to it by Revelation and the law of conscience.

From George Allen
Ms: JMC

Newark,
Delaware
February 20, 1840

Dear and Honored Sir,

I have delayed writing until I could report some progress—I was forever in getting McVickar's book. At last, I got Mr. Converse[1] to pull out *his* copy and send it by mail. I wrote to Seabury[2]—not at all expecting he would print—but I received a *very* favorable letter from him Tuesday evening. He thinks Coleridge's Philosophy *non compos*, and is friendly (he says) to McVickar—but he is willing "his book should have a [. . .][3] and (*mischief!*) he mentions and offers to send me McVickar's old articles in the Churchman. I have written to get them.

I have been grievously delayed—for want of the book—occupations—toothache—but have done and am doing the very best I can, and *most cheerfully*. I expect to send off Number one Saturday, to appear a week thereafter. I am more prolix than I could wish, and rather more mischievous and ironical than you will like—but I am in a hurry and in earnest, and cannot help it.

I expect B.B. Newton here soon. I told him to call at Gould Newman's[4] and ask if there were a copy there for me. I perceive I shall rub up my Coleridge learning a little by this means. Thank Mr. Goodrich for the title, etc to your new edition.

Seabury begs me not to "butcher McVickar to death" (I had written a very murderous letter) and I wrote to him, that he should not be *killed*, only *kilt*. But he uses the Oxford-tract dialect as incorrectly as he does that of Coleridge; so I propose to Seabury that we twain should kill him outright.

"For ill-pronouncing Shibboleth"—as Milton hath it.[5]

I *think* McVickar will have such a dressing as he will not wish to have repeated. It shall not be "come [. . .] of" but perhaps I shall err by *overdoing*.

Remembrances to Faculty and friends

Ever most truly Yours—
G.A.

1. John K. Converse (1801–80), Dartmouth Class of 1827, Princeton Seminary 1830, served various congregations in Burlington, Colchester, and Milton, Vermont.
2. Samuel Seabury (1801–72), a High Church Episcopalian and supporter of the Oxford Movement, was editor of *The Churchman* (1833–49).
3. Allen's script, as he remarked himself to Marsh, is often illegible in the holograph. Brackets in this letter so indicate.
4. Gould, Newman, and Saxton were booksellers and publishers in New York City.
5. Judges 12:6.

From Henry Nelson Coleridge
Text: *Remains*, pp. 156–157.

April 1, 1840

My dear Sir

Pray accept my thanks for both your letters, which were very interesting to me. The principal object of this note, however, is to say that I have never seen the New York edition of the Aids to Reflection to which you refer. Mr. Pickering's[1] name is usurped in the title page, neither he nor I having any knowledge of the publication; and if it is so used as to induce readers to believe that the edition has any peculiar sanction from us in England, I think it an unfair transaction. Professor McV. I conjecture only to be Professor McVickar. I do not know whether he is the gentleman who used to be known to Mr. Southey, and whose son I met in London about a year ago.[2] Of the merits of the New York edition, or the propriety of the preface, I can of course say nothing in my present ignorance, except that I should not agree with any denial of your having rendered a great service to the cause of sound philosophy as involved in the principles taught by Mr. Coleridge. My uncle was born and bred, and passed all his later life, and died an affectionate member of the church of England; but the fact of church membership would not in and of itself have influenced one of his conclusions. He was a member of the church, because he believed that he had ascertained by observation and experience that it presented the best form of Christian communion, having regard to primitive precept and practice, social order, and the development of the individual mind. I am sorry there should be any parties among Christ's disciples; though increasing in strength, they still need union in their warfare.

If you should find a fair opportunity, I should be much gratified with a copy of your reprint of the Aids. I have nothing to send you at present; but am closely getting on, as I find leisure, with an edition of the Biographia Literaria, with notes, biographical and others.

Mr. Green means very shortly to beg your acceptance of a copy of his Hunterian Oration with notes and appendices and another Lecture he is publishing in a volume under the title of Vital Dynamics.[3]

Pray excuse this short note, which I write amidst much occupation, wishing you to believe me, my dear sir,

Yours very faithfully,
H. N. Coleridge

1. William Pickering (1796–1854), the English publisher.
2. McVickar himself went to England in 1830 well-equipped with letters of introduction and met many prominent English literary and ecclesiastical figures, including Robert Southey (1774–1843), the poet and and friend of Coleridge who, in 1795, had married Edith Fricker, Sarah Coleridge's sister. H. N. Coleridge could very well have also met McVickar's son.
3. As Hunterian Orator at the College of Surgeons, London, in 1840, Joseph Henry Green delivered his "Lecture on Vital Dynamics" in which he attempted to connect modern science and Coleridge's philosophy. See note 1, letter of February 25, 1839.

To Henry Nelson Coleridge[1]
Ms: University of Texas

Burlington
July 16, 1840

My dear Sir,

I am greatly obliged to you for your note in relation to the New York edition of the "Aids."[2] I did not myself indeed indulge any fear that you would in any case do me less than full justice in respect to the agency I might have had in promoting the influence of that work. I only claimed to have thought freely and to have written what I thought at a time when all ecclesiastical influences as well as all philosophical institutions in the country were adverse to Coleridge's views and when to speak in their favour was hazardous to a man's reputation either for sound sense or orthodoxy. That being the case you would not wonder perhaps if I were somewhat moved at an apparent attempt now that Coleridge's works are becoming known and their influence acknowledged to set me aside as a "sectarian" writer and unfit to have my name associated with that of a son of the Church or to be read by a Churchman. I however resolved to say nothing and to leave it to others to determine whether anything ought to be said. I have not been disappointed in the result except that more has been said than I anticipated and far more ascribed to my bold adventure in authorship than I should ever have claimed for it. I venture to send you Mr. Allen's Letters in The Churchman with Dr. McVickar's Essay and his piece in The Churchman of 1832. It is but fair to say that Mr. Allen was a favourite pupil of mine and a warm personal friend and that much may be indited to his partiality. Other leading papers however and several of the Quarterlies have briefly noticed the matter and all take the same general view of Dr. McVickar's proceeding. Even the editor of The Churchman[3] wrote to Mr. Allen decidedly approving the severity of his criticisms though at the close as you will see he still seeks to turn the edge of them and to make the most of Dr. McVickar's edition as a good one "for the Church." However I rejoice sincerely that by means of it the work will gain currency in that communion far more extensively than could otherwise have been expected. Nor have I any fear that the younger men who study and imbibe the spirit which the editor seems to me to manifest. Indeed I take my own views on the *general principles* of Church government and on the Church to be much nearer those of Coleridge than Dr. McVickar's.

I fear you may think me more *malicious* than I really am in sending you Dr. McVickar's article in The Churchman of 1832. He alludes to it in a note to his Essay and it will show you how far he is correct in saying that Churchmen needed no vindication of Coleridge's philosophical views when he himself wrote that article years after my Essay was published. His reference to Mr. Van Buren[4] in that article was a blunder the occasion of which is not worth explaining. He was introduced to Mr. Coleridge by a Mr. Kerr from this country who wrote to N. P. Willis[5] at the time a glowing report of Coleridge's conversation apparently with a view to awaken Willis's religious feelings. I mention this to show what sort of conversation it was of which McVickar has given such an account. But I have said quite too much I fear upon topics that have a personal relation to myself. My only apology is that I supposed you might have some curiosity in regard to the diffusion now becoming so known and valued that the ordinary interest of the Book Trade will supply the market and there will be found I have no doubt more and more of a soil congenial to the seeds which he has sown. His views indeed are taught ex cathedra only here[6] but in all our Colleges and Theological schools his works are read and have a daily increasing influence. In all our Theological controversies and they abound in every denomination the want of a higher stand-point is becoming continually more manifest and more distinctly felt. I told the parties to a heated controversy in Connecticut[7] years ago that if they would lay aside the dispute and study Coleridge and Tholuck earnestly for six months they would see the whole controversy to be idle and useless. They are disputing still but some of them I believe begin to see that the matter cannot be settled by this method of discussing it. The Unitarians at Boston have a controversy among themselves in which the "Old School" adhere to the sensualism of Locke and singularly enough have become zealous assertors of miracles and inspiration, while the "New Lights" profess a spiritual philosophy but instead of coming back to the truth as it is in Christ are falling I fear into a mystic Pantheism. The last of their pamphlets which I have seen aimed to maintain the *theism* of Spinoza. The Oxford Tracts are creating divisions in the Episcopal Church but of its position in relation to that matter I only know that a Bishop of Maryland has been recently elected—Dr. Whittingham[8]—who is opposed to the Tracts and who was an early advocate of Coleridge's works.

I am glad to see that in England too the influence of Coleridge's higher views is felt where perhaps it would not be distinctly acknowledged and that the doctrines of Paley are no longer unquestioned at Cambridge. I allude to the Sermons of Mr. Whewell[9] which were preached there and have been republished in this country.

Our edition of the "Aids" of which I send you a copy was published simultaneously in New York by Gould, Newman and Saxton. It is not as well done as I could wish and a few typographical errors need an apology. The first and last sheets were printed in my absence when suddenly called away by the sickness of one of my family and were not attended to as they should have been.

Appleton and Co. of New York are about publishing the whole of Coleridge's Prose Works in ten volumes 12mo to correspond with the Boston edition of his Poetical Works in three volumes published in 1835. It is to be printed in Boston and in the same style which is the best *American.* I shall inform them of what you are doing with the Biographia and hope they will wait for your edition. I hope you will make the biographical notes as full as the circumstances of the case will admit and in saying this I refer to a remark of yours in the Preface to the Table Talk.[10]

I wrote this in the expectation of sending it with a package by Mr. Atkinson[11] a gentleman from London. He is now here but is not going immediately as I had supposed. I conclude therefore to send the letter by mail and the packet which he very kindly offers to take you will probably receive he tells me in November. I had intended to send you a copy of Dr. McVickar's edition but the fear of taxing Mr. Atkinson's kindness by sending so large a bundle induced me to send only his Essay which you will find with a copy of our Edition here as also Mr. Allen's letters and Dr. McVickar's reply. My knowledge of Mr. Kerr's letter to Willis is derived from a friend who had read it but I have not myself seen it.

The gentleman by whom I send the package is George Atkinson, Esq., 21 Eustace Square, St. Pancras, London. He is confident that he shall carry it free of duty, if not you may receive it with a charge attached to it.

The title of Dr. Green's work[12] indicates topics upon which I have thought much and I look for it with great interest.

Yours very truly,
J. Marsh

1. An edited version of this letter appears in Wells, pp. 158–59.

2. *Aids to Reflection*, by Samuel Taylor Coleridge, with the author's last corrections. Edited by Henry Nelson Coleridge, Esq., M.A. To which is prefixed, a preliminary essay, by John McVickar, D.D., Professor of Moral Philosophy in Columbia College, New York (London: William Pickering; New York: Swords, Stanford, and Co., 1839).

3. Samuel Seabury.

4. McVickar's supposed "blunder" was in associating the American Coleridgians with a political point of view that somehow reflected President Martin Van Buren's elegant Jacksonianism. As Marsh should have recognized after Van Buren's response to

the Canadian Rebellions of 1837–38, McVickar was not far wrong for Van Buren in fact acted along lines Marsh approved.

5. N. P. Willis (1806–67), the colorful journalist and short-story writer, had been very friendly with a Mr. Carr, not Kerr, in 1832 when Willis met him during a tour of Europe. Carr was the American consul at Tangiers and when Willis travelled in the Mediterranean before going to England Carr gave him a letter of introduction to Coleridge.

6. UVM.

7. The Taylorian Controversy.

8. William Rollinson Whittingham (1805–79) had been professor of ecclesiastical history at the General Theological Seminary, New York (1836–40), before he was consecrated bishop of Maryland.

9. William Whewell (1794–1866) was professor of moral theology, Trinity College, Cambridge (1848–52). His Bridgewater Treatise, delivered as a lecture "on the power, wisdom and goodness of God as manifested in the creation," was published under the title *Astronomy and General Physics Considered with Reference to Natural Theology* (London, 1839).

10. " . . . for the purpose of general elucidation, it seemed not improper to add a few notes, and to make some quotations from Mr. Coleridge's own works; and in doing so, I was in addition actuated by an earnest wish to call the attention of reflecting minds in general to the views of political, moral and religious philosophy contained in those works." *Table Talk, The Works of Samuel Taylor Coleridge*, ed. W. G. T. Shedd (New York, 1853), VI, p. 231.

11. The Atkinsons were prosperous merchants and land developers in the vicinity of Bellow Falls, Vermont. John Atkinson (1742–1823) came to Vermont from London, by way of New York City, and developed the Bellow Falls Canal. His brothers and their sons, among them George Atkinson, remained in England, but capitalized and continued to support Atkinson enterprises in Vermont well into the second quarter of the nineteenth century.

12. See above, letter of April 1, 1840, note 3, and letter of February 25, 1839, note 1.

From Henry Nelson Coleridge
Text: *Remains*, pp. 157–58

My dear Sir

I trust you will excuse a very few lines in acknowledgment of your last letter. And I wish to mention that several months ago I sent to Mr. C. Goodrich a copy of the last edition of the Friend, which, from your silence, I almost fear he cannot have received. I already possess a copy of Dr. McVickar's edition of the Aids. I trust that you are to be the editor of the new edition of the other works.[1] I am going tomorrow morning for a ramble on the continent; but hope to get out soon after my return the little volume of which I believe I spoke to you—The Confessions of an Inquiring Spirit. You are aware that there are editions of all Mr. Coleridge's prose works, except the Biographia. With the Friend, Mr. Green sent you a copy of his Hunterian Oration. I hope both have been received. Mr. Allen[2] sent me all his letters and Dr. McVickar has lately sent me his. The Editor[3] seems to me totally unfriendly, not to you only, but to Coleridge. Believe me, my dear Sir,

Yours very faithfully,
H. N. Coleridge

1. Marsh planned new editions of other works by Coleridge. However, it was left to his student, William Greenough Thayer Shedd (1820–94), UVM Class of 1839, Andover 1843, to produce the long-standard 1853 edition of *The Complete Works of Samuel Taylor Coleridge* in seven volumes.
2. George Allen.
3. John McVickar.

To Joseph H. Myers[1]
Text: *Remains*, pp. 146–48

Burlington
October 2, 1840

My dear Sir

I have but this moment received your letter, and too late, I fear, for you to get an answer before tomorrow morning. However, I will do my best to have it reach you. I shall not probably have occasion to use the long discourse which you have, within a few weeks, and you are quite welcome to keep it. The sermon which I inquired for has appeared, so that I shall not need to ask for your copy.

I fear I can hardly give, in a letter and in so much haste, a series of subjects for discussion that will be of service to you. I will, however, give an outline that may be filled afterwards. It will be connected, as you will see, with the philosophical views which must of necessity determine the method of a theological system; but at the same time I would discuss each topic under the practical aspect which it assumes in the word of God.

1. Anthropology. Man, as a created, a dependent, a responsible, and therefore a free or self-determined, a spiritual and personal being; his relation to the absolute and universal law of truth and duty, his primitive or ideal character and condition as formed in the Divine image, his fallen condition by nature, and relation of the finite free will to an individual nature on the one hand, and to the redemptive power of the Word and Spirit of God on the other.

In connection with these topics, study carefully the Epistles of Paul, especially that to the Romans, with Usteri's Paulinische Lehrbegriff,[2] Tholuck's Commentary on Romans, Heinroth's Anthropologie and Psychologie, Coleridge, and I will venture to add, my sermons. Right views of these subjects are indispensable to all that follows, as pertaining to the Christian system.

2. The doctrine of revelation, of inspiration, etc., and the true idea of these as connected with anthropology and psychology. The whole subject connects itself with our views of the relation of the understanding to the reason on the one side, and to sense on the other. You will find valuable helps in the latter part of both works of Heinroth to which I referred above, as well as Coleridge. Coleridge's work on Inspiration is not yet published. The common works, your teachers can refer you to. Nordheimer and Henry[3] can probably help you to the German books.

3. The doctrine of Redemption. Distinguish its subjective and objective necessity. The former, as already considered under the first head. The latter is a vexed question, and you will do well to study it as presented by different systems of Theology and as treated by Tholuck and Coleridge, neither of whom, however, is very explicit. See Tholuck's Commentary on Romans, fifth chapter. This is, of course, closely connected with the work of Redemption in the same relations as subjective and objective, or relative to the subject redeemed, and to the necessary requisitions of the law and character and God. The common method is to treat first, as connected with this whole subject, of the person and character of Christ, his relation to man and to God, and so to the several offices which he bears, as connected with the work of redemption.

4. The effects wrought in the redeemed—regeneration, faith, repentance; and so all the fruits of the Spirit. This will involve, again, the relation of the believer to Christ, and the agency of the Spirit of God. The doctrines of justification and sanctification, and their relation to each other, you will find points of much controversy, and requiring careful study. Read St. Paul for yourself, and with all the help you can get. This topic lies at the bottom of some great divisions among theologians and is connected, as you will see, with the main topic under the previous head.

The church, or the relation of believers to each other, as one in spirit, and to Christ, as their common head, and as constituting the spiritual church, governed by a spiritual law, and co-operating to a spiritual end. The visible church, as grounded on and deriving all its life and power and authority from this, and so a mere lifeless and spiritless and unmeaning semblance, except as it expresses the actual and living presence and power of Christ in his members—his body, which is the church.

The future state of believers and unbelievers, future rewards and punishments, the spiritual world, the judgment and its consequence, etc. Theology in its limited sense—the rational idea of God—grounds of a rational conviction of his existence—mode of existence—personality, triunity, relation to nature or the material universe, and to the spiritual world, or spiritual existences.

But I have made out a longer list than I intended; yet I could think of no better way, than to put the subjects in the form of a systematic outline. Many things, however, are left out, as you will perceive, which are necessary to a complete system. I believe you will find what I have given to be subjects that have a systematic relation to each other, and you can take up more or less, and more or less minutely as you choose. For the purposes of the pulpit, I would discuss everything in a practical form, and carry nothing there simply speculative. My own more elaborate sermons are not such as I would approve for common use. There is so much of speculative interest in all our schools, that the plain, practical preaching of the gospel is likely to be lost sight of. Pray you rise above this; and let your sermons breathe and utter forth the solemn earnestness and the yearning love for the souls of men, that characterize the gospel itself. Whatever may be the character of my own sermons, the exhibition of such a spirit is, in my deliberate judgment, the only preaching.

Yours truly,
J. Marsh

1. Joseph H. Myers (1817–90), UVM Class of 1837, Union Theological Seminary, New York, 1841, was professor of ancient and modern languages at the University of East Tennessee (1846–51), and moved, during the following years, between New York State and Florida teaching in various locations.

2. Leonard Usteri, *Entwickelung des Paulinsichen Lehrbegriffe* (Zurich, 1831).

3. Isaac Nordheimer (1809–42), Ph.D., Munich, 1834, came to America in 1835 and taught at Union Theological Seminary, New York City, and New York University (1838–42).

4. C. S. Henry.

From George Ripley
Ms: UVM

Boston
October 17, 1840

My dear Sir

I was truly grieved that it was not in my power to see you again during our Commencement Week; but my distance from Boston deprived me of that pleasure; and I can now only hope that your winter vacation will give me the opportunity of continuing our acquaintance. I have just learned from Mrs. Bradford[1] that you take some interest, as a spectator, in looking at the movements of our "new lights" and "literary radicals" in Massachusetts; and I therefore take the freedom to request your acceptance of the first two numbers of the "Dial,"[2] which attempts to tell how high the sun is according to their observation. I cannot presume on your sympathy for much of its contents; indeed, there are many things which I could wish otherwise myself; but I trust you will find its freedom is not without the companionship of reverence and love. We know well our own wishes and are not unconscious of our defects, while we are sure that we have no aim but the spread of a more generous culture and the illustration of cleaner and more healthy relations between man and man.

I should be much gratified, and so I am sure would all our fellow-workers, by the contribution of any articles from your pen. We are heretics and radicals ourselves; so much must be confessed; but we have large sympathies with ideal conservatives in church and state; and some individuals of that character feel that they can write with us and for us without compromise or inconsistency. Your views in theology or metaphysics would always be welcome in the pages of the "Dial." We have no speculative novelties to assert now, but love rather to see the old made fresh and living. Our next great heresy will probably be a practical one, namely, the attempt to see how literature and labor will fare together, or the union of a scholar's life with a farmer's.[3] Many have arrived at this faith—that mind and body will both be greatly rewarded by the return to a simpler life and that the culture of the earth is the best foundation for the culture of the soul. Our present social state is sick almost unto death; our finest and truest minds too weary of this hot race for physical good; almost every profession demands compliances at which a just sense of morality hesitates; and those who are thus led to utter a peaceful protest, according to the signs seen just now, will ere long look to the land for its support and realize on its acres the desired union of a contemplative and practical life.

I also enclose you a letter which I have recently addressed to my society, which though almost entirely personal, may have some interest for your mind as a slight indication of the times.[4]

I shall rejoice to hear from you, and if I can be of any service to you in the accomplishment of any of your literary plans do not hesitate to command me. With the sincerest esteem.

I am, dear Sir, ever yours
Geo. Ripley

1. The wife of George Bradford (1807–90). He intended to translate Fenelon for Ripley's *Specimens*.
2. The first number of *The Dial* (July 1, 1840) included pieces by Charles, Edward and Ralph Waldo Emerson, Margaret Fuller, Henry David Thoreau, Ellen Tucker, Samuel Gray Ward, and Bronson Alcott.
3. Begun April 1, 1841, in West Roxbury, Massachusetts, by Ripley and a group of his friends in the "West Street circle," within six years Brook Farm had acquired 120

members on its rolls, some like Charles A. Dana, having bought shares in the enterprise. Emerson, Bronson Alcott, and Margaret Fuller avoided full membership, which did include, however, Hawthorne, Charles A. Dana, recently graduated from Harvard, Isaac Hecker, subsequently founder of the Paulist Fathers, George Curtis, George P. Bradford, and Charles King Newcomb, a young mystic from Providence. Harvard students, farm and city girls, laborers and Boston Brahmins at one time or another resided at Brook Farm. George and Sophia Ripley, R. H. Dana's younger sister, worked ten hours a day in field, garden, laundry, and lecture room, he teaching philosophy, she giving classes in history and Italian. Charles A. Dana gave classes in Greek and German. A stage twice-a-day to Scollay Square was their omphalos to the world of the civilized. Van Wyck Brooks's account in *The Flowering of New England*, Chapter XII, "Alcott, Margaret Fuller, Brook Farm," remains the most readable sketch of the people, the impulse, the event.

4. "A Letter Addressed to the Congregational Church in Purchase Street" (Boston, 1840), written October 4, 1840, declared Ripley's faith in transcendentalism, which he identified with Christianity. Ripley scolded his congregation for their moral and intellectual sins and said that if the church really performed its duty, oppression, war, jails, violence, and ruthless competition would be eliminated.

From Henry P. Tappan[1]

Ms: UVM

New York
November 16, 1840

Reverend and dear Sir

Your letter of the fifth together with your discourse[2] were left with me a few days since. I am exceedingly gratified with the perusal of both. You have clearly expounded your system. The idea of Coleridge that a *nature is introduced into the will*, as he expresses it and as you expound it, I am not prepared to receive. Freedom seems to me inseparable from the will under all its possible conditions. I cannot see how the will can even by its own self determination get rid of its freedom, any more than the Reason can lose its capacity of perceiving truth. The evil habits engendered by a course of disobedience —of pandering to the passions exhibit the will under a sort of nature and weakened in its causative energies—but like Sampson awaking from his sleep when his locks were only braided and pinned, it can rouse up again its innate strength. Augustine and Calvin will admit that evil had its origin in the free will, in the free will of Adam. And the whole race are guilty because as comprehended in Adam or as represented by him they sinned in him or by him. Coleridge contends and so do you that the origin is truly in the will of each individual—each originates it for himself and therefore each one is personally guilty. But as to the effect of the original sin you seem to agree. Augustine and Calvin make Adam to have lost all freedom and ability by his sin. They might say in accordance with their system that Adam by an act of self determination introduced a nature into his will, i.e. his will under a law of Cause and Effect, after his first sin, necessarily gave out sinful volitions. And as the race sinned in him, they in him introduced this nature into their wills likewise. Coleridge makes each individual to fall like Adam, and like him to introduce a nature into the will; but now on his system as well as on Augustine's all the subsequent developments of the being are the *necessary effects of this nature*. Again Coleridge does not determine by actual consciousness, the fact that this nature was introduced (Aids etc. American Edition, p. 173, 1829); neither does Augustine in respect of the race. Adam alone knew when he sinned. I have psychological objections to this theory. It avoids indeed the absurdity of sinning in Adam or by Adam, but I cannot conceive how the will can introduce a nature into itself and destroy its feedom. And besides it does not seem to me to be a present fact of consciousness that all present acts are enveloped in a governing purpose and this again is an ultimate and common priciple of depravity lying in the Will. The connection between the present act and the purpose, and between the last and the ultimate principle being necessary. The very idea too of original sin is that of sin beginning to be, and therefore cannot be thrown out of all relation to time as Coleridge insists it should be. And how is it that I have by an act of selfdetermination introduced this portentous nature into my will without any consciousness of the fact. Was it done in the womb or in early infantile weakness? Why is it a universal fact? Coleridge calls original sin as he explains it a mysterious fact, but I cannot rest with him here. My theory is not I take it like Dr. Taylor's.[3] I am not familiar with his writings and therefore shall not speak confidently. I have been inclined to think that he verges towards Pelagionism and really denies original sin altogether. My theory is that when Adam sinned he introduced depravity into his Sensitivity, he drew it out its sphere of subordination to the Reason and made it a governing faculty. I say with you he took its enjoyments as his governing aims and placed it in a position where all run to excess and become deformed into selfishness. But the Will retained its integrity and freedom as Simple Causality, even as the Reason retained its capacity as simple intelligence. This corrupt Sensitivity is inherited—this I take as an obvious fact. This corrupt sensitivity affording the chief supply of temptation to the Will lays a ground of probability that the Will will sin—and now as confirmed by the experience of many generations becomes a moral certainty. It does not appear to me a small evil that this corruption should exist —and although I believe that the man can by a change of purpose make a self regenerative act—still I do not believe either on the ground of human experience or the word of God that this act will effect the regeneration of the Sensitivity by itself alone. The Holy Spirit can alone effect this. But under the light of Conscience, the free will can struggle for purification, and place the Man in a position where the promise finds him. "Every one that seek shall find etc." I have written my dear Sir in a great hurry and I fear in rather a rambling manner. The discussion is one of deep interest and I should esteem it a great privilege to renew it with you in personal conversation, or by letter if it be possible. I seek for truth. I am willing to be his servant. With great respect

Yours very truly
H. P. Tappan

1. Henry P. Tappan (1805–81), graduate of Auburn Theological Seminary (1827), taught at New York University (1832–37) and was president and chancellor of the University of Michigan (1852–63).

2. Marsh's ms. treatise on the Will was finally published by Torrey, *Remains*, pp. 368–90.

3. Nathaniel Taylor.

From Henry J. Raymond[1]
Ms: JMC

Office of the New Yorker
30 Ann St., New York
January 14, 1841

My dear Sir:

On coming to this city some weeks since I found your kind letter awaiting my arrival; and I fear my long continued neglect to comply with your request that I should speedily inform you of my arrangements, will seem but a poor acknowledgement of your many favors. But I am sure that you will acquit me of any intentional neglect to express my thanks and to avail myself of the privilege you offered me.

After remaining for some weeks at home[2] and finding it quite inpracticable to obtain any employment thereabouts I came hither and have made engagements to remain with Mr. Greeley[3] in the literary department of the The New Yorker for at least a year. I am sure that I have taken in this the wisest course: and yet it was the only or at least the best which seemed open to me, and I find many advantages connected with the situation. I am under the necessity of devoting but slight attention to the lightest literature of the day, and I have my evenings and occasional portions of the day at my own command. I am not quite decided as to the most profitable way of spending my leisure: I am very desirous to study German, and I presume that I could enter a class which Professor Nordheimer[4] is forming quite advantageously. But if I do so, by reason of the little time that I have for study, I must almost entirely relinquish my classical studies—which I am very unwilling to do.

Which course will be most wise for my permanent interest? I have been considering with no little anxiety for a few weeks what profession I ought, in view of my circumstances, to study. Nearly all my wishes are in favor of Theology, and I am almost inclined to believe it my duty to prepare for the active ministry. And yet my pecuniary circumstances and those of my father are such as to make it incumbent upon me to regard expediency in this matter somewhat; if I should decide upon studying Law, I could enter my name in an office very soon, and enter upon the practice of my profession at least two years sooner, and with far better pecuniary prospects than I could in case I should study Theology. Will you not favor me with some instructions upon this point also?

I find myself in rather a singular atmosphere—morally and intellectually. Mr. Greeley is professedly a Universalist—but in consequence of some remarks which I made in a notice of the New York Review, he avowed his adhesion to the doctrines of the "Dial": he inclines to materialism and said that he believes the mind to be the *result* of the body! He is also an out and out utilitarian and in all his aims seeks only to make the outward condition of his fellows comfortable. He is strongly opposed to all classical studies and values science and, I presume religion, only so far as they tend to some immediately beneficial result. In conjunction with several others he intends shortly to publish a new paper having for its object the reorganization of Society upon a new basis![5] Their plan is a sort of revivification of those of Owen and Fourier,[6] except that they profess to respect the sanctity of the marriage relation, to interfere with no one's theological opinions, to regard the rights of property and to preach no crusade against the interests of any particular class. Their object they say is not destructive but constructive. Mr. Greeley showed me his 'leader' today. The *Great Truth* which they propose to establish and unfold is that "the great principle of associated, organized effort which had been so *efficiently* and advantageously resorted to in National defense, and in commercial enterprises, may be with far greater efficiency and beneficence to Industry, engaged in Agriculture or Manufacturing employment." They propose that 2 or 300 families should "club together," live in the same house, possess the same fields, eat at the same tables, work the same hours and equally divide "the spoils": and thus they expect that "Labor may be ennobled, Production vastly increased, Waste infinitely diminished and Industry rendered attractive."

Our Dr. Brisbane,[7] from Philadelphia, is the real father of the scheme. He appears to be a conceited fellow—anxious to become notorious in some way or other. He said in our office the other day that Lord Brougham[8] in his opinion was like *Cicero*, nothing but a "bag of wind"! It is certainly ludicrous to see a pert, flippant brainless young man gravely attempting to remodel the framework of Society, to suit his own notions of propriety.

But there are abler men than he engaged in this scheme. I believe that Bryant[9] is concerned in it and Brownson in his last Quarterly Review extends to them the right hand of his fellowship.[10] Greeley is an able and popular political writer: but by this new alliance he will destroy the only commanding influence which he possesses. I think however that his motives are unquestionably good.[11]

I find that with a certain class of readers—such as read the *better part* of the light literature—Emersonism is exceedingly popular. They take up the doctrine quite zealously promulgated—especially by the Unitarians (among the most able of whom is Rev. Mr. Bellows)[12] that *our opinions are independent of the will*, and that therefore we are not accountable for them. Out of this they make whatever they choose: the most of them not quite content with having no opinions at all.

If your leisure will permit, I would be deeply obliged to you if you would write me a letter exposing the grounds of error with the Boston Transcendentalists. I would like it most especially for my own benefit—and if you are willing, for that of Mr. Greeley and the readers of The New Yorker.

On many accounts I am very comfortably situated. I have my old friend Mann[13] for a roommate and frequent opportunities to see Myers.[14] I am told that Mead[15]—a son of U.V.M.—recently left the city for South America in a very discreditable manner. He had been for some time in connection with one of the Theatres and managed to elope with a portion of their funds. The New York Review has doffed its episcopal character—not formally but in effect: and I gathered from one of the morning papers that Professor Henry had left it.[16] If this be true I presume we may soon expect another new one. Professor Lewis[17] is publishing some very fine articles in a little Monthly brought out by the University students. I suppose you have of course seen Coleridge's Confessions of an Enquiring Spirit:[18] else I should send it to you.

If there should be any opportunity for me to do you a favor in the city, I need not say that I shall be most happy to do so. Mr. Mann desires me to present to you his respectful regards. Please to remember me kindly to the other gentlemen of the Faculty and believe me ever desirous of remaining your

deeply obliged and
grateful pupil
H. J. Raymond

1. Henry Jarvis Raymond (1820–69), editor and politician, UVM Class of 1840, worked for Horace Greeley on *The New Yorker* and *The Tribune*, eventually leaving Greeley and finally going on to help found *The New York Times* (1851).
2. Raymond was from Lima, New York.
3. As an undergraduate Raymond had corresponded with Greeley, who encouraged him in writing and signed on Raymond as his agent in northern New England and northeastern New York. In 1838 Raymond wrote a two-installment review of Gillman's *Life of Samuel Taylor Coleridge* for *The New Yorker.*
4. Isaac Nordheimer (1809–42) came to America in 1835 from Munich. While teaching Oriental languages at Union Theological Seminary and New York University (1838–42), Nordheimer published his important *Critical Grammar of the Hebrew Language.*
5. In early 1841 Greeley was planning to publish a penny paper in New York with a Whig point of view somewhere between the sensationalist *Herald* and the staid *Evening Post.* Greeley's *New York Tribune* first appeared April 10, 1841.
6. Robert Owen (1771–1858), the Welsh social reformer, with the publication of his *New View of Society* (1813) began a campaign to reform social structures and eventually established a reformed community at New Harmony, Indiana.

Francois Marie Charles Fourier (1772–1837), French social theorist, proposed a plan to harmonize social relationships by arranging society into *phalanges*, units of 1,500 people, each unit to live in a common dwelling. Each trade and profession would be represented in a *phalange*, a minimum wage paid, and surpluses distributed, thereby reconciling individual and communal interests.
7. After a grand tour of six years in Europe, Albert Brisbane, of Batavia, New York, returned to New York City in 1834 troubled by the competitive chaos of an emerging industrial society. Having studied under Charles Fourier in Paris, Brisbane believed he had the answer to America's social problems—organize humanity into compact cells of 1,620 people, "phalanxes," as Fourier called them, and plan the communal economy on this basis. Shortly before the first issues of Greeley's new *Tribune* appeared in 1841, Greeley met Brisbane, read his *The Social Destiny of Man*, and printed for Brisbane his magazine *The Future, Devoted to the Cause of Association and a Reorganization of Society.* The first issue of *The Tribune* advertised *The Future* and, beginning March 1, 1841, the left-hand column of the front page contained a

feature: "Association; or, Principles of a True Organization of Society. / General View . . . No. 1." Brisbane bought the space for $500, although Greeley's partner subsequently claimed that the bill was never paid.

8. Henry Brougham (1778–1868), first Baron Brougham, was with Canning one of the great, though sometimes eccentric, parliamentary orators of his time.

9. Parke Godwin (1816–1904), William Cullen Bryant's brother-in-law and associate editor of *The Evening Post*, was at this time writing fiery editorials for Bryant's paper in which he claimed that "the few rich are becoming more and more rich, the unnumbered many are becoming poorer. . . . Our modern world of industry is a veritable Hell, where disorder, discord, and wretchedness reign."

10. Orestes Brownson was well aware of the need for social reform long before he heard Fourier's name and readily gave Brisbane full opportunity in the pages of his quarterly to argue for the substitution of some form of attractive industry for the current system of wages and labor. Like Brisbane, Brownson was convinced that the system must embrace the principles of association into units larger than the family, but smaller than the state. Unlike Brisbane, however, Brownson did not think Fourier's plan the soundest because it subordinated the spiritual to the material. Cf. "Social Evils and their Remedies," *Boston Quarterly Review*, 4 (1841), 265–71.

11. Raymond had less faith in Greeley's motives after Greeley began reducing Raymond's literary department in *The Tribune* soon after it was founded. In 1843 Raymond left Greeley to go with *The Courier* when Greeley failed to meet his competitor's offer of a $5.00 weekly raise to Raymond.

12. Henry Whitney Bellows (1814–82) was pastor of the First Unitarian Church, New York City (1839–82).

13. Alexander Mann (d. 1860) had persuaded Raymond to attend UVM.

14. Joseph Henry Myers, UVM Class of 1837.

15. UVM records contain no mention of a Mead.

16. *The New York Review* apparently ran out of funds and died in 1842.

17. Tayler Lewis (1801–77) was professor of Greek at New York University (1838–50).

18. Samuel Taylor Coleridge, *Confessions of an Inquiring Spirit*. Edited from the Author's Ms. by Henry Nelson Coleridge (Boston: James Munro, 1841).

From George Allen
Ms: JMC

Newark, Delaware
January 18, 1841

Dear and Honored Sir,

I hardly know how to account for this long silence. I can at least say, however, that it has not been towards you alone. The unsettled state in which our affairs for a long time continued to be, I suppose, as it furnished me with nothing certain to tell, so it kept me from writing altogether. You have probably heard from Father[1] before this what our present prospects are. If the Old School men do not use their power, while they have any, to break up the management, I do not doubt that we shall have students enough. I could have wished for a New England Congregationalist, but perhaps nothing short of a decided understanding with this new party could secure our existence, as things go here. I took the liberty to speak of our friend, Mr. Smith,[2] and I have no doubt they would have held some correspondence with him, but that Mr. Gilbert[3] comes as the avowed candidate of the New School party, with their written pledge to support him. You have met Mr. Gilbert, it appears; and you know him therefore as well as I do. He is likely to be a popular President, and an agreeable man to be associated with. He is no scholar, however, and has very shallow notions of education. Besides, he comes as the President of the Philadelphia Historical Association and will be expected to manage matters according to *their* notions. Now they will be much more anxious to have two prayer meetings a week and to have a famous revivalist get up there and not to make the College pulpit the premises of a College. But let that stand thus until time proves the truth or falseness of the prediction. As to my own situation, all is fair weather now, and I do not doubt the sincerity of Mr. Gilbert's favorable expressions; but however human nature is human nature, and expecially New School-Presbyterian human nature is New School Presbyterian human nature; and it is not likely that an unevangelical, transcendental, semi-high-churchish Episcopalian can always be comfortable or always be an object of *peculiar* love to men who wish that to be done in a college which can be done only by "exhorting" professors, and who cannot know how to estimate what can be done by a scholar. I therefore—with perfect good feeling, on *my* part, towards the present arrangement—look upon myself as having no very long or strong hold upon my place here; and the sooner I leave it the happier I shall be.

I know of nothing in the way of news that can interest you. Even as to my McVickar crusade, you must have been much more in the way of hearing the result of it than myself. I am out of the world and know nothing. It must be McVickar that wrote on Coleridge's Pantheism etc in the New York R.[4] It is his style, his logic, his narrowness, and his *thinness* of thinking. He does not smell the real difficulty of the case. People have not said, that Coleridge called himself a Pantheist, or that his avowed creed was Pantheism, but that his *principles*—his tendency—was pantheistic. Now such a charge cannot well be met by quoting Coleridge's disclaimers or his confutations, and doing nothing more. As to claiming Coleridge to be a High Churchman, according to New York standard, and proving it by particular extracts, what could be more absurd. I once wrote you, by the way, a long letter, the fruit of vexation at some of Coleridge's foolish ways; but I burnt it. See how he behaves about Baptism, e.g. he demonstrates that no spiritual effect (no effect on the will) can be asserted of Baptism without absurdity; yet he tries hard to make something out of that sacrament from his predetermination to agree apparently with the Church of England; and what does he make out but mere assertion (as in the next to the last Edition of the Aids to Reflection) with a confession behind the scenes that he could not well say what he would say.[5] It is lucky that this vexation is felt by "one of us." If an enemy had such knowledge of Coleridge as I have, he could cut him up terribly—and, upon the whole, *unjustly*. I have just read his "Confessions"[6] and *that*, I like. It does not contain a word, however, which those who had learned to think in his spirit had not either seen, or thought into, his other works. Mr. Reed[7] lent me his Literary Remains Volume 3, which I have just read, and with the greatest interest. Likewise his Church and State.[8] I wish H. N. Coleridge did not run into that wishy-washy, "gelatinous" mystic prettiness of style which appears to constitute the dialect of second-rate Coleridge-men. It is too like Dr. McVickar's stuff. Between us, I do not think H. N. Coleridge coins very heavy metal—well-read and well-meaning as he is. Was not that an evil article in Blackwood. Coleridge's plagiarisms?[9] It was, to be sure, unjust; I wish there had been no truth in it. *My* explanation and defense is that Coleridge wrote his Biographia Literaria in 1814–16, when he must have been *morally* the worse for his opium. But is it not absolutely astonishing to hear him speak in his Table Talk of his discussion in Chapter last, Volume II, of the Biographia Literaria as being composed without apparently the slightest misgiving as to his propriety therein![10] But I must not give way, longer, to the humour of fault-finding, which a bad cold has been generating in me.

This winter I have to hear the President's recitations, and I am deep in Paley, Whateley, Kames and Brown.[11] I have made my boys read the second volume of the Biographia Literaria, Wordsworth's Prefaces and a part of his Poems. I have also dug away in Krug, and am preparing a syllabus of his Authori Divisi[12] as a compromise to an ex tempore translation to my class. Krug suits my present state of knowledge very well but I wish much to be able to get at the giants themselves—Kant, Fichte, Schelling and Hegel. I got hold of Mr. Emerson's "Nature"[13] lately, and I like it the best of his things. It is very pretty reading. I was particularly struck with his view of Reason as being what Coleridge calls Imagination.[14] If they had one strong, manly writer amongst them, those Dialists might do a good deal. But who would read such stuff as most of those contributors furnished? As old Judge Turner[15] would say, they put too much water with their rum. There is too much pretension, without power of performance—not one complete back-bone to the whole set. Yet I have always felt inclined to side with *Emerson* (at least) partly because I like the man partly because those ignorant orthodoxists behave so ruffianly towards him, and partly because his Unitarian friends back him so like Sir John's followers.[16] It is delightful to hear *them* crying out infidel and Athiest—the fools! Of the Norton and Ripley controversy, I saw only the first number of each side.[17] I liked Ripley very well, and hated the other man most cordially. I did not see why Ripley was not perfectly in the right in the greater part of his piece.

I am doing nothing in the way of writing this winter, except that I have promised a Lecture to a Society in Wilmington, which if I make out well and can afford to sink a little money, I may print. I hope this winter vacation finds you with the press in prospect. Matter so well cut, and piled, and dried might easily be set on fire, I am sure. More than I am longing to see the blaze.

I owe Mr. Torrey a letter, and would write if I had anything to say. We were upon Greek metres, but from want of books, I have gone but little further than when I wrote to him last. I sometimes think now I will prepare a College Greek Syntax out of Thiersch, to which de Sacy's General Grammar[18] would furnish a good Introduction. If I thought I could do it tolerably and could make a little money out of it, I would try to have it ready by next winter. I should like to see a few of Plato's Dialogues, too, well edited for Colleges. But *I* do not expect ever to be equal to doing that well. I wish Mr. Torrey was at some such work instead of Neander[19]—important as that undertaking certainly is.

May we not hope to see you here? There are several of us New Englanders here, all of whom consider themselves acquainted with you, and would do all they could to make a visit agreeable. Remember me to the Faculty, and to all Burlington friends.

I remain, dear Sir,
Faithfully yours,
G. A.

1. Heman Allen (1774–1844) in 1841 was one of the most prominent lawyers in Vermont.
2. Worthington Smith.
3. Eliphalet Wheeler Gilbert, alternatively president of the Board of Trustees of Newark College and president of the College (1834–35 and 1840–47).
4. The author of the article is unidentifiable, although he sounds McVickarish at one point when he says that there is not in Coleridge any form of "that falsely appropriated epithet, 'Evangelical,' elevating the written word at the expense of the Christian Sacrements" [*New York Review*, 7 (1840), 403–29].
5. Some fourteen pages in the first American edition of *Aids* and sixteen pages in H. N. Coleridge's edition of 1838 (three pages were added from the unpublished notebooks) discuss the arguments pro and con Infant Baptism. Coleridge argues that there is no historical or logical evidence for Infant Baptism having been practiced in Apostolic times, but that there are perfectly good historical and spiritual reasons for practising the rite as it is done by the Church of England in modern times. *Aids to Reflection*, *The Complete Works of Samuel Taylor Coleridge*, edited by W. G. T. Shedd (New York, 1853), I, pp. 333–49.
6. Samuel Taylor Coleridge, *Confessions of an Inquiring Spirit*. Edited from the Author's Ms. by Henry

Nelson Coleridge (Boston: James Munro, 1841).

7. Henry Hope Reed (1808–54), professor of rhetoric and English literature at the University of Pennsylvania (1835–54), was the foremost American disciple of Wordsworth.

8. Samuel Taylor Coleridge, *On the Constitution of the Church and according to the Idea of Each* (London, 1830).

9. The question of Coleridge's "plagiarism" from Schelling had first been broached in *Tait's Magazine* by Thomas De Quincey a few weeks after Coleridge's death. The article in *Blackwood's Magazine*, 47 (1840), 289ff., discusses mostly the chapters on imagination and associational psychology in the *Biographia Literaria* and remarks the similarities between what Coleridge said in Chapter XII of the *Biographia* with portions of Schelling's *System des Transcendentalen Idealismus.*

10. Walter Jackson Bate's discussion of Coleridge's "plagiarism" is perhaps the most sensible and balanced. See *Coleridge* (New York, 1968), pp. 131–38.

11. William Paley (1743–1805), English theologian and author of the famous *Evidences of Christianity* (1794) and *Natural Theology* (1802).

Richard Whately (1787–1863), Archbishop of Dublin, author of treatises on logic (1826) and rhetoric (1828), was one of the founding figures in the Broad Church Movement.

Henry Home Kames (1696–1782), Scottish philosopher, author of the widely read *Elements of Criticism* (1762).

Thomas Brown (1778–1820), Scottish philosopher, was a colleague of Dugald Stewart at Edinburgh University and attempted to reconcile Hume's skepticism to religion.

12. Wilhelm T. Krug, *Etwas, das Herr Adam Müller gesagt hat, über Etwas, das Göthe gassagt hat, und noch Etwas das Luther gesagt hat. Zur Nachfeier des Reformazions-Jubiläumus* (Leipzig, 1817). A reply to Müller's *Etwas das Göthe gesagt hat.*

13. Only ninety-five pages, Emerson's *Nature* was published in September 1836.

14. "The Imagination may be defined to be the use which the Reason makes of the material world." Section VI, "Idealism."

15. Bates Turner (1760–1847), a prominent Vermont lawyer, had been a justice on the Vermont Supreme Court (1827–28).

16. *Henry IV*, Part I, Sc. ii, lines 12–52 and lines 70–74.

17. In a pamphlet entitled *A Discourse on the Latest Form of Infidelity* (Boston, 1839), Andrews Norton (1786–1853), formerly Dexter Professor of Sacred Literature at Harvard (1819–30), attacked the "modern German School of Infidelity," chiefly Hegel, De Wette, and Schleiermacher. Norton defended the validity of the proof-from-miracles argument against German "higher criticism." George Ripley replied anonymously with *"The Latest Form of Infidelity" Examined* (Boston, 1840), defending Spinoza, Schleiermacher, and De Wette. Norton replied with *Remarks on a Pamphlet Entitled "The Latest Form of Infidelity" Examined.* Ripley subsequently published two more letters. The culmination of the debate came when Norton published a reprint of two articles from *The Biblical Repertory* by

James W. Alexander, Albert Dod, and Charles Hodge, entitled *Transcendentalism of the Germans and of Cousin and Its Influence on the Opinion in this Country* (Cambridge, 1840).
18. Friedrich Wilhelm Von Thiersch, *Griechische Grammatick* . . . (Leipzig, 1818); Silvestre de Sacy, *Principles of General Grammar*, trans. D. Fosdick (Andover, 1834).
19. Torrey's translation of J. A. W. Neander's *Allgemeine Geschichte der christliche Religion und Kirche* (Hamburg, 1825) was entitled *History of the Christian Religion and Church* (Boston, 1848).

To Henry J. Raymond
Text: Wells, pp. 166–68

Burlington
March 1, 1841

My dear Sir

I hope you will have ascribed my long delay in answering your letter to some good cause and will not need a very long apology. The simple fact was that it came soon after I had gone to Boston, and I only found it on my return, the day before yesterday. I had, indeed, intended to write you from Boston and on some of the topics you mention, but found myself too much occupied then to do so. Some numbers of your paper[1] had fallen in my way (and I am obliged to you for those you have sent) from which I began to fear you were yourself getting a little infected with visions which, in one so young as you indeed, might be tolerated, but which seem to be quite unpardonable in one of mature years. The schemes cherished in New York[2] are very nearly of the same character, I suppose, as those which Mr. Ripley and others are going to commence near Boston on the first of April[3] (an ominous day); and it may be prudent for the New Yorkers to wait the result of their experiment. Those engaged at Boston are men, so far as I know, of good spirit, and as well qualified to realize such schemes as any men can be who are visionary enough to entertain them seriously at all. Ripley says it requires men of Christian spirit, above the grovelling selfishness of the world; and the grand error I take to be in the hope which he indulges of finding men in this world sufficiently under the law of pure reason, or even sufficiently raised by divine grace above the selfishness of human nature, to live together on such terms as they propose. Every scheme of social existence that does not assume the principles of self-seeking, as giving law practically to the conduct of men in their intercourse with each other, and form its arrangements on that assumption, will and must fail. It would be just as rational to propose mechanical theories without taking into account the law of gravity.

Now it is the business of the Christian philanthropist to aim at ends which require men to overcome and rise above that principle, but he must provide for its being overcome. And this is, in fact, the great purpose of christianity itself; to redeem men from the bondage and limitations of the natural self-will, and bring them into that spiritual freedom in which each shall do freely and from the heart that which is for the best good of all—in which the universal shall overpower and control to its own higher ends the individual and self-seeking principle in each. But christianity is, and professes to be, in a state of continuous warfare with the natural will of man and with the spirit of the world, which is the natural will generalized. In this view christianity is a perfectly rational system—its means are adapted to its ends—it assumes the facts as they are, and works accordingly—waving a mighty weapon, and sweating great drops of blood. These reformers, on the other hand, hope to redeem the world by a sort of dilletanti process, to purge off its grossness, to make a poetical paradise in which hard work shall become easy, dirty things clean, the selfish liberal, and the churl a churl no longer. Ask Mr. [Greeley] how many out of the first hundred men he meets he would be willing to live with on the terms proposed, of having common granaries, and a common purse, in expectation that each would limit himself to his own share of the common stock—that there would be none willing to eat who did not work; and how long it would probably be before in his little world all the fences for protection of individual right would be needed, which he now finds in the great world.

Even among Unitarians the practical conviction of the original sin of selfishness is so strong that "the colony," backed as it is even by Dr. Channing,[4] is the theme of severe ridicule and sarcasm almost universally. Yet on their system it ought to be practicable. But common sense and common experience are too strong for theory in most minds. The whole of Boston transcendentalism I take to be rather a superficial affair; and there is some force in the remark of a friend of mine that the "Dial" indicates rather the place of the moon than of the sun. They have many of the prettinesses of the German writers, but without their manly logic and strong systematizing tendency. They pretend to no system or unity, but each utters, it seems, the inspiration of the moment, assuming that it all comes from the universal heart, while ten to one it comes only from the stomach of the individual.

I spent more than a fortnight in Boston in the domicile of my old friend, Choate,[5] now gone to the Senate, and spent two evenings with Allston, one with Channing, Ticknor, Bancroft,[6] and other literary men. I heard also the discussion before the Board of Overseers in the Senate Chamber, on the extension of what they call the voluntary course at Cambridge. The argument, I confess, did not meet my objections, but seemed to me to rest upon a quite superficial view of the whole subject of education. It was however, adopted, and henceforth students, at the end of freshman year, may pursue the classics farther or not at their option, "with a full knowledge" (as one of the resolutions has it) on the part of the boy and his parents of the course left, and of the one taken as a substitute. How they are to get the knowledge, we are left to our Yankee privilege of guessing.

J. Marsh

1. In March 1841 Raymond was still with Greeley's *New Yorker* and would be named his chief assistant on *The Tribune* in April.
2. See above, letter from Henry Raymond, January 14, 1841, note 8.
3. The Brook Farm venture. See above, letter from Ripley, October 17, 1840, note 3.
4. Both William Ellery Channings, the "great Unitarian" (1780–1842) and his nephew the poet (1818–1901), supported Brook Farm.
5. Rufus Choate (1799–1859) served out Daniel Webster's term in the Senate and was reelected for one term (1841–50).
6. Washington Allston, the painter; Edward Tyrell Channing (1780–1856), Boylston Professor of

Rhetoric at Harvard; George Ticknor (1791–1871), who was then writing his *History of Spanish Literature*; and George Bancroft (1800–91), who had by 1841 completed the third volume of his *History of the United States.*

From Joseph Henry Green[1]
Text: *Remains*, pp. 160–63

King's College, London
March 5, 1841

My dear Sir

When I contrast the date of this letter with that of your welcome communication, I am truly ashamed of having so long delayed the acknowledgment of the great pleasure it afforded me, not only on its own account, but as an earnest (which I trust it is) of our better acquaintance and of the support which we may mutually give each other in the establishment of the philosophy of ideas, of which in the present age Coleridge was unquestionably the reviver and re-originator. And if the "Vital Dynamics,"[2] with your approbation of which I am highly flattered, should at all contribute to enlist scientific men in the cause and to infuse a more vital philosophy into science, especially physics, I shall derive the high gratification of having been one of the instruments, under Providence, of promulgating the truths of a spiritual philosophy and of rescuing the pursuits of noble minds from the taint of errors, which I fear are too apt to arise under the dominant influence, hitherto prevalent in physics, of a philosophy, the tendency of which is assuredly to place all reality in sensuous intuition, consequently to withdraw the mind injuriously from super-sensuous truths, and in confounding faith with belief, to substitute conjecture, probability, and the subjective condition of the believer's mind, for the proper evidence of the great truths upon which the whole moral life of man is based. We may, indeed, discern an order of Providence in the development of physical science; and we can scarcely doubt that it could not have advanced in connexion with the imperfect nature of the human mind, which sees only in part, except under the condition of a too exclusive attention to the senses, and to the forms of sense, which it mainly owed to Descartes and Gassendi;[3] whilst we cannot but admit that physical science and natural knowledge are important elements in the cultivation of man, both as it respects the development of his intellect and the creation of the means and instruments of civilization and of a common participation by the whole race in the blessings granted to any one more favored portion. We have indeed learned a better creed than that derived from a sensuous philosophy, which mistakes means for ends; and viewing the acquisitions of science in relation to the moral man, of whom the intellect is after all but a fragment, we press onwards to the goal at which the intellect, with its noblest product, science is still to be subordinated to the moral will in that moral life of the whole man, head and heart, in which philosophy even must await its final and complete vivification. I fear that you estimate too highly the labors of the English so called natural philosophers, and I should hesitate to ascribe to them generally a higher merit than the talent of generalization; at all events, the perception of law in the spirit of a true dynamic philosophy has scarcely more than dawned upon some few of my countrymen; and had I not been prompted by a deep sense of the momentous nature of the truths which I have endeavored to inculcate in my oration, I should hardly have ventured with those auditors and readers to whom it was addressed, to cast my bread upon the waters. Should you think that an advantageous impression might be made by its publication on your side of the water, I pray you to dispose of it as you may see fit; and well convinced I am that a preface from your pen would incalculably aid its effect both there and in this country.

There is, however, one passage in your letter, which has excited an apprehension in my mind that I may have been misunderstood, and that in respect of the relation of God to nature you may be disposed to infer that my doctrines are tainted by the erroneous tendency of Schelling's philosophy to Pantheism; for that such is its tendency, notwithstanding his declaimer, I cannot doubt. Now if there was any one point on which above all others Coleridge manifested the utmost anxiety, it was that of preventing the possibility of confounding God with nature; and perhaps no better evidence can be offered than the formula, which he was frequently in the habit of repeating: World – God = 0: God – world = Reality absolute; the world without God is nothing, God without the world is already, in and of himself, absolute perfection, absolute reality. And this doctrine of genuine Theism he has most nobly vindicated, in its inalienable connection with the doctrine of the Trinity as it is set forth in the Nicene Creed, by establishing as a truth of reason the Personality of God; a doctrine which is the very foundation of moral truth, as is the dominant principle of Coleridge's system, but to which Schelling's philosophy is inadequate; and I do not think that I am asserting too much in saying that its inadequacy to the attainment of the idea is virtually confessed in its utter improgressiveness after a certain period long since passed, and that it is this inadequacy which has probably prevented Schelling's long promised completion of his philosophy in a systematic form.

I send you herewith a small brochure, just published, on a subject which now is agitating the medical profession in this country; and though you can take no part in its particular object, yet I have thought that its general scope and design might not be unacceptable to you, and that it might interest you as a specimen of reasoning by ideas. It will at least show that I am not idle, though drawn off for a time from what I must ever consider as the main business of the remainder of my life—the exposition in a systematic form of the philosophy of my great and excellent teacher.

With my fervent wishes for your welfare, and my sincere prayers for the continuance of your successful labors in the cause of truth, Believe me, my dear Sir,

Yours ever very
sincerely,
Joseph Henry Green

1. See above, letter of February 25, 1839, note 1.
2. See above, letters of April 1, 1840, note 3, and February 25, 1839, note 1.
3. René Descartes (1596–1650), French rationalist philosopher and mathematician, the "father of modern philosophy"; Pierre Gassendi (1592–1655), French philosopher and mathematician, an early critic of Descartes.

1838–1842 To Nancy Swift[1]
Text: UVM[2]

Burlington
March 17, 1841

Dear Miss Swift

I have repeatedly been asked to make out a course of study and suitable text-books for young ladies in the department to which you refer but have never been able to do so to my own satisfaction. We have very few books in the language that seem to me quite upon the right track and those not of such an elementary character as to answer your purpose in a school. I meet indeed with the same difficulties in my college classes and am obliged to patch up a course as well as I can, partly with text-books and partly without. What we need in these studies with our pupils is first a right philosophical *method* by which every part of what pertains to philosophical knowledge shall be put in its proper place and have its due proportion to the whole. This being clearly understood we should be able to judge how much is appropriate to pupils in different stages of discipline and beginning in the right place to secure them from the necessity of unlearning what they have once gained. As it is, departments of study which I regard as quite distinct and belonging to different stages of advancement are so confounded together in the usual textbooks that a pupil cannot be put upon the simplest, without being at once involved in the most difficult. It is desirable as far as may be to carry students along from the first elements by such steps that they may always have the necessary data and the requisite discipline for advancing the next step without unreasonable perplexity . . . yet again the different stages of progress in the knowledge of our own inward being are so connected from the inherent unity and interpenetration of its living powers that nothing can be adequately known till we are prepared to contemplate each in its relation to the whole.

The comparatively outward and sensuous agencies are however first in order, and though they cannot be adequately understood in themselves alone, are the necessary condition for apprehending those higher powers by which they are themselves in turn made intelligible.

But I am talking rather obscurely I perceive, and shall gain my purpose better perhaps by sketching in order my view of the method to be pursued in this department of study. It must of course be very general and I fear necessarily too vague to be of much service.

In the first place then, I would distinguish the sphere of sense as containing the immediate and primary conditions of self-knowledge and as first offering itself to our observation in the sphere of consciousness. Drawing the line between physiology and psychology we may leave out what pertains to the former in the organic structure of the several organs of sense and confine ourselves to that of which we are conscious in the affections of the several senses.

Here we have then as the first object of attention the manifold affections of the outward senses in their immediate relations to their correlatives and outward objects, which correlatives again are the conditions of our experience. With this too, we may connect the sensual appetites awakened by the presence of their proper objects in the sphere of sense and we may dwell here distinguishing and classing phenomena ad infinitum. Such writers as Brown[3] give themselves infinite trouble and take great credit for marking distinctions here which are after all of little moment as belonging *only* to the sensuous and conditional. Yet we may profitably employ young pupils a good deal in studying and distinguishing in immediate affections of the several senses and the conditions of their occurrence, and there is much to be said here not said by Brown or Abercrombie.[4]

We may distinguish here from the empirical affections of the outer senses the presentations of pure sense, or space or extended forms in space, as the common condition of all outward affections of sense.

Here we have also the power of presenting pure space void of all that affects the senses empirically and so the conditions of geometry as determining the possible forms of space itself.

From the outward senses we may distinguish also the inner sense—as designating under the relations of time the *immediate conscious* presentation of the inward affections and agencies of our being, whether arising from antecedent affections of the outer sense or the agency of higher powers. Thus the representations of the images of outward objects or of past experiences as spontaneously reproduced and retaining the individuality of that which they represent is still to be regarded as belonging to *sense* and distinguished from the *conceptions* of the *understanding*. I include here the spontaneous agency of association and all that is passive or involuntary in the presentations of the inner sense.

In the *second place* I would distinguish the *understanding*, or the faculty of voluntary reflection by which we consciously and freely represent the phenomena of sense and form *conceptions* essentially *general* in their character and thus progressively bring the manifoldness of sense within the grasp of conscious thought.

This is a power by which we are raised above the sphere of sense, freed from the blind necessity of brute nature—made capable of conscious knowledge and of a conscious self-proposed purpose in the pursuit of which we use and direct the powers of our sensual nature. The understanding of course cannot be conceived separate from a free will though its laws of thought may be studied and this study constitutes Logic in its widest extent. In this I embrace not merely therefore the process of reasoning expressed by syllogism, but the formation of conceptions by attention—abstraction—generalisation—etc.—the nature of conceptions so founded as expressed by words, the whole structure of language, as the utterance of the understanding and its outward birth, judgment, ratiocination with the inherent and necessary laws by which all the agencies are determined.

Thus the study of Logic taken in this extent is an essential part of an education both as discipline of the understanding for acquiring precision and distinctness of conception and in the use of terms, I regard as indispensable and absolutely so for the intelligent study of the higher philosophy.

It is much to be desired that we had a course of discipline devised in the study of our own language which should as far as may be, secure the same end that is aimed at in College by the study of Latin and Greek. I think it might be attained with young ladies in a great degree by pursuing analysis of words, sentences and discourses, though it would be difficult to present as good problems for the purpose as they have in every sentence of Latin and Greek.

On the same grade with the understanding as an object of study are the desires, the passions and purposes which, as distinguished from the instinctive impulses and appetites of sense arise from reflection upon our experience, are grounded in our self-conscious being and referrible to the will or *identity* of the individual man—as a free self-controlled and responsible agent.

Here again we see how the understanding and will as constituting the unity and identity of the finite and individual *free intelligence* in having the conditions of its development in the outward the sensuous and conditional experience of sense in the world of sense become a sensuous and conditional understanding and will—under bondage to nature and self-subjected to the limitations of sense—the mind of the flesh and the will of the flesh—and need to be, the one enlightened by the unconditional truths of the universal reason—the other redeemed from bondage to an alien law and, quickened by the spirit, go forth freely in the pursuit of those ends which the law of the spirit requires as of universal obligation. In this enlightening of the individual understanding by the truths of reason we have the standpoint of pure science and in the consciousness of its ultimate principles and to that unconditional form of presentation in which being and knowing are recognized as identical and absolute. This is philosophy—and the identity of will with the universal law of practical truth revealed in the conscience, or a free and joyful coincidence of all its purposes and aims with the will of God is *religion*.

Now the light of the understanding as individual comes from above and out of the universal. So the quickening power and life of the will by which it overcomes the power of nature and its own self-imposed limitations to mere natural and selfish ends also must come not from nature but from a higher source, from the redeeming word and spirit of Christ by which we are made partakers of his life. In the relation of the individual and conditional to the universal and absolute are found all the difficult questions both in philosophy and religion. What that relation is every one must learn upon reference to his own higher consciousness, and to make scholars attain this higher self-consciousness is the great difficulty. In regard to the *practical* however, every one knows till some false speculation blinds him, the relation of his individual will, his purposes and motives to the universal law of duty in the conscience, and here we have the strong ground for moral and religious instruction. To keep the mind awake and alive to the distinct consciousness of this relation seems to me the sum of our duty as moral teachers, and this is important also as habituating to reflection in its relation to speculative philosophy and ultimately guarding against false speculative principles. For the speculative is grounded in the practical and not the reverse, as sensualism would teach us.

But I have attempted more than is possible in a letter and I fear have failed of any good purpose in answering your inquiries. However I consider the general division of what is promiscuously jumbled in English text-books into psychology-logic and Philosophy, though I have very imperfectly marked their boundaries, as of great importance for the teacher even when the pupil is limited to the first and second divisions. Psychology in its widest extent would of course embrace all the powers of the soul in their living relations to each other under the same general heads of sense, understanding and reason and their co-ordinates; natural appetites, natural or conditional will, and the rational will.

Brown and the other writers of that school have indeed but little beyond the proper sphere of empirical psychology, and as such, a good deal of their books may be used with advantage. Only it is difficult with their method and language to guard against the sensualizing and fatalistic tendencies of their works. Cousin's psychology translated by Henry[5] as an introduction to philosophy is a very good book, though some of his other volumes are quite pantheistic. The prospects of our College are still good and improving though we are always mendicant.

Yours truly
J. Marsh

1. Nancy Swift was the daughter of Judge Samuel Swift of Middlebury, Vermont, and ran the sabbath school in the Middlebury Congregational church.
2. The text of this letter suvives only in a typescript copy at UVM.
3. Thomas Brown (1778–1820), Scottish metaphysician, argued in *Cause and Effect* (1804) that Hume's skepticism and denial of causation could be made compatible with religion.
4. John Abercrombie, M.D. (1780–1844), Scottish physician, believed that mental problems were solely neurological in origin. His *Inquiries Concerning the Intellectual Powers and the Investigation of Truth* (Edinburgh, 1830) and *Philosophy of the Moral Feelings* (Edinburgh, 1833) were immediately published in the United States. An unoriginal thinker, Abercrombie clearly owed a great deal to Brown.
5. Victor Cousin, *Elements of Psychology: Included in a Critical Examination of Locke's Essay on the Human Understanding*. Translated by C. S. Henry (Hartford, 1834).

John Wheeler to Washington Allston
Ms: Massachusetts Historical Society

Burlington
July 3, 1842

My dear Sir

Will you pardon my intrusion upon your retired and studious life to say that our beloved Professor Marsh has gone from us to take his place in the glorious company to which he had long been united in spirit. He died this morning, at half past four o'clock, having retained his senses and the discriminating powers of his mind to the last—remarking even this morning, "It is as I could have wished, to die of a Sabbath morning."

At no time of his life has his view of spiritual truths been clearer, or his hopes more sustaining, or his faith more immovable, than during his protected illness.

His manuscripts, which will be found, I fear, very incomplete (he was but forty eight years old, and for several years has been in comparatively ill health, with a load of College duties on his shoulder), are committed to Professor Torrey for selection, revision and publication. This is to be accompanied, as I suppose, with a memoir. It would be desirable to have this accompanied by a good engraved likeness, but it is doubtful whether it could be done. We have a portrait taken by an itinerating artist, which has given his forehead well, and some other feature, but not the whole expression of the face. There is also a Daguerreotype likeness, and we hope to have a cast of the head, but it is uncertain as yet.

Were it possible, there is a great desire for a good portrait of him, but we suppose it impossible, as no artist has seen him to know him of late. Yourself is the only one that has seen him, so far as I know, for many years, and that not under such conditions as would lead me to hope that the hand that had so successfully placed the features and the character of Mr. Coleridge on the canvass could think of attempting the same for his admirer and worthy commentator. But I forget myself, and close by expressing my own, and if his living voice were here, Professor Marsh's *hearty thanks* to you for giving "Monaldi"[1] to the publick. Mrs. Wheeler and my daughters read, and reread, and talk of it, and will not let it die out of mind, nor even rest quietly there, because of constantly alluding to it. With kind regards to Mrs. Allston I am, with great respect,

Very truly yours, etc.
J. Wheeler

1. Washington Allston, *Monaldi* (1840), a Gothic romance.

Index